DISCARD

VOICE AND DICTION
Phonation and Phonology

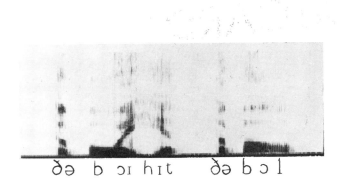

MERRILL'S
International Speech Series

under the editorship of

John Black
Ohio State University

Paul Moore
University of Florida

VOICE AND DICTION
Phonation and Phonology

John W. Black
Ohio State University

Ruth B. Irwin
Ohio State University

CHARLES E. MERRILL PUBLISHING COMPANY
A Bell & Howell Company
Columbus, Ohio

PN 4162
, B55

Standard Book Number: 675-09422-4

Library of Congress Catalog Card Number: 70-89553

1 2 3 4 5 6 7 8 9 10—73 72 71 70 69

PRINTED IN THE UNITED STATES OF AMERICA

Preface

Voice and Diction: Applied Phonation and Phonology recognizes that there is substandard speech and that society generally will be helped by any improvement that can be brought to bear on this speech. Importantly, speech improvement is not a topic for only economically disadvantaged and culturally deprived people. It is a topic for everyone, all who speak and all who listen.

This book explores and supports the following conclusions: First, a modification of speech behavior is more likely to occur if a person understands the system with which he is producing speech. An awareness that speaking is muscularly controlled motor activity contributes to the reasonableness of systematically developed series of exercises. Second, this same degree of understanding should be sought and encouraged with regard to the elements of oral language that are being used in speech. Third, the modification of speech to the extent that many people envisage for themselves is an enormous and long task which flourishes best in an environment that encourages having fun as one works with his speech. In this introduction to an adult life of continuing improvement of personal speech, the many exercises suggested are intended to lead to insight about one's speech and to do so in manners that induce fun.

As a basic skill for communication, speech is probably the most important tool for giving information and is vital in achieving effective use of one's abilities as well as satisfactory social adjustment. This book provides the motivation for better pronunciation and the exercises for achieving it.

Contents

1

Your Speech and Your Life

Have you ever thought how the ability to speak affects your life? With speech, you convey thoughts to your friends; you inform or instruct; you express your needs or desires; you communicate emotions; you greet your friends with a "good morning"; and you have the pleasure of listening to yourself talk. Listening to the speech of others is an important part of the total communicative process. As you improve your listening abilities, you will also improve communication. Good listening leads to improved speaking habits as well as understanding between people.

Every person wants favorable responses from others. How to influence people to think and act in the way you desire is one of the primary purposes of effective speech. You are eager to win a favorable response whether it be to cause a customer to buy a hat, to persuade people to vote for you in an election, to effect some moral change in a character, to chastise a child, or to make others think well of you. Hardly any activity in American life is without need for proficient speech.

To win favorable responses from others, you need to understand what people want and appeal to them through such avenues as money, love, preservation of life, and social security. The fulfillment of these goals will be determined not only by what you say, but by how you speak. Is your voice pleasant? Is your articulation free from error? Are you intelligible? Could you be as effective, for example, with a deep husky voice and unintelligible speech as you would if your speech were pleasant and intelligible? Standards of good speech will be discussed in Chapter 2; particular aspects of speech will also be discussed in later chapters.

IMPORTANCE OF GOOD SPEECH

Speech is a basic skill—means for the communication and exchange of thought. In the present-day world, speech is probably the most important tool for giving information. Considering that almost every situation during the day requires speech, effectiveness in talking is quite essential. "Good" speech is not only important to persons in their daily occupational activities, but also in social situations.

If you are afraid to talk, you may have experienced some of the following symptoms or feelings before, during, or after speaking: dryness of throat and mouth, forgetting, tension in the abdominal region, inability to produce voice, stuttering or stammering, tremors of knees and hands, weak voice, excessive perspiration, accelerated heart rate, speech rate too slow or too fast, stomach upset, difficulty in breathing, inability to look at audience, feeling of disapproval by an audience, inability to finish speaking, excessive hesitation, and dread before speaking.

Your speaking behavior will, in a large measure, determine your environment of personal attitudes and reactions. People may react differently toward you if you evidence some of the symptoms listed above than if you appear at ease during your speaking. Feelings of insecurity may develop if persons in your environment treat you as the "shy" one who is afraid to talk. Moreover, these symptoms of stage fright tend to stimulate further fear of speaking. It is assumed in the following discussion that "good" voice and articulation will assist you in making better use of your abilities and more satisfactory social adjustment than if your speech were unsatisfactory or deviant.

Effective Use of Your Abilities

Removal or decreasing of distracting speech deviations and the improvement of intelligibility of speech and vocal efficiency and pleasantness should improve your chances to use your specific social and occupational talents more effectively. Although you may have intelligence and a specific kind of aptitude in a profession or business, unintelligibility of speech or an unpleasant voice might prevent you from advancing your education or profession according to your capabilities. Any special abilities you have socially, politically, or as a leader in the community would be enhanced through the use of proficient speech.

Earning Your Living. Almost any profession or occupation requires some speech. With inadequate use of speech, the individual may not advance as rapidly as his occupational knowledge and skills might warrant. The student, afraid to talk, may seek a research or laboratory position in which very little speech is required. The person with inadequate speech is often discouraged and may take a job where the necessity for speech is limited. One twenty-three-year-old woman with unintelligible speech, for example, chose to work in a lens factory where she needed no speech. A forty-five-year-old plumber who stuttered severely worked with his brother. The stutterer worked but left all of the talking to his brother.

Not all persons, obviously, can attain "perfect" speech but some improvement in the use of articulation and voice can usually be expected for everyone who is motivated to improve and practice new skills. For those without noticeable articulatory or vocal deviations, any degree of speech improvement will certainly lead to more favorable reactions of others than if he had distracting speech mannerisms. Such favorable reactions should improve the speaker's chances for success in his profession or occupation.

Fulfilling Your Rights as a Citizen. The person with effective voice and speech can do much to shape the policies of his community and nation. He may work with organizations promoting the welfare of the community. His participation in political activities may lead to important laws for the nation. A statesman and public leader can use his speech in molding opinions; his ideas are important, but his articulation and voice may cause listeners to react favorably or unfavorably to his ideas.

Satisfactory Social Adjustment

The effective use of voice and articulation may improve your (1) interaction with the environment, (2) understanding of the environment, (3) control of the environment, and (4) adjustment to the environment. With speech, you explain to the waitress what you want to eat. The attendant at the gas station learns through speech what you want. By telephone, you use speech to order groceries or make dental or hair appointments. Although many of the modern self-service stores have reduced the need for speech to the minimum in some instances, it is still a necessary tool for interaction with one's fellow men in most daily situations.

Understanding Your Environment.   Through speech, you learn much about people and countries in which you live. To many people, the spoken word takes precedence over the written work as a means for securing information. Through mass instruction by way of the radio and television, the importance of proficient speech has gained momentum. The visual aspect of television enhances the meaning of the spoken word. Conversing with others also leads to mutual understanding of common problems in a particular environment.

Controlling the Environment.   You can often control difficult situations in your environment through speech. The speaker, for example, may help the listener to relax and feel at ease through the controlled use of his voice. The irate father may be quelled by the teacher who responds in a manner-of-fact way, "Mr. Brown, let's sit down and talk this over." The president of the university may be able to calm an angry mob of students by his slow, deliberate, low-pitched speech.

Walt Whitman must have been aware of the influence of voices when he wrote the following poem.

Voices

Now I make a leaf of Voices—for I have found nothing mightier
      than they are,
And I have found that no word spoken, but is beautiful, in its
      place.
Oh, what is it in me that makes me tremble so at voices?
Surely, whoever speaks to me in the right voice, him or her I shall
      follow,
As the water follows the moon, silently, with fluid steps, anywhere
      around the globe,
All waits for the right voices:
Where is the practis'd and perfect organ? Where is the develop'd
      Soul?
For I see every word utter'd thence has deeper, sweeter, new
      sounds, impossible on less terms.
I see brains and lips closed—tympans, and temples unstruck,
Until that comes which has the quality to strike and to unclose,
Until that comes which has the quality to bring forth what lies
Slumbering, forever ready, in all words.

Leaves of Grass
Walt Whitman

Adjusting to Environment.   Adequate speech should assist you in adjusting to others with less difficulty than if your voice and articulation were substandard. Feelings of security are enhanced as you become aware of your own speech adequacies; you then do not feel conspicuous because of speech deviations.

The person with noticeable speech problems may feel the need to adjust to the reactions of others to his inadequacies. Bill, for example, had difficulty adjusting to his environment because of the /l/ substitution for /w/; John seldom talked because people made fun of his stuttering; and Mary withdrew from social situations because people had difficulty understanding her. Although Bill, a pilot, was 28 years old, he said "wed" for "led." He would say, "I wode in the airpwane." As the result of his speech inaccuracy, people stared at him and often made fun of his speech. Bill gradually lost interest in social groups. He lost confidence in himself. His enthusiasm and resourcefulness in his work dwindled. After Bill was taught to say a good /l/ by a speech clinician, his whole attitude changed. As he learned how to use the sound correctly in conversational speech, he gradually assumed his rightful role in his vocation according to his abilities.

The individual who has not learned to meet his problems realistically and objectively will usually reflect the effects of attitudes of others toward his inadequacies. Physical beauty, well-adjusted personality, and an excellent speaking voice decrease a person's maladjustment. He gains confidence as he feels the satisfactory personal reactions of others toward him. In a way, an individual can make his own environment by causing others to react positively.

It is somewhat obvious to the observant listener that speech may affect his general impression of an individual speaker. A person with a weak, whiny voice may impress the listener as a sick or tired individual. The loud, boisterous voice may appear to belong to another stereotype. Characters in plays utilize articulation and voice effectively in the portrayal of characters. Your speech or voice reveal more of *you* than you realize. You tell people what you are by what you say and how you say it.

WHAT IS SPEECH?

Speech is often used interchangeably with language and communication. *Communication* is a form of interaction in which one organism acts as a stimulus for the behavior of another. In verbal communication, a spoken (or written) word serves as the stimulus to arouse relevant symbolic processes in the hearer (or reader). In verbal communication, information or stimulus for action is transferred from one person to another. *Language,* a tool of communication, is concerned with the meaningful use of written or oral symbols by which individuals communicate with each other or with themselves. *Speech,* also an instrument of communication, is spoken language concerned with production as it leaves the mouth. Speech refers to both the expressive (speaking) and the receptive (listening) aspects of spoken language. *Speech* is defined by the committee on language of the American Speech and Hearing Association as "the process of producing the sounds, stress, rhythm, and intonation by which oral language is spoken."

Speech Is Learned

Imagine that you were placed on some isolated island at the age of six months. No other human being lived on this island. You heard only the noises of animals and birds. Would you have learned to talk? No, not in the language of other human beings. You would need and learn the language of the animals; you would learn no human speech. In other settings where both animals and humans lived, you would speak as humans.

If Romulus and Remus had been left with the wolves and woodpeckers, their language and speech would certainly have been affected. Roman history would have been different. Instead, a swineherd found them where they had been cast away by Roman officials; he sent them to school where they were well instructed in letters and other accomplishments "befitting to their birth." Accounts of children associating only with animals indicate that these feral individuals developed without language and other forms of human culture.

Deaf children do not learn to talk or use spoken language meaningfully because they do not hear speech. Such children need special instruction before they can learn the symbols with which to speak. They must also learn how to utter the sounds effectively so others will understand them.

You will also learn to speak the language which you hear. Suppose you were born of English-speaking parents living in Alaska. Your parents died while you were only four months old. Your only human companions spoke the Eskimo language. What would you learn? English? No, you would have learned to talk as the Eskimos do.

Lack of speech and language development often results from extreme social isolation of children. Isabelle did not learn to talk in the normal way because she was imprisoned with a mute and uneducated mother. She did not talk until she was six and one-half years old, after a speech clinician had worked with her. The mother had used only crude gestures with her. Kingsley Davis writes about two victims of extreme neglect. Anna and Isabelle were unable to speak at age six and appeared mentally retarded. At ten, Anna "talked mainly in phrases but would repeat words and try to carry on a conversation."

Although the child may learn speech, inadequate models of speaking may cause the child to learn poor speech. If the mother talks in a high-pitched voice, for example, her daughter may also learn to talk in the same way. A twenty-year-old girl with inarticulate speech came from a home in which the father and two older brothers spoke inaccurately. The child born in disadvantaged areas will learn to speak as his parents, brothers, sisters, and friends do. His speech behavior may differentiate him from that of the speech of persons in middle-class society.

Quintilian, a Roman rhetorician, born about 35 A.D., emphasized the importance of the early model for the child's learning of speech. He stated:

> Above all see that the child's nurse speaks correctly. . . . No doubt the most important point is that they should be of good character: but they should speak correctly as well. It is the nurse that the child first hears, and her words that he will first attempt to imitate . . . As regards parents, I should like to see them as highly educated as possible, and I do not restrict this remark to fathers alone. As regards the boys in whose company our budding orator is to be brought up, I would repeat what I said about nurses.

Although parents are probably the most important as models for the early teaching of oral language, teachers, particularly in the early grades, exert much influence on the child's speaking patterns. Quintilian also mentioned the teacher as well as the parents for helping in the formation of speaking habits. He stated that "the teacher should therefore be as distinguished for his eloquence as for his good character, and like Phoenix in the Iliad be able to teach his pupil both how to behave and how to speak."

Proficient Speech Is a Miracle

Although imitation is an important part in speech learning, parents and teachers often do little or nothing to teach talking. It is really a miracle that you talk as well as you do when none of your physical structures function basically for speech purposes. The intelligence which differentiates you from animals is in your favor. With adequate intelligence, normal physical structures, and socially stimulating environment, you should learn to talk like those with whom you associate.

No part of the anatomy was primarily intended for use in speaking. The teeth and lips are used for the intake, biting, and chewing of food. The throat functions in the swallowing of food. Not even the larynx functions basically as a speech organ. The vocal folds are used to prevent small food particles or gaseous elements from entering the trachea where they might choke you. Speech, an overlaid function, has been superimposed upon structures biologically intended for chewing, sucking, swallowing, and breathing.

DEGREE OF SPEECH PROFICIENCY

In the general population, persons will vary considerably as to their speaking abilities. There is the garrulous speaker who talks about anything and everything or the speaker who seldom talks. Another person may be so careless and indistinct that he cannot be understood. To an employer may come the weak and fearful speaker who appears to be incompetent because he lacks forcefulness in his speech. Then there is the monotonous speaker who talks about uninteresting details, speaking in the same pitch, time, and rhythmical patterns. There is the person with the unpleasant voice which may be nasal, hoarse, harsh, or breathy. You may occasionally meet a person with an exceptionally pleasing voice and excellent diction.

As a means of establishing a frame of reference for speech improvement, the variations in speech proficiency may be estimated to approximate the distribution used by psychologists to demonstrate various intellectual levels. You will note in Figure 1 that the majority of persons fall within the normal range of speech adequacy. A similar pattern of

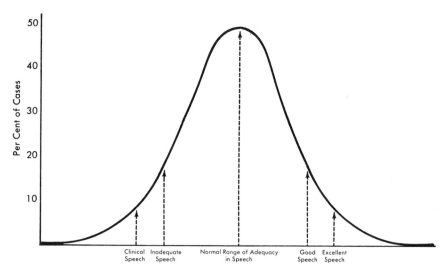

Figure 1. The range of speech proficiency approximates a normal distribution.

normality will be evidenced by individuals with adequate speech. Roughly, fewer than 8 per cent of the general population are estimated to have excellent speech and vocal characteristics. Some individuals may have good speech with no known attempt at speech training. The other 92 per cent of the persons in the population are estimated to have varying degrees of adequacy in voice and articulation. About 17 per cent have "good" speech at the upper end of the continuum, and 17 per cent have inadequate speech or "poor" speech at the lower part, as represented in Figure 1. From 5 to 10 per cent of the general population are estimated to have clinical speech deviations. The large majority of all persons, or approximately 50 per cent, fall in the middle group or within the normal range of adequacy in voice, articulation, rhythm, and language. The standards for good speech will be discussed in Chapter 2.

For many individuals, adequate speech which may be described as neither "good" or "bad" may be satisfactory for coping with most situations arising in life. The person with speech within the normal range of adequacy will probably function in speaking situations without awareness of the possible increased effectiveness of his life through the use of proficient speech.

The preceding discussion of speech proficiency has been in terms of the general population. What can you expect of students in the university? You may find a similar pattern of speech proficiencies there as represented in Figure 1. In any voice and diction class, you will probably find individuals falling along the entire range of speech proficiencies with the majority having speech within the normal range of adequacy.

Although the clinical population may not exceed 4 per cent of the students in the university, it may be assumed that the majority need some form of the speech improvement in order to handle effectively the communicative requirements of their educated culture. Inadequate or "near normal" speech may have some of the characteristics, however in lesser degree, of the speech in need of clinical attention. For this reason, the clinical types of speech inadequacies will be discussed.

SPEECH INADEQUACIES

On the abscissa of Figure 1 are tallied percentages of individuals with degrees of proficiency in speech. What can you expect of students in the university? In a ten-year survey of speech disorders among 33,000 students at the University of Michigan, Morley found the average incidence of speech disorders to be 3.8 per cent, which is much lower than usually cited for the general population of the children in the elementary grades.

Several reasons may account for this difference, among which are factors of maturation, speech therapy in the schools, and the stimulating environments of the selected group going to the university.

If you happen to be among this lower clinical group of roughly 5 per cent of the college population, you will need special help with your speech. In general, the speech disorders may be classified as those involving irregularities of (a) voice, (b) articulation, (c) rhythm, and (d) language. These clinical speech problems, according to Van Riper, may call attention to themselves, may interfere with communication, or may cause the individual to become maladjusted. The individual who substitutes /θ or ð (th)*/ for /s/ has speech which calls attention to the speaker. The unintelligible speaker is unable to communicate effectively, and the stutterer may not only have speech which attracts attention and interferes with communication but also may have speech which causes him to become maladjusted.

The cerebral-palsied person may have speech which is noticeable by its unintelligibility; the physical handicap plus the inability to express himself understandably may cause him to become socially maladjusted.

Vocal Inadequacies

Vocal problems, constituting 15 per cent of the clinical population in the university according to Morley, are usually defined in terms of inadequacies in pitch, intensity, duration, and quality. The pitch may be inappropriate for age, sex, or situation—too high or too low; the intensity may be unsuitable—too soft or too loud; duration of vowels may be too short or too long; there may be harshness or hoarseness; pitch, intensity, or rate may be monotonous. Too much or too little nasal resonance may also be a distracting characteristic of the speaker.

Articulatory Deviations

Disorders of enunciation or articulation involve substitutions, omissions, or distortions of sounds. Of the students with clinical problems in the university, Morley found that 50.7 per cent of them had articulatory inadequacies. Substitutions of one sound for another might be illustrated by the use of /w/ for /r/ as in the "wittle wed wagon" for "little red wagon." You may see someone protruding his tongue when he says "see," resulting in "I *th*ee you" or "Y*eth*, I can go." Omissions of sounds occur frequently at the ends of words. You may be able to say the sounds, but are careless in saying them during speaking or reading. A distorted

---

* Phonetics will be treated in Chapter 8.

speech sound is poorly produced, sometimes approximating the correct sound, and at other times is recognizable as any sound known to the speaker's language. Some unintelligibility of speech may occur through speaking too rapidly with slurring of final consonants and inadequate grouping of thought units. This type of unintelligible speech is sometimes called cluttering.

Inadequacies of Rhythm

Disfluencies may be characterized by (a) interjections of sounds, syllables, words, or phrases; (b) repetitions of part-words, words, or phrases; (c) unvocalized intervals; or (d) prolonged sounds. The severe stutterer may exhibit one or more of these characteristics and also have accompanying overt symptoms such as facial grimaces or handshaking which advertise his awareness of the problem. The stutterer may suffer penalties from society in that some may laugh at him, some may want to help him, and some may feel sorry for him. The person who reacts noticeably and unfavorably to his nonfluencies may need clinical attention. Although the student in a voice and diction class may not give evidence of clinical disfluencies, he may read or speak with irregular or spasmodic rate.

Disorders of Language

"A language deviation," according to the committee on language of the American Speech and Hearing Association, "is a condition in which the child has not acquired the code of his linguistic community or in which the child or adult loses the code after acquiring it."

Disorders of language are usually associated with brain-damaged conditions. The adult who has suffered a stroke or cerebral hemorrhage may lose his ability to speak or to understand language. The child may never learn to talk because of possible neurological damage. If he does talk, some inadequacies in symbolic formulation and expression may occur.

Students in the university will not have major disorders of language. They may, however, have limited vocabulary or inadequate syntactical structures in speech. Verbalization may be excessive or lacking in spontaneity.

SUMMARY

Proficient speech may improve the effective use of any vocational talents which you possess or aid you in making satisfactory social adjustment. Speech is a learned process; it is a form of communication concerned with hearing and speaking an oral language; it is superimposed on physical structures biologically intended for sustenance of life. Approximately 5 per cent of the students in the university may be expected to have clinical speech problems (articulation, voice, rhythm, language); all others, with the exception of possibly 5 to 10 per cent with excellent speech, may profit from some type of speech improvement.

Exercises

1. Prepare a one-minute speech on the possible value of "good" voice and diction to one of the following persons:

a physician	a stenographer
a lawyer	a society woman
a college professor	an army officer
a college student	a teacher
a mother	a saleswoman

2. If a speech clinic is available, visit and listen to the various types of speech deviations. Write a report of your visit with an analysis of the speech you heard.

3. Prepare to read aloud some paragraph in this chapter.
   a. substituting /t/ for /k/, /θ/ for /s/, or /w/ for /r/.
   b. stuttering on all words beginning with /s/.
   c. omitting final consonants.
   d. nasalizing vowels as in h*a*t.

4. Correct the speech irregularities of these sentences. What are the substitutions?
   a. Mawi had a witte wam.
   b. He had a witte wed wagon.
   c. She wanted to do to de sidy.
   d. I thee it on de table.
   e. You goin' to go to de tore.

5. Read the following story aloud. Only one sound is defective, the /s/. Since the /s/ sound is used so frequently in the English spoken language, any deviation may interfere seriously with communication. Note how the one substitution of /θ/ for /s/ affects the speech.

The Lisping Hobo

One morning, a middle-aged man stopped at a farmer's house. He asked Mrs. Brown, the farmer's wife, for some breakfast. Mrs. Brown, thinking the hobo should pay for his breakfast, said, "Did you see that woodpile as you came in?"

The hobo started running. When he got to the gate he stopped and yelled, "Yeth, you thaw me thee it, but you ain't goin' to thee me thaw it."

6. To understand the close association between posture, "state of well being," and speech, try this exercise. Slide down in your chair. Feel sorry for yourself. Then, try to say "My! I feel wonderful! On top of the world!" It would be much easier to say, "Oh my . . . *what* a day!"

7. Read and discuss the following passage concerning the uses of speech:

> The general use of speech is to transfer our mental discourse into verbal, or the train of our thoughts into a train of words, and that for two commodities, whereof one is the registering of the consequences of our thoughts, which, being apt to slip out of our memory and put us to a new labour, may again be recalled by such words as they were marked by. So that the first use of names is to serve for 'marks,' or 'notes,' of remembrance. Another is, when many use the same words to signify by their connection and order one to another what they conceive or think of each matter; and also what they desire, fear, or have any other passion for. And for this use they are called 'signs.' Special uses of speech are these: first, to register what by cogitation we find to be the cause of anything, present or past; and what we find things present or past may produce, or effect; which, in sum, is acquiring of arts. Secondly, to show to others that knowledge which we have attained, which is to counsel and teach one another. Thirdly, to make known to others our wills and purposes, that we may have the mutual help by playing with our words, for pleasure or ornament, innocently.
>
> *Of Man, Being the First Part of Leviathan*
> Thomas Hobbes

8. Read aloud the following passage from "The Golden Sayings of Epictetus". Epictetus was born about the middle of the first century A.D. Discuss the relationship of listening to speaking and how the content of the message and the sincerity of the speaker may affect the listener.

> "Epictetus, I have often come desiring to hear you speak, and you have never given me any answer; now if possible, I entreat you, say something to me."
> "Is there, do you think," replied Epictetus, "an art of speaking as of other things, if it is to be done skillfully and with profit to the hearer?"
> "Yes."
> "And are all profited by what they hear, or only some among them? So that it seems there is an art of hearing as well as of speaking . . . To make a statue needs skill: to view a statue right needs skill also."
> "Admitted."
> "And I think all will allow that one who proposes to hear philosophers speak needs a considerable training in hearing. Is that not so? Then tell me on what subject you are able to hear me."

"Why, on good and evil."

"The good and evil of what? a horse, an ox?"

"No; of a man."

"Do we know then what Man is? what his nature is, what is the idea we have of him? And are our ears practised in any degree on the subject? Nay, do you understand what Nature is? can you follow me in any degree when I say that I shall have to use demonstration? Do you understand what Demonstration is? what True and False is? . . . must I *drive* you to Philosophy? . . . Show me what good I am to do by discoursing with you. Rouse my desire to do so. The sight of the pasture it loves stirs in a sheep the desire to feed; show it a stone or a bit of bread and it remains unmoved. Thus we also have certain natural desires, aye, and one that moves us to speak when we find a listener that is worth his salt: one that himself stirs the spirit. But if he sits by like a stone or a tuft of grass, how can he rouse a man's desire?"

"Then you will say nothing to me?"

"I can only tell you this: that one who knows not who he is and to what end he was born: what kind of world this is and with whom is associated therein; one who cannot distinguish Good and Evil, Beauty and Foulness, . . . Truth and Falsehood, will never follow Reason in shaping his desires and impulses and repulsions, nor yet in assent, denial, or suspension of judgment; but will in one word go about deaf and blind, thinking himself to be somewhat, when he is in truth of no account. Is there anything new in all this? Is not this ignorance the cause of all the mistakes and mischances of men since the human race began? . . ."

"This is all I have to say to you, and even this against the grain. Why? Because you have not stirred my spirit. For what can I see in you to stir me, as a spirited horse will stir a judge of horses? Your body? That you maltreat. Your dress? This is luxurious. Your behavior, your look?—Nothing whatever. When you want to hear a philosopher, do not say, 'You say nothing to me'; only show yourself worthy—or fit to *hear,* and then you will see how you will move the speaker."

9. Read and discuss these "Sayings of Confucius."

   a. "To keep silence to him who has ears to hear is to spill the man. To speak to a man without ears to hear is to spill thy words. Wisdom spills neither man nor word."

   b. "The whole end of speech is to be understood."

   Prepare your own sayings based on information in this chapter.

   c.

   d.

   e.

10. Read the following passages aloud. Discuss each in terms of your reactions.

   a. It is . . . true that in a certain sense the individual is predestined to talk, but that is due entirely to the circumstance that he is born not merely in nature, but in the lap of a society that is certain, reasonably certain, to lead him to its traditions. Eliminate society and there is every reason to believe that he will learn to walk, if, indeed, he survives at all. But it is just as certain that he will never learn to talk, that is, to communicate ideas according to the traditional system of a particular society. Or, again, remove the new born individual from the social environment into which he has come and transplant him to an utterly alien one. He will develop the art of walking in his new environment very much as he would have developed it in the old. But his speech will be completely at variance with the speech of his native environment. Walking, then, is a general human activity that varies only within circumscribed limits as we pass from individual to individual. Its variability is involuntary and purposeless. Speech is human activity that varies without assignable limit as we pass from social group to social group, because it is a purely historical heritage of the group, the product of long-continued social usage. It varies as all creative effort varies—not as consciously, perhaps, but none the less as truly as do the religions, the beliefs, the customs, and the arts of different peoples. Walking is an organic, an instinctive, function (not, of course, itself an instinct); speech is a non-instinctive, acquired "cultural" function.

Edward Sapir*

b. Language is man's greatest invention. It is a social tool more important than the community, the state, the law, the church, or the school. It is an intellectual tool as important as observation and experiment, and more important than logic. It is more important than all the physical tools invented in the last two thousand years. These assertions may well seem extravagant, but they can be justified.

E. L. Thorndike**

c. Animals . . . are one and all without speech. They communicate, of course, but not by any method that can be likened to speaking. They express their emotions and indicate their wishes and control one another's behavior by suggestion. One ape will take another by the hand and drag him into a game or to his bed; he will hold out his hand to beg for food, and will sometimes receive it. But even the highest apes give no indication of speech.

Philosophy in a New Key
Susanne K. Langer

11. Prepare to read the following passage aloud. Discuss in terms of the discussion in this chapter on stage fright.

From Doghouse To Doctorate

I remember taking part in one of those programs when a school was visiting us. I felt as though I had a persimmon in my throat, a dry, green one at that . . . and juiceless. My heart pounded so that

* From Edward Sapir, *Language: An Introduction to the Study of Speech*. New York: Harcourt, Brace & World, Inc., copyright 1921, renewed 1949 by Harcourt, Brace & World, Inc.
** E. L. Thorndike, *Man and His Works*. Cambridge, Mass.: Harvard University Press, 1943.

I felt as though others would hear it, if it didn't break a rib. I chose a selection which some of you might remember, Trowbridge's "Charcoal Man." It was a humdinger . . . for an elocutionist . . . but not for me. It gave every opportunity in the world for maneuvers, but I was rigid as the Charcoal Man on the coldest winter's night. It went something like this:

> Though rudely blows the wintry blast,
> And sifting snows fall thick and fast,
> Mark Haley drives along the street,
> Perched high upon his wagon seat:
> His somber face the storm defies,
> And thus from morn till eve he cries,
>   CHARCO! CHARCO!
> While echo faint and far replies,
>   HARK, O! HARK, O!
> Charco! Hark, O! Such cheery sounds
> Attend him on his daily rounds.

Well, I got through the thing, but I didn't make the most of my opportunity. To some of us, undertaking a recitation on an occasion like that was like trying to fire a bazooka . . . you don't know if it is going to blow up or backfire or explode in front the way it should.

Lee Emerson Bassett*

References

Brown, Charles T. and Charles Van Riper, *Speech and Man*. Englewood Cliffs, N.J.: Prentice-Hall, Inc., 1966.

Davis, Kingsley, "Extreme Social Isolation of a Child," *American Journal of Sociology*, 45 (1940), 556-65.

Fisher, Hilda B., *Improving Voice and Articulation*. Boston: Houghton Mifflin Company, 1966.

Hahn, Elise, Charles W. Lomas, Donald E. Hargis, and Daniel Vandraegen, *Basic Voice Training for Speech*, 2d ed. New York: McGraw-Hill Book Company, 1957.

Irwin, Ruth Beckey, "Teaching a Deaf Child to Talk," *Journal of Speech Disorders*, 9 (1944), 131-33.

Johnson, Wendell, Spencer Brown, Clarence W. Edney, James F. Curtis, and Jacqueline Keaster, *Speech-Handicapped School Children*. New York: Harper & Row, Publishers, 1967.

Johnson, Wendell, *Your Most Enchanted Listener*. New York: Harper &

---

* Given before the Western Speech Association, 1949, by Lee Emerson Bassett, Professor Emeritus, Stanford University. Printed from Mouat's *Guide to Effective Speaking*.

Row, Publishers, 1956.

Mason, Marie K., "Learning to Speak after Six and One-Half Years of Silence," *Journal of Speech Disorders,* 7 (1942), 295-304.

Morley, D. E., "A Ten-Year Survey of Speech Disorders Among University Students," *Journal of Speech and Hearing Disorders,* 17 (1952), 25-31.

Mouat, Lawrence H., *A Guide to Effective Public Speaking.* Boston: D. C. Heath & Company, 1953.

Negus, Sir V. E., *The Mechanism of the Larynx.* London: William Heinemann, Ltd., 1929.

Van Riper, Charles, *Speech Correction Principles and Methods.* Englewood Cliffs, N. J.: Prentice-Hall, Inc., 1963.

2

Standards for Your Speech

"What is the standard for good speech?" or "How do I know whether I am speaking correctly?" These may be questions which you are asking. It is not much wonder that you may be confused somewhat concerning "good" or "correct" speech. On the one hand, you may hear about artistic speech and how to "correct" or "beautify" your speech and voice; others will tell you to "Let your speech alone. Whatever you do is all right. Haven't you always done all right with the speech you have?" These two points of view represent opposite ends of the continuum concerning standards of speaking. As an educated person, you will probably want to find a realistic standard which will fall someplace between these two extreme goals of speech improvement. Standards may involve the consideration of pronunciation, vocal quality, and articulation.

CRITERIA FOR STANDARD SPEECH

Pronunciation, voice, and articulation should be appropriate, intelligible, and nondistracting. "Good" speech is easily understood in terms of loudness, rate, phrasing, and emphasis. The speech is also nondistracting in vocal quality, pitch, loudness, articulation, in rhythm, or any aspect of rate, or language. In addition to specific speech characteristics defining the standards for proficient speech, the effective speaker must please others through visual factors emanating proper enthusiasms, poise, posture, gestures, and facial expressions. An effective speaking voice is produced with the minimum of effort, with the maximum results, and with the most pleasing effect on the listener and observer.

Appropriateness of Speech

Pronunciation, voice, and articulation must be appropriate to the speaker, the speaking situation, the social environment, and the geographical region in which the speaker lives.

The Speaker. Pitch, an attribute of voice, is usually described in terms of its suitability to the speaker's age, sex, and size. A young girl's voice is higher in pitch than the woman's voice; some girls, however, continue to talk like little girls after they reach maturity. When recordings are played back, these individuals might exclaim, "That sounds like a little girl." In some instances, grown daughters and their mothers both sound like little girls.

The male student may also present symptoms of inappropriate pitch; he may sound more like a woman over the telephone than he does like a man. His voice might give evidence of preservation of his boy's voice, although his vocal mechanism is capable of producing a masculine voice. Size is also a factor in the consideration of appropriateness of pitch or intensity. Imagine a husky football player with a weak, breathy voice or a small frail girl with a deep, husky voice.

Voice, articulation, and pronunciation are usually fitting for the occupation or profession to which the speaker belongs. Whether your profession is to be theatre, radio, teaching, engineering, medicine, or law will in a large measure serve as motivation for the cultivation of "good" voice and diction. All educated speakers will probably want speech which is more than acceptable.

If you plan to be a radio announcer or an actor, for example, your voice and diction must definitely meet high standards. The instructor of speech or the speech clinician must know not only the characteristics of "good" speech but how to use speech effectively. The speech clinician is often called upon to give speeches to parents and educators in the community; he is looked upon as "the speech teacher" and consequently expected to portray the very epitome of excellency in speech production. The classroom teacher is also obviously in need of the very best voice and diction possible, since children, particularly in the lower grades, listen to the same teacher several hours each day. In general, the more educated the speaker the more important is a "good" speaking voice with no distracting visual or auditory behavior. As speaking requirements for the educated person increase, so does the necessity for "good" practices in voice, articulation, and pronunciation.

The Speaking Situation. Standards for speech are also determined by the speaking situation. There may be "good" speech for (a) informal conversation, (b) formal conversation, (c) public speaking, (d) radio and television, (e) theatre, and (f) oral reading. Four principal styles of good spoken English for practical purposes are designated by Kenyon: familiar colloquial, formal colloquial, public speaking, and public reading. The various levels of usage, disregarding effects of differences due to geographical regions or occupational fields, are represented by Fries* in Figure 2. The figure may be interpreted through use of the following explanation.

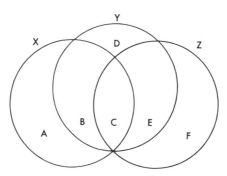

Figure 2. Usage levels and dialect distribution (from Charles C. Fries, *The American College Dictionary,* Clarence Barnhard, ed., New York: Random House, 1951, p. xxx).

> X—formal literary English, the words, the expressions, and the structures one finds in serious books.
>
> Y—colloquial English, the words, expressions, and the structures of the informal but polite conversation of cultivated people.
>
> Z—illiterate English, the words, the expressions, and the structures of the language of the uneducated.
>
> B, C, and E represent the overlappings of the three types of English.
>
> C—that which is common to all three: formal literary English, colloquial English, and illiterate English.

* From Charles C. Fries, "Usage Levels and Dialect Distribution," *The American College Dictionary,* Clarence Barnhard (ed.). New York: Random House, 1951, p. xxx.

B—that which is common to both formal literary English and colloquial English.

E—that which is common to both colloquial English and illiterate English.

A, D, and F represent those portions of each type of English that are peculiar to that particular set of language habits.

In general, speech for informal speech situations does not require the rigid patterns often necessary for formalized speaking. The public speaker, for example, will usually find that speech is effective when spoken in short phrases, long pauses, clear-cut articulation, and with a variety of inflection, intensity, and pitch. The casual speaker can usually be understood with less effort than the public speaker is required to use. Consequently, the student of voice and diction may need to learn how to speak in various types of speaking situations.

The Social Environment. Poverty and isolation from educated persons will affect the speech and language. People living in culturally and economically deprived areas will probably continue to use public language and speech which is adequate for the community in which they live. These people, however, will need to learn a formal type of speech and language if they expect to move from their social group to another.

Geographical Region. Your speech and language must be appropriate for the region in which you live. A standard dialect refers to the most acceptable speech or that spoken by the best educated people of a large geographical dialectal region. "Dialect," as used here, refers to the common features of the most acceptable speech of any group of people living in one large geographical area. The three traditional regions of pronunciation as represented in Figure 3 of the United States are Eastern, Southern, and General American.

The ten major areas of dialectal pronunciation, as defined by Thomas, are presented in Figure 4 as Eastern New England, New York City, Middle Atlantic, Southern, Western Pennsylvania, Southern Mountain Central Midland, Northwest, Southwest, and North Central. Lack of communication with others may limit opportunity for hearing standard speech of any large area. The people living, for example, in the Ozarks or the Appalachian Mountains often have characteristic dialects of their own.

The diversity of speech patterns in the various areas of the United States may be illustrated by a passage from *The Grapes of Wrath:*

"I knowed you wasn't Oklahomy folks. You talk queer kinda—
That ain't no blame, you understand."

Figure 3. The three major regions of dialectal pronunciation as observed before 1940.

Figure 4. The ten major regions of dialectal pronunciation: A: Eastern New England, B: New York City, C: Middle Atlantic, D: Southern, E: Western Pennsylvania, F: Southern Mountain, G. Central Midland, H: Northwest, I: Southwest, J: North Central (after Charles K. Thomas, *An Introduction to the Phonetics of American English*, 2nd ed., The Ronald Press Company, 1958, p. 232).

"Ever'body says words different," said Ivy. "Arkansas folks says
'em different, and Oklahomy folks says 'em different. And we seen
a lady from Massachusetts, an' she said 'em differentest of all.
Couldn' hardly make out what she was sayin."

The Grapes of Wrath
John Steinbeck

Visitors who use General American dialect often have difficulty in
understanding directions as spoken by natives. For example, do you
understand the following directions on how to reach the historic Adams
home in Boston?

You sawr an old white bann back theyah? Turn right. That'll take
you to Quincy Squahah. Turn again at a morden bank building and
you ott to be able to pack your ka. You wunt get lost again.

"Charlestonese" words also give trouble to the visitor to the historic
city of Charleston, West Virginia. The following words and their definitions are among those prepared by Ashley Cooper of the *News & Courier:*
air, what you hear with; beckon, meat from a pig and often eaten with
aigs for brakefuss; mine eyes, salad dressing; snow, to breathe loudly
and heavily while sleeping.

The large colonial groups determined somewhat the speech styles of
the various areas of the United States. People who came from the South
of England, for example, did not pronounce their /r's/ so the early
settlers in New England were influenced to omit the prevocalic and post-
vocalic /r/ in their speech. Those who came from the counties in North
England and later from Ireland and Scotland spoke words retaining the
/r/ sounds. These people settled in areas of the United States now using
General American speech. Although the speech of the early settlers had
great influence on the development of the styles of speech in the United
States, the influence of England is no longer as great as it once was. At
first, an attempt was made to standardize the speech according to that
spoken by the eastern settlers.

Certain factors work for similarities in speaking styles. Radio, television, cinema, and travel are influencing speech patterns. The prepon-
derance of General American speech used by speakers on radio and
television will undoubtedly tend to work toward some uniform standard
of speech in the United States. Since speech is learned by hearing speech,
General American speech may be learned by the majority of listeners.
Travel from one state to another also affects the speaker. Transportation,
particularly since World War II, has increased opportunities for movements and assimilations of peoples all over the United States. Certain
groups, however, remain in relatively confined communities and tend to

retain their dialectal pronunciations. The Pennsylvania Germans, the Milwaukee Germans, the French Canadians in New England, the Louisiana French or Cajun of the Gulf area, the Orientals in the large urban centers, the Mexicans in the Southeast, and the Negroes in the South may have specific speech characteristics because of the somewhat isolated environments where the language of a particular group is "locked in." In spite of several factors interfering with the development of uniform pronunciations in the United States, it would seem that a standard speech is arising spontaneously from the people rather than being imposed upon them as was attempted in the early day.

Intelligible Speech

Probably the most important single factor necessary for standard speech is intelligibility or understandability. A speaker must be heard and easily understood if the message is to be received. Such intelligibility involves the adequate use of vocal intensity, precise articulation of consonants, suitable rate of speaking, appropriate phrasing and emphasis.

Nondistracting Speech

Articulation and voice should be nondistracting to the listener in terms of vocal quality, pitch, intensity, production of specific sounds, rhythm, and language. Vocal quality should not call attention to itself because of hoarseness, harshness, or breathiness. Pitch should not be too high or too low; intensity should not be too loud or too soft. Specific sounds should be produced in such a way as not to distract the majority of the listeners. Rhythm that is staccato or irregular will be distracting; repetitious sounds, words, or phrases also attract undue attention to the speaker. The choice of words, the inadequate structure of sentences, and the poor use of grammar are factors which may be distracting to the listener. Speech inadequacies have been discussed in Chapter 1.

Visual Factors

Accompanying speaking are such visual factors as bodily activity, posture, facial expressions, and gestures. Effective speaking involves more than the mere movement of the lips and the tensing of the vocal folds. In all types of speaking, the body acts as a whole to convey the poise and enthusiasm of the speaker. Effective bodily action occurs as the result of the speaker's personality and experience in speaking, his ideas, and the reactions of his audience to his speaking.

Posture, facial expressions, bodily movements, and gestures will depend upon your sex, age, formality of the situation, nature of communication, and your intellectual and emotional involvement in the communication. In public performances the inexperienced speaker will want to assume a comfortable and natural standing posture which allows for ease of movements. Standing with arms and hands to the side of the body allows for freedom of action. All gestures need to be natural, unobtrusive, definite, and motivated by an idea.

Some of the "do nots" in posture are (a) do not stand on too wide a base, (b) do not teeter back and forth as you speak, (c) do not lean toward the audience, (d) do not lean backward, (e) do not keep hands in pockets continuously or folded in front of you, and (f) do not fiddle with fingers, keys, money, or jewelry. In general, visual factors should not detract from the communicative process.

SUBSTANDARD SPEECH

Substandard speech may be defined as that speech which does not meet the criteria described above for standard speech. In other words, substandard speech may be (a) inappropriate for the speaker, the speaking situation, the social environment, or the geographical region; (b) unintelligible; and (c) distracting. Substandard speech is usually spoken by uneducated or culturally disadvantaged people. Within each of the large dialectal regions are pronunciations which identify a person as belonging to a specific city or part of a state. Consequently, his pronunciation is often conspicuous when he moves to another part of the same general dialectal area. "Sub-cultural language," according to the committee on language of the American Speech and Hearing Association, "refers to any acquired linguistic code which is not in correspondence with the standards of the dominant linguistic code of the community."

Unusually rapid speech with slurring of words may cause your speech to be unintelligible and thereby substandard. You may be able to say each of the consonants but you do not do so in your rapid speech. Adding to this unintelligibility is the lack of phrasing or pausing between thought units.

Some of you may have difficulty in the production of such sounds as /r, l, θ, s, z/ or you may not be able to differentiate between the way you say the /ɑ/ as in f*a*ther and the /ɔ/ as in *a*ll. Such deviations may interfere with communication and may contribute to the evaluation of your speech as substandard. Although your speech may be intelligible as far as articulation is concerned, the vocal factors of pitch, intensity, or quality may not meet the standard criteria. Further attention will be given to standards of pronunciation in Chapter 11.

SUMMARY

In this chapter, the standards for good speech have been discussed. An effective speaking voice, which is appropriate, intelligible, and unobtrusive, is produced with the minimum of effort, with the maximum results, and the most pleasing effect on the listener. To achieve this efficient speech, you will want to strive toward the following criteria:

1. Appropriateness of speech for speaker, the speaking situation, the social situation, and the general geographical region.

2. Intelligibility of speech in terms of loudness, rate, phrasing, and emphasis.

3. Nondistracting speech and vocal characteristics.

Substandard speech refers to that speech which does not meet the particular criteria outlined above. It is speech which may not be appropriate, may be unintelligible, or may be distracting to the listener.

Trends in the development of a general speaking standard appear to be growing spontaneously from the people themselves. The tendency toward the use of General American speech is influenced by the large numbers of people speaking General American speech and by the radio and television. The ease with which people move from one area to another tends to lead to common speech habits. Some influences, however, will continue to mitigate against the attainment of a universal standard of speech: racial and national groups, impoverished peoples, and geographical isolation.

You will want to strive to develop the best speech spoken by the educated people of the region in which you live. Your speech standards will vary according to professional goals and speaking situations. Specific characteristics of "good" speech include a pleasing vocal quality, understandability, appropriate pronunciation and diction, adequate intensity, suitable pitch, flexibility, and animation. Good speech is free from any noticeable deviations in articulation, voice, or rhythm.

Exercises

1. Discuss how each of the following conditions have influenced your speech:
   a. the place where you live,
   b. your education,

c. your travels,

d. early speech training in your home,

e. other factors.

2. Discuss the pros and cons of a standard pronunciation for America.

3. Explain the meaning of the following statement: "There are different standards for speech according to the uses made of speech."

4. Define the following terms: speech intelligibility, articulation, voice, diction, enunciation, and pronunciation.

5. Read the following passages as you would to a (a) small informal audience, (b) small formal audience, (c) large informal gathering, and (d) large formal group. How do vocal patterns and bodily activity vary with each?

> a. And now ye shall hear from me a plain extemporary speech, but so much the truer. Nor would I have ye think it like the rest of Orators, made for the Ostentation of Wit; for these, as ye know, when they have been beating their heads some thirty years about an Oration, and at last perhaps produce somewhat that was never their own, shall yet swear they compos'd it in three days, and that too for diversion: whereas I ever lik't it best to speak whatever came first out.
>
> *The Praise of Folly*
> Desiderius Erasmus

> b. Today the guns are silent. A great tragedy has ended. A great victory has been won. The skies no longer rain death—the seas bear only commerce—men everywhere walk upright in the sunlight. The entire world is quietly at peace.
>
> *The Surrender of Japan,*
> September 2, 1945
> Douglas MacArthur

> c. Build thee more stately mansions, O my soul,
> As the swift seasons roll!
>
> *The Chambered Nautilus*
> Oliver Wendell Holmes

> d. He who knows and knows that he knows,
> He is wise; follow him.
>
> *Arabian Proverb*
> Anonymous

6. Talk on any topic using one of the following styles: (a) familiar colloquial, (b) formal colloquial, or (c) public speaking.

7. Read the following passage and discuss in terms of speech standards.

> Usage remains to be discussed. For it would be almost laughable to prefer the language of the past to that of the present day, and what is ancient speech but ancient usage of speaking? But even here the critical faculty is necessary, and we must make up our minds

what we mean by usage. If it be defined merely as the practice of the majority, we shall have a very dangerous rule affecting not merely style but life as well, a far more serious matter. For where is so much good to be found that what is right should please the majority? The practices of depilation, of dressing the hair in tiers, or of drinking to excess at the baths, although they may have thrust their way into society cannot claim the support of usage, since there is something to blame in all of them (although we have usage on our side when we bathe or have our hair cut or take our meals together). So too in speech we must not accept as a rule of language words and phrases that have become a vicious habit with a number of persons. To say nothing of the language of the uneducated, we are all of us well aware that whole theatres and the entire crowd of spectators will often commit *barbarisms* in the cries which they utter as one man. I will therefore define usage in speech as the agreed practice of educated men, just as where our way of life is concerned I should define it as the agreed practice of all good men.

Institutes of Oratory
Quintilian

8. Read and be prepared to discuss the factors which may contribute to substandard speech.

What then is the duty of the teacher whom we have borrowed from the stage? In the first place he must correct all faults of pronunciation, and see that the utterance is distinct, and that each letter has its proper sound. There is an unfortunate tendency in the case of some letters to pronounce sufficiently, substituting others whose sound is similar but somewhat duller. For instance, *lambda* is substituted for *rho,* a letter which was always a stumbling-block to Demosthenes; our *l* and *r* have of course the same value.* Similarly when *c* and *g* are not given their full value, they are softened into *t* and *d*. Again our teacher must not tolerate the affected pronunciation of *s*** with which we are painfully familiar, nor suffer words to be uttered from the depths of the throat or rolled out hollow-mouthed, or permit the natural sound of the voice to be over-laid with a fuller sound, a fault fatal to purity of speech; the Greeks give this peculiarity the name (plastered over), a term applied to the tone produced by a pipe, when the stops which produce the treble notes are closed, and a bass note is produced through the main aperture only. He will also see that final syllables are not clipped, that the quality of speech is continuously maintained, but when the voice is raised, the strain falls upon the lungs and not the mouth, and that gesture and voice are mutually appropriate. He will also insist that the speaker faces the audience, that the lips are not distorted nor the jaws parted to a grin, that the face is not thrown back, nor the eyes fixed on the

---

* The misspelling of *flagro* as *fraglo* exemplifies the confusion to which Quintilian refers.

**Quintilian perhaps alludes to the habit of prefixing *i* to initial *st, sp, sc* found in inscriptions of the later Empire.

ground, nor the neck slanted to left or right. For there are a variety of faults of facial expression. I have seen many, who raised their brows whenever the voice was called upon for an effort, others who wore a perpetual frown, and yet others who could not keep their eyebrows level, but raised one towards the top of the head and depressed the other till it almost closed the eye. These are details, but as I shall shortly show, they are of enormous importance, for nothing that is unbecoming can have a pleasing effect.

Institutes of Oratory
Quintilian

9. In the following exercises, try to coordinate speech with total bodily activity. Start first with pantomimic action, then add speech appropriate for the character and action.

  a. Walk across the classroom
    1. in your own way,
    2. as an old man,
    3. as a model showing off an evening wrap,
    4. as a football player in his uniform,
    5. as a fat woman or man in a hurry.

  b. Without words, convey to the audience what you mean by the following:
    1. I implore you.
    2. No, not for you.
    3. Horrible, horrible.
    4. I am King!
    5. Justice must be done!

  c. Read the words in Exercise b and use total bodily action.

  d. Using bodily activity, read the following lines:
    To bed, to bed! there's knocking at the gate.
    Come, come, come, come, give me your hand.
    What's done cannot be undone. To bed, to
    bed, to bed!

Macbeth
William Shakespeare

Macbeth's Vision

Macbeth: Is this a dagger which I see before me,
    The handle toward my hand? Come, let me clutch thee:
    I have thee not, and yet I see thee still.
    Art thou not, fatal vision, sensible
    To feeling as to sight; or art thou but
    A dagger of the mind, a false creation,
    Proceeding from the heat-oppressed brain?
    I see thee yet, in form as palpable
    As this which now I draw.

Macbeth
William Shakespeare

10. The following passage from Basset's "From Doghouse to Doctorate"*
will provide an opportunity for you to practice the use of bodily activity
in speaking.

> ... I attended a program given by a middle-aged lady of good
> proportions, who had learned some poems and things. I remember
> one was about the troublesome corn she had. During her reading
> she sat down on the stage, took off her shoe, and rubbed her foot,
> groaning all the time and complaining about that corn. I heard
> another reader in Los Angeles, in the auditorium before a large
> audience ... I forgot what the occasion was, but this young lady
> came out in a diaphanous garment that looked like the garb of a
> Halloween fairy. She recited, of all things, "The Splendor Falls on
> Castle Walls." She did it this way ... and I am not exaggerating
> (faintly in a light, high singsong manner with arm moving a descrip-
> tive gesticulation throughout).
>
>> The splendor falls on castle walls
>>   And snowy summits old in story;
>> The long light shakes across the lakes,
>>   And the wild cantaract leaps in glory.
>> Blow, bugles, blow, set the wild echoes flying
>> Blow, bugle; answer, echoes, dying, dying, dying.
>>   (M-m-m-mm, faint, and fainter, with hand cupped
>>   to ear for intent listening attitude)
>
> Now that sort of thing shocked people of culture and taste, yes,
> and common sense. The term "elocution" was anathema among
> people concerned with genuine education. That can be readily
> understood. So far as colleges and universities were concerned the
> exhibitionist and attitudiner was in the doghouse. We can respect
> them for that attitude, but it was tough on those who recognized
> the value of training in honest and sincere utterance and the disci-
> pline that brings skill. If not all were in the doghouse together, all
> were under suspicion, even the best.

References*

Bronstein, Arthur J., *The Pronunciation of American English* (An Introduction to Phonetics). New York: Appleton-Century-Crofts, 1960.
Carrell, James and William R. Tiffany, *Phonetics: Theory and Application
to Speech Improvement.* New York: McGraw-Hill Book Company, 1960.

---

* From Mouat's *Guide to Effective Public Speaking,* pp. 249-250.
* Here and subsequently some of the references of an earlier chapter are
applicable. However, a standard textbook in one of the academic areas treated
in the present book is cited only one time. The reader is urged to read as many
treatments of each topic as possible.

Fries, Charles C., "Usage Levels and Dialect Distribution," *The American College Dictionary,* Clarence Barnhard (ed). New York: Random House, Inc., 1951.

Gray, Giles W. and Claude M. Wise, *The Bases of Speech,* 3d ed. New York: Harper & Row, Publishers, 1959.

Kantner, Claude E. and Robert West, *Phonetics,* rev. ed. New York: Harper & Row, Publishers, 1960.

Kenyon, John S. and T. A. Knott, *A Pronuncing Dictionary of American English.* Springfield, Mass.: G. & C. Merriam Company, Publishers, 1944.

————, *American Pronunciation,* Ann Arbor, Michigan: George Wahr, Publisher, 1935.

Thomas, Charles K., *An Introduction to the Phonetics of American English.* New York: The Ronald Press Company, 1958.

3

Modifying Your Speech Behavior

Quintilian (A.D. 35-95), a famous Spanish-born Roman rhetorician, said that speech training should begin at birth and continue throughout life. Much emphasis was placed upon speaking ability during that period. A young man's success in public affairs often hinged upon his oratorical ability. Throughout the years, speech has held varying degrees of importance according to changing educational goals. The importance of speech proficiency has increased as radio and television have become accessible to the general public and as education has become more widespread.

The aim of education is not necessarily learning for the sake of learning but rather for the utilization of knowledge and skills for solving the fundamental problems of human existance. If speech is to be useful, it must be an effective medium for helping the individual to use his abilities, adjust and cooperate with others, earn a living, and to control his environment. Speech which is free from noticeable deviations or substandard diction and pronunciation is desirable for the most effective use of speech. Success in various vocations and social activities is often mentioned in relationship to good speech.

Since speech is a learned process as indicated in Chapter 1, it is assumed that new habits may be learned or old undesirable ones may be changed for new patterns of speech or behavior. Speech is learned through various sensory avenues: auditory, visual, and kinesthetic. Through hearing, the speaker obtains standard patterns for sound production or pronunciation of words. As he produces the sound or word, the speaker listens to himself and compares his sound with the production as heard spoken by someone else. If the sound appears different, he may try to change his production.

The speaker also visually observes the functioning of the articulatory mechanisms in the production of sounds as another speaker produces them. With the use of a mirror, he may compare his production of the sound with that of his model and make any necessary corrections. The kinesthetic avenue of perception may provide some help if changes from old patterns are necessary. After the change is made, the speaker may indicate that the sound does not feel right; but he needs to learn how the production feels in order for it to sound right to the listener. In time, the feeling seems right during the accurate acoustic production of the sound.

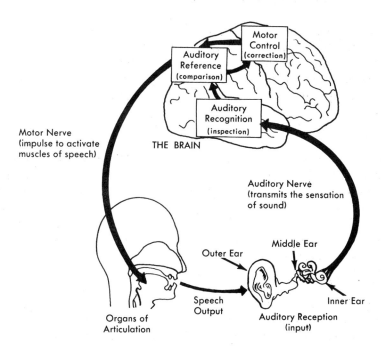

Figure 5. The auditory feedback loop (after Hilda B. Fisher, *Improving Voice and Articulation*, Houghton-Mifflin Company, 1966).

The auditory feedback loop is illustrated in Figure 5. As the subject says "wed" instead of "red," for example, the sound waves are conveyed to his ear through the air and by bone conduction. The message is conveyed to an area in the brain where he recognizes the word as he said it (audition). Under normal learning conditions, the subject would hear the sound as he actually produced it ("wed" instead of "red"). He would also be aware of tactile and kinesthetic factors involved in the production of the sound, such as the rounding of the lips for /w/ instead of the movement of the tongue for /r/ (tactition). He might also be aware of the pressure used by the lips to form the /w/ (kinesthetic sensation). Following this inspection by the "normal" subject or one who has had speech therapy, comparisons of his production of "wed" will be made with his internalized model of "red" which is the preferable pronunciation. The next step in the corrective process occurs when impulses are sent to the subject's articulatory mechanisms to articulate "red" instead of "wed."

FACTORS AFFECTING SPEECH IMPROVEMENT

The prognosis for speech improvement is dependent upon a number of factors. Obviously adequate intelligence and the normal functioning neurological and structural mechanisms are important. If you expect to achieve noticeable improvement in speech proficiency, you also need motivation to improve an adequate personal adjustment.

Motivation

Without a desire to improve articulation, voice, or pronunciation you cannot be successful. Motivations will vary from individual to individual according to his needs and abilities. As a student, you may be motivated to change your pronunciation or inflection. Others may not accept your speech. In fact, many may ridicule you. One of the strongest motivators is the need to be like your peers; you may want to talk as others in your general linguistic community do.

You may be a student who has been advised to improve your voice or eliminate some articulatory deviation if you are to continue your studies. It depends on how much you want to be a doctor, a teacher, or a business man whether changing your speaking habits will be worth the effort. In some instances, poor speech may interfere with obtaining a position. The student should have many reasons for improving his speech.

For those who are not students, there are also many possible motivations. The mother, for example, may want to improve her speech or voice so as to be a good speaking model for her children. The housewife may need to improve her communicative skills in order to earn a living. Sometimes, general self-improvement is enough motivation for some adults to work on speech improvement.

Personal Adjustment

It is assumed that the type of person you are may have some effect upon the kind of speech and voice you have. Personal factors may affect intelligibility, rate of speaking, intensity, pitch, resonance, and quality of the voice. Tensions may be reflected in the pitch of your voice or the rate at which you speak. If you are a fearful person or feel insecure in speaking situations, you may speak too quietly to be heard. Your voice may be breathy. If you are tense or an unusually aggressive type of person, your voice may give evidence of harshness.

The improvement of personal and social adjustment tends to have a favorable effect upon speech and voice; improvement in speech also affects the attitude and personal adjustments of the individual. Intelligible speech and a pleasant voice tend to elicit favorable reactions from the listener. As speech improves, the speaker may observe that others react more favorably to him. Improved speech may lead to improved attitudes and behavior since listeners are reinforcing the speech with attention. This reaction may be in marked contrast to his behavior as a listener when the speaker's skills were inadequate. In many instances of vocal inadequacies, vocal training and speech rehabilitation need to progress concurrently with attention to social and personal adjustment if any lasting results are to be achieved in the improvement of the speaking voice.

Positive Attitude. The positive attitude is one in which you recognize that you can do something to change your speech if you so desire. "I can" or "I will" should be the general attitudes toward speech improvement rather than "I can't," or "I never could talk," or "This is the way I'm supposed to talk." The positive attitude is represented by working toward realistic goals constructively in an active way. A strong motivation to improve your speech will also affect your attitudes positively. You must want to speak better; you must believe that it is important to speak effectively; and you must have faith in the ultimate success of your program in speech improvement if followed conscientiously under the guidance of your instructor.

Negative feelings involving rationalizations or defensiveness for your present speech will only result in failure. Fear of speaking will result. A positive attitude toward yourself, your speech, and the speaking situation will help to reduce your anxiety about speaking. To speak effectively, fear must be reduced to the minimum since the vocal mechanisms cannot function adequately if the muscles are tensed through fear. The more severe the stage fright, the more numerous and stronger are the symptoms of fear.

Knowing what takes place during speaking may aid the speaker to change or reduce the symptoms of stage fright which are listed in Chapter 1. It is encouraging to know that a certain amount of fear or anxiety is normal and felt by almost all speakers. You may reduce your fear of speaking by knowing your subject well, by being interested in the topic, being interested in the listeners, and repeating your speaking experiences.

An interesting and familiar topic should result in reducing your fear of the speaking situation. Suppose, for example, that you were asked unexpectedly to give a five-minute talk to your class on a topic not familiar to you. Would you experience more fear in this situation than if you were to talk to the class in voice and diction on your major study in the university? The chances are that you would feel quite uncomfortable in the first situation. Anxiety would be increased with an audience of strangers who appeared hostile.

Eye contact will help you to establish more effective communication with your audience. As you improve your communication with the listener through eye contact and bodily movement, your tensions during the speaking process will diminish. For each repeated speaking experience, you will also find a reduction in your anxiety.

Remembering that no two speech experiences are really alike may help to reduce anxiety. Neither you nor your listeners are the same today as you were yesterday. You may, however, talk to the class in much the same way and with the same fears as you did several years earlier. The concept that no two situations ever remain the same is illustrated in Figure 6.

Substituting positive action and thoughts for negative behavior may result in feelings of security. Assume, for example, that you are president of a large university. How would you say, "How are you?" Now try to assume that you are a poorly paid clerk in a grocery store. Say again, "How are you?" Do you note any difference in your attitude, speech, or behavior?

Objective Attitude. An objective attitude refers to your ability to observe events as they really are, not as your emotional reactions cause you to see, hear, or think. An objective attitude in regard to your speech will contribute much to your success in the improvement of speech.

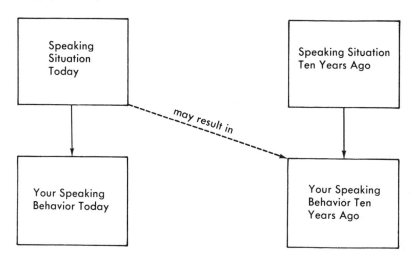

Figure 6. Speaking behaviors change with speaking situations.

Objectivity will assist you in accepting constructive criticism from others, recognizing realistically your own speech needs, and facing speaking situations unemotionally.

You may fall within or above the normal range of acceptability in speech proficiency. If you do not, are you willing to recognize and accept your possible need for speech improvement? Can you face your problems objectively, devoid of emotional factors such as rationalization, defensiveness, or resistance?

Your Objectives. Your general objectives in speech improvement are (a) to learn about speech and the structures used in speaking, (b) to improve intelligibility or understandability of your speech, (c) to develop speech appropriate to the standard of the general speech community in which you live, (d) to eliminate or reduce the distracting speech behaviors, and (e) to learn how to use speech skills effectively in various types of speaking situations. You will want to develop general criteria for evaluating speech of others (Chapter 2). Specific goals for yourself may be formulated with the aid of your instructor following the analysis of your speech needs.

Speech improvement usually occurs as the result of certain sequential steps, although some may overlap. These periods of speech improvement are as follows: (a) appraisal of speech behavior, (b) acquisition of basic information, (c) improving perceptual skills (auditory, visual, and kinesthetic), (d) acquiring speech proficiency, (e) habituating improved characteristics of speech in various types of speaking situations.

Appraisal of Speech Behavior

Discovering your speech needs and abilities is the first step in the speech improvement program. At the beginning of the program in speech improvement, information concerning your attitudes, speech and vocal skills, auditory perceptual abilities, intelligibility, and pronunciation are desirable. A questionnaire concerned with your speech experiences and attitudes toward these experiences may help in analyzing your present feelings toward the improvement of your speech. Though instructors will differ in procedures and tests used, suggested materials are contained in the Appendixes.

Your instructor will probably evaluate your voice, articulation, language, rhythm, and behavior in several types of speaking situations. Auditory perceptual skills will be considered. How well do you hear as measured by pure-tone audiometry? How adequately can you identify or discriminate among various speech sounds or voices? Some of the same tests may be repeated again at the end of your program of speech improvement. Such procedures will provide concrete evidence of your progress and needs for continuing practice.

Acquisition of Basic Information

Basic information is needed in the speech processes, the linguistic environment, and speech sounds.

Speech Processes. An understanding of the six "shuns" (audi*tion,* respira*tion,* phona*tion,* resona*tion,* articula*tion,* and pronuncia*tion*), will aid in the development of speech proficiency. Detailed discussion of the physiological and physical bases of speech is presented in Chapters 4 to 8. You need to study these chapters carefully in order to understand how (a) tone is produced in the larynx; (b) tone becomes speech through resonance; (c) pitch, time, loudness, and quality affect the effectiveness of the speaking voice; (d) articulation of consonants and vowels is affected by movement of lips, mouth, and soft palate; and (e) hearing is related to speech. An understanding of these processes will facilitate your insight and self-improvement.

Although the mechanisms you use for speech production may be without organic defects, the most effective use of expiration, vocal folds, resonating cavities, and articulatory mechanisms in the production of speech is dependent upon a number of factors. Learning how to superimpose speech on the outgoing breath stream often requires much practice for some students. Adequate breath support to initiate tone in the vocal folds is part of the task of learning to use breath efficiently for speech.

Proper posture places the larynx in a position for the most effective production of voice. Try saying "This is a fine day," for example, in a slouch-sitting position with jaw protruding so the throat is tense. The voice is likely to sound "tight" and unpleasant. Now stand at the door with body and back of head touching the edge of the opening. Walk away with body at ease but in position. Try again to say, "This is a fine day." Is it not easier to produce pleasing vocal quality on the second trial?

A third element making for the effective use of the vocal mechanism on the production of pleasing quality is relaxation. The best relaxation is that which comes as the result of personal adjustment rather than being artificially imposed. The practice, however, of differential relaxation often provides an opportunity for the student to compare states of tension with those of relaxation. For example, you could imagine that you are lifting a heavy load. Feel the tensions in your body. Now let go! Feel the "letting go" in contrast to the previous tenseness. If you try to talk during the relaxed and tense states, you will notice the different effects on your voice. With practice, the student can learn to assume voluntarily a relaxed state conducive to best speaking.

Another element for effective speaking might be described in terms of effort or energy. To avoid inarticulate or "lazy-lipped" speech, the speaker will often need to make the effort to move his articulatory mechanisms. Such attention to the articulators plus added breath pressure will result in increased efficiency of the speaking voice.

Linguistic Environment. Some knowledge and understanding of the various linguistic environments, as discussed in Chapters 2 and 11, will serve as guides for making any desirable changes in order to conform to the "standard" used by the best educated people of your general community.

If you live in Ohio, for example, you will want to listen to General American speech as spoken by the educated population. If an analysis of diction identifies you too definitely with a certain section of the state, steps should be taken to adopt acceptable speech patterns of the general linguistic community. The student who lives in one region and goes to school in another general dialectal region will notice differences in his speech. If he expects to return to his home to live, his goal should be to develop the best speech suitable for his native dialectal community.

Speech Sounds. The International Phonetic Alphabet is a tool for the study of voice and diction. In addition to the study of the symbols of speech sounds, you will learn how the individual sounds are made. Consider, for example, the articulatory mechanisms involved in the produuction of /f/: the lower lip is moved upward toward the upper teeth and air is blown over the lip; no voice is used.

Through the study and application of phonetics, you may learn to hear your own speech more accurately, recognize unsatisfactory speech patterns of others, hear differences between pleasant and unpleasant voices, improve your speech without affectation, and use the pronouncing dictionaries. Phonetics will also serve as a continuing aid throughout life in the maintenance of speech proficiency. Detailed study of the speech sounds is presented in later chapters.

Improving Perceptual Skills

Although auditory skills are usually considered the most important of all the sensory avenues in the perception of speech, you will want to consider also the values of kinesthetic and visual feedbacks. Critical listening, feeling, and watching will aid in comparing productions of sounds with standard patterns. If your production is not similar, you may need to change. As you produce the sound or vocal pattern, try to feel what happens. Compare this with what you learn is the "right" way to produce the sound. With the use of the mirror or some visual feedback from your instructor or friend, you may utilize the visual aspects of the production in your analysis, comparison, and correction.

In the early stages of your speech improvement program, you will probably need guidance from your instructor in the evaluation of your speech production. Record your speech. While playing back the recording, listen to your speech critically. During the next recording, try to improve your production.

In the world of radio and television, spoken word prevails as a constant stimulus to the listener. Much of the audible stimulation, however, is not perceived by the auditor. Although words are heard and comprehended, the nondiscriminating listener does not observe the differences which differentiate "good" speech from "poor" speech. One of the early goals in your speech improvement program is to develop discriminating listening. As you learn to listen critically, you will hear variations among speech sounds and voices more effectively.

How effectively do you use the mechanisms for hearing? Does your ear tell you when voices are nasal, harsh, low-pitched, or pleasant? Can you hear, for example, the difference between an /æ/ as in cat and the /ɑ/ as in cot? The study of phonetics will add to your ability to hear these speech-sound differences. Not until you are a discriminating listener to the speech of others will you be able to evaluate your own speech effectively. You may observe that someone talks differently from you. How? In what way? You may, for example, be aware that you are the only one among your friends who uses the vowel /ɑ/ in f*a*ther or John. The others use the /ɔ/ to rhyme with jaw or taught. Which sounds are usually spoken in your linguistic community?

Acquiring Speech Proficiency

Your goals may involve the improvement of one or more of the following: your pronunciation, articulation of sounds, intelligibility, or voice.

Improving Your Pronunciation. Your instructor will help you to decide about changes you should make in your pronunciation. From your study of Chapter 2, you may have decided that your present speech is substandard for the general linguistic community in which you live. If you expect to live and work in one of the standard dialectal regions different from the one in which you learned your present speech, you may feel the need to learn to use the diction and pronunciation of the adopted community.

The constant influence of the spoken language will have an effect upon your speech without your awareness. One graduate student who came from Alabama to Ohio had excellent speech according to Southern Standard speech, but her speech sounded definitely out of place in Ohio. Without any conscious attempt on her part, her speech gradually lost many of its characteristic southern speech patterns. This student later moved to California. If she were to move back to Alabama, her family and friends would no doubt notice many changes in her speech.

Additional help on improving your standard of speaking will be found in the chapters on speech sounds and pronunciation. Improvement of pronunciation hinges on your ability to hear and apply phonetic differences to your own speech. The use of phonetic dictionaries will also guide you in learning cultivated colloquial English pronunciation which is acceptable to your standard dialectal region. You are cautioned to read the introduction in the dictionary carefully before incorporating any specific pronunciation in your speech. Akin writes that "early realization that there is not complete agreement on pronunciation among lexicographers should help the learner to be tolerant when he hears a pronunciation that differs from his."

Improving Specific Articulatory and Vocal Skills. Students with major speech or vocal inadequacies will need to see a specialist for treatment. The specialized therapy required for such treatment is beyond the scope of this book. An instructor can usually refer persons needing such assistance to the proper source.

For any one speech skill, a series of steps must be mastered. In general, you might expect to establish new speech or vocal patterns in the following sequential steps: (a) in an isolated sound or syllable, (b) in a word containing the sound practiced in the first step, (c) in a phrase containing the same word, (d) in a sentence, (e) in a paragraph or verse, (f) in a written form of speech (unemotional), (g) in a written form of speech (emotional), (h) in conversational forms of speech (unemotional), (i) in a conversational form of speech (emotional), and (j) in everyday conversation with automatic application of skills.

Regular periods for practice of speech exercises should be established. Two or three fifteen-minute periods each day will be better for learning new habits than a longer period. Working on one problem at a time in any speech exercise is enough. According to the analysis, your voice, for example, may be breathy; the /s/ sound may be hissy; and you may talk too fast. Obviously, you cannot concentrate on all three of these problems at once. Following the first consultation with your instructor, you will probably know which aspect of speech improvement to tackle first. Work on that. Add others as you gain success.

Stabilizing Improved Skills in Various Types of Speaking Situations

It is not enough to know how to produce a pleasing voice and adequate articulation in a controlled classroom situation. You must be able to use your voice effectively in all types of speaking activities, such as informal conversation, public discussion, oral reading, and public speaking. The goal is not to perfect the use of the various speech forms but to use the types of speaking activities as a means for practicing specific skills in voice and articulation. Each form of your speech activities, however, will grow in effectiveness as you learn to use your speech skills.

The same skills used in effective formal speaking activities are also utilized in informal situations. The intensity of the voice, however, may vary according to the size of the room and the nature of the listening situation. Speech intelligibility is always important, but extreme precision of articulation is not needed in small conversational groups as much as in platform situations.

In the beginning, all situational practice (oral reading, discussion, public speaking, conversation) should be structured or planned carefully. Learning to read a written speech, for example, should precede extemporaneous speaking. More attention may be given to the application of speech skills when written material is used than during spontaneous speaking. After becoming proficient in applying speech skills to poetry, plays, or written speeches, structured conversational situations may be practiced. As you learn through practice, each new speaking situation may be increased in difficulty. To stabilize the use of your new speech skills in various types of speaking situations, refer to Chapters 12 and 13 for further exercises.

YOUR SPEECH NOTEBOOK

You may profitably keep a notebook of the various phases of your study and practice of speech improvement. By preparing your own speech notebook, you may individualize your instruction to meet your specific needs and abilities. This notebook may also be used effectively for continued practice after you have completed the formal aspects of the speech improvement program.

The notebook may be divided into sections such as the following: (a) class assignments, (b) speech evaluations and progress reports, (c) specific exercises suitable for your practice, (d) observations concerned with listening to self and others, (e) selections and exercises suitable for stabilization of acquired skills in various speaking situations, (f) log of listening and practice (language laboratory), and (g) plan of speech improvement for the future.

Class Assignments

At the end of each chapter in this book, and frequently scattered througout the chapter, speech activities are suggested. Copies of assignments may be placed in the notebook. Examples of exercises might include a list of words transcribed phonetically along with definitions of any words which you want to add to your vocabulary, an analysis of five "good" speaking voices using suggestions in Appendix B, or an outline of a discussion which you prepared.

Speech Evaluations

At the beginning of the course, an analysis of your voice and articulation will probably be made by your instructor, and possibly by your classmates. Evaluations and comments may be placed in your notebook. As the result of your instructor's and your own critical listening to your recorded speech, you may plan a program of speech improvement.

Evaluative Materials

All tests, schedules, questionnaires, and forms used in the study of your speech should be in your notebook. At the end of the course, comparisons may be made between the "before" and "after" scores of those tests which are administered both at beginning and end of the course.

Specific Exercises

Although many exercises are included in this notebook, you may want to copy for your notebook those which have particular value for your needs. This is an opportunity to make your own anthology of materials for practice from poetry, prose, drama, and excerpts from speeches. This part of your notebook might well be the part to which you would refer for practice materials after the course is over. A short statement with each selection regarding the specific reasons for your choice will always be helpful.

Log

A log of practice sessions with evaluations may also be recorded. The results of the final evaluation of your speech based on your review of the final recording and your instructor's comments may be entered in this part of your notebook. In the final evaluation of your progress in speech improvement this log of your evaluative sessions will be tangible and satisfying evidence of your work and progress.

PLANNING YOUR FUTURE PROGRAM

Since speech improvement is a continuous process, you will need to continue your consideration of speaking effectiveness in order to maintain what you have learned or to stabilize some skills which are not sufficiently reinforced. Some plan of practice could be established. Setting aside fifteen minutes each day for reading aloud with particular attention to the speech skills which need continued reinforcement may help to maintain some of the speaking proficiency which you attempted to achieve in the speech improvement program. In short conversational periods with a friend, some attention to the use of certain skills may also be an effective means of continued attention to your speech. You will certainly want to continue your use of dictionaries in guiding your choices of acceptable pronunciations.

At the completion of your formal speech improvement program, you will want recommendations from your instructor about future steps to take in the further development of speech proficiency. It may be that courses in public speaking, dramatics, discussion, or oral reading may be indicated for you.

SUMMARY

The purpose of this chapter has been to help you plan a program of personal speech improvement. Since speech is a learned process, it is believed that you can modify your present speaking habits. Factors, besides intelligence and normal physiological process, which often affect the improvement or change of speech behavior are motivation to improve and attitudes toward self, others, and speech.

The general objectives in the speech improvement program are to understand basic processes used in speaking, to improve intelligibility of speech, to acquire pronunciation appropriate for the standard used in your linguistic environment, to eliminate or reduce distracting speech behavior, and to use acquired vocal and articulatory skills in various types of speaking situations. In order to meet these general objectives, the speech improvement program is planned to progress sequentially, sometimes overlapping through these stages: appraisal of speech behavior, acquisition of basic information, improving perceptual skills, acquiring speech proficiency, and stabilizing improved characteristics in various types of speaking situations.

A speech notebook containing various records and materials related to the speech improvement program is suggested. Habits of speech behavior cannot be changed without much diligent practice.

Exercises

1. Record the following passage, "People Never Hear Their Own Voices" on tape or disk, using the procedures suggested in Appendix B. This paragraph may be used by the student for recording his speech at the beginning and end of the course. Other paragraphs for recording may be found in Appendix A. Ask your instructor to assist you in the analysis of your speech.

People Never Hear Their Own Voices

—I wish you could once hear my sister's voice,—said the school mistress.

If it is like yours, it must be a pleasant one,—said I.

I never thought mine was anything,—said the school mistress.

How would you know?—said I. —People never hear their own voices,—any more than they see their own faces. There is not even a looking-glass for the voice. Of course, there is something audible to us when we speak; but that something is not our own voice as it is known to all our acquaintances. I think, if an image spoke to us in our own tones, we should not know them in the least.

*The Autocrat of the
Breakfast Table*
Oliver Wendell Holmes

2. Read and discuss the following examples of plans for speech improvement. Relate your discussion to topics presented in this chapter. Write an

essay on your own plan. Include in your discussion the factors which may have affected your present pronunciation, articulation, and voice.

a. *My Speech Program*

In analyzing my speech it is clear that many areas need improvement. Generally, my voice is too soft, nasal, too fast, and monotonous in pitch and loudness. I also need more oral activity and expression to improve intelligibility. Since my problem areas are widespread and numerous, an overall program of improvement is needed.

The first phase of my speech program is to learn the basic mechanics of speech. This is being done with the aid of the textbook, class lectures, taped instruction, and lab sessions. Particular attention is paid to my teacher-appraised problems and in this way I am also acquiring perceptual skills in appraising speech attributes.

While learning and appraising the mechanics of speech the time spent in taping my voice provides practice in imitating the standard speech, thus helping my speech to become a more conscious and controllable mechanism.

My specific program for pitch at present is to practice going up in pitch at the end of phrases, speaking longer at higher pitches, and practice extending my functional pitch range both in oral reading and conversation. Listening to myself on tape has allowed me to realize the lack of color in monotonous pitch. Therefore, another exercise will be adding inflection to color my conversation and recitations.

Nasality seems to be related to my lack of oral activity and loudness. My plans are therefore to work on these two areas and then appraise my voice for nasal quality.

My program for loudness is to stress proper initiation of tone. I believe my poor volume is due to a weak supply of starting sound. It has also been learned that proper loudness has the effect of animating speech and this is another incentive to speak out.

The intelligibility of my speech behavior is often poor and is due to substandard oral activity, expression and loudness. I plan to increase my oral activity by practicing over-articulation of consonant sounds on applicable tape programs and structured reading. For expression I will consciously try to use more emphasis and inflection in my phrases.

Increasing my rate control will be helped by using pauses to bring out the thought content. By practicing rate variation and making distinct contrasts my expression program will provide a means to exercise rate control. Poetry and prose reading can be used to increase my expressive qualities.

After the overall improvement program has been accomplished my aim is to establish a more specific program to correct my most difficult problems. Along with this a constant, habitual awareness of good speech is hoped to provide a continual standard to guide my speech behavior.

b. *My Plan for Speech Improvement*

Because I have no serious speech defects, my plan for speech improvement will consist of working to improve all of the areas of speech a little bit, hopefully to achieve a more interesting, and above all, pleasing voice to listen to. Up until the time I started this course in voice and diction, I had never had the opportunity to listen to my voce on tape. When I finally did, I was surprised, and a little bit disappointed, in fact, that I did not sound as I thought I would. My speech was not distinct enough and no matter what I said, everything sounded the same. At first I tried as hard as I could to say things with more expression, but the words still came out in a monotone. Finally, I decided that my problem is that I have a very low degree of inflection. I plan to try to correct this by slowing my speech down a bit. If I control my breath more and take more pauses in my speech, I will not sound as though everything I am saying is coming from the same breath. Also, I should try to accent my consonants better. On most of the tapes I found that I slurred many of my /d's/ and /t's/. I should definitely concentrate on making them more distinct.

Probably my most embarrassing speech difficulty is that of stage fright. I become too nervous and my rate quickens. And along with the quickness in rate comes my trouble with inflection and slurring sounds. My main program for improvement in this area will be practice. I should take every opportunity to speak in front of people, even if it is just answering questions in my classes.

3. Discuss your experience as a speaker. Indicate your present attitudes and feelings in various types of speaking situations. Do you feel extreme stage fright in formal speaking events? If so, describe your feelings, the situation, and how you propose to reduce this problem.

4. Read the selections below. Relate the ideas to the discussion in this chapter to your feelings as a speaker. Discuss implications for developing "proper attitudes."

    a. In a speech to a group of journalists in London, the famed British cartoonist, David Low, stated that every time he had to make a speech he felt as if he had a block of ice, nine inches by nine inches, right in the pit of his stomach.

       After his speech he was approached by one of the audience, a Mr. Winston Churchill. "Mr. Low," asked Churchill, "how large did you say that block of ice is?"

       "Nine inches by nine inches," replied Low.

       What an amazing coincidence," replied Churchill. "Exactly the same size as mine."*

    b.   A Fable

       The mountain and the squirrel
       Had a quarrel,
       And the former called the latter 'Little Prig';
       Bun replied,
       'You are doubtless very big;
       But all sorts of things and weather
       Must be taken in together,

---

* Jeff Keate, *Reader's Digest,* May, 1955, p. 210.

To make up a year
And a sphere.
And I think it no disgrace
To occupy my place.
If I'm not so large as you,
You are not so small as I,
And not half so spry.
I'll not deny you make
A very pretty squirrel track;
Talents differ; all is well and wisely put;
If I cannot carry forests on my back,
Neither can you crack a nut.'

A Fable
Ralph Waldo Emerson

5. Prepare a two-minute speech, playing the role suggested by one of the following passages:

"I am monarch of all I survey."
"I am king! Obey me!"
"I'm only the kitchen maid."
"I can't."

6. a. Using the same outline which you used in the analysis of your own voice (Exercise 1, a) analyze the speech of three speakers you see and hear on television. Indicate what you liked and did not like about each voice. Do you think the visual elements affected your judgments? How?

   b. Listen to the speech of three students. Evaluate in terms of their pronunciation, articulation, and voice, using the same outline.

7. Contrast the differences between the tense and relaxed states of bodily tension as you do the following exercises:

   a. Tense your body all over—now let go!

   b. Stand up—lean over and pretend you are lifting a heavy weight as high as your waist—not let it drop. Do you feel differences in tension and relaxation?

   c. Lift a heavy load again. Do you feel tension at the throat and jaw? Try tensing this area without actually acting out the lifting process.

8. Initiate tone as the result of abdominal pressure which forces the sound out through the open relaxed pharyngeal and oral cavities. The grunt will help you to sense the feel of the pressure.

   a. Grunt as you say *ah, oh, aw, oo, ay.*

   b. Try initiating tone through the use of abdominal pressure as you say
      1. Mumbo Jumbo, god of the Congo.

The Congo
Vachel Lindsay

2. O wind a-blowing all day long.
3. Alone, alone, all, all alone,
   Alone on a wide, wide sea!

The Rime of the Ancient
Mariner
Samuel Taylor Coleridge

4. Heigh ho! heigh ho! it's home from work we go!
5. Who has seen the wind?

9. Reinforcement of tone or resonance occurs through the proper use of resonating cavities. Resonance may be developed through stressing production of nasal consonants, adequate adjustment of oral cavities for production of vowels, and prolongation of vowels and some consonants.

   a. Prolong nasal consonants in these passages.

It was many and many a year ago,
   In the kingdom by the sea,
That a maiden lived, whom you may know
   By the name of Annabel Lee;
And this maiden she lived with no other thought
   Than to love, and be loved by me.
I was a child and she was a child,
   In this kingdom by the sea;
But we loved with a love that was more than love
   I and my Annabel Lee,
With a love that the wingèd seraphs of heaven
   Coveted her and me.
And this was the reason that, long ago,
   In this kingdom by the sea,
A wind blew out of a cloud, chilling
   My beautiful Annabel Lee;
So that her high-born kinsmen came,
   And bore her away from me,
   To shut her up in a sepulcher,
   In this kingdom by the sea.

Annabel Lee
Edgar Allan Poe

The king was in the counting house,
Counting out his money.
The queen was in the parlor,
Eating bread and honey.
The maid was in the garden,
Hanging out her clothes;
Along came a bumblebee
And stung her on the nose.

Mother Goose

   b. Prolong vowels and stress voiced consonants.

The day is cold, and dark, and dreary;
It rains, and the wind is never weary;

The vine still clings to the mouldering wall,
But at every gust the dead leaves fall,
And the day is dark and dreary.

The Rainy Day
Henry W. Longfellow

c. Then I heard the boom of the blood-lust song

Mumbo-Jumbo will hoo-doo you.

The Congo
Vachel Lindsay

d. I dwelt alone
In a world of moan
And my soul was a stagnant tide.

Eulalie—A Song
Edgar Allan Poe

10. The vocalized sigh is a technique for superimposing voice on the outgoing breath stream. Try sighing "Ah," "Oh," and "Oo."

a. Stretch and sigh "How are you? "Who are you?" "Where are you?"

b. Try to sense a feeling of relaxation as you read the following passages. Use the sigh technique if you feel the need to coordinate speech with the outgoing breath.

1. We shall walk in velvet shoes:
Wherever we go
Silence will fall like dews
On white silence below.
We shall walk in the snow . . .*

2. The fog comes on little cat feet.

Fog
Carl Sandburg

3. Jes' a-sorto' lazin' there . . .
S'lazy, 'at you peek and peer
Through the wavin' leaves above,
Like, a feller 'ats in love
And don't know it, nor don't keer!
Everything you see and hear
Give some sort o' interest . . .
Maybe find a blue bird's nest
Tucked up there conveniently
Fer a boy 'ats ap' to be
Up some other apple tree!

Watch the swallows skootin' past
'Bout as peert as you could ast;
Er the Bob-white raise and whiz
Where some other's whistle is. . . .

Knee Deep in June
James Whitcomb Riley

References

Akin, Johnnye, *And So We Speak: Voice and Articulation*. Englewood Cliffs, N.J.: Prentice-Hall, Inc., 1958.

Anderson, Virgil A., *Training the Speaking Voice* (2nd ed.). New York: Oxford University Press, Inc., 1961.

Garbe, Joanne S., "A Study of the Auditory Perceptual Skills of College Students Enrolled in a Voice and Diction Course." Unpublished master's Thesis, The Ohio State University, 1965.

Hanley, Theodore D. and Wayne L. Thurman, *Developing Vocal Skills*. New York: Holt, Rinehart & Winston, Inc., 1962.

Lee, Irving J., *Language Habits in Human Affairs*. New York: Harper & Row, Publishers, 1941.

Seymour, Harry, "An Evaluation of a Voice and Diction Course at Shaw University," unpublished master's thesis, The Ohio State University, 1969.

4

Speech Production: The Physical Impetus

One feature of speech is that it is acoustic; it is sound; and it is audible. It has a property of *loudness*. The driving motor that accounts for speech and for loudness is exhaled air. This air flow is also the source of power in normal whistling, in snoring, in laughing, in singing, and for the sound of the trumpet and other wind instruments. Some of these are very human sounds. There are other forces that set up sound; for example:

> a hammer hits a piano string, a stick hits a drum, air rushes from a toy balloon, a foot hits a floor, a stick is drawn along a serrated surface, a bow vibrates a string, a pick plucks a string, exhaled air blows the lips apart, rushing air vibrates a reed, water sizzles on a stove, water boils, large waves hit a coast line, an aircraft breaks the sound barrier, a saw cuts through wood, and the like.

In each instance there is a source of power and it contributes to the distinctive sound of the system. We learn to identify the system aurally: one system becomes equated with one kind of sound. Speech is more complex. The exhaled air activates different sound-generating systems. It blows the vocal folds apart to produce a tone; it rushes through an aperture with audible friction to make an /s/; and it drives the lips apart and explodes into a /p/. The varied systems that enter into speech production generate tone, bursts, and gusts, and are powered by a single source, exhaled air.

THE PROCESS OF RESPIRATION

Breathing is inhalation (inspiration) and exhalation (expiration); in medical parlance this is *ventilation*. The breathing process seems simple, no matter how complicated the chemistry and the control of this physiological process may be. For example, there is nothing unusual about air rushing from a toy balloon nor in inflating the balloon again by coupling it to a compressed air system. These homely and familiar processes have analogies in respiration. Figure 7 is a stylized represen-

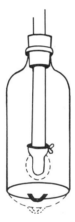

Figure 7. An illustrative device to show the flow of air with changes in environmental pressure.

tation of these simple occurrences. The parts are a cylindrical glass bell, A; a glass pipe, B, which is inserted through the top of the bell; and a toy rubber balloon, C, tied to the lower end of B. A taut sheet of rubber, D, with a handle attached, covers the bottom of the bell. The space within A and outside B and C is tight and contains "trapped air." The air within B and C, however, is part of the environmental air E. If one pulls the handle of the rubber sheet downward, the sheet is distended from point D to D_1 and a partial vacuum is set up in C. In this circumstance, air rushes into pipe B until the rubber balloon C takes the position C_1 and equilibrium is again established between the pressure of the trapped air and the environmental air.

Recapitulating, the external influence was applied at point D. The remainder of the action was only a matter of balancing air pressures. When the air pressure of C was less than the air pressure of E, air rushed into the pipe until the pressures C and E were equal. Now, if the operator releases his hold on D_1, the rubber sheet returns to D, the balloon returns to C, and air passes out through B. The external effort—the driving force—was exerted on the rubber sheet. All else was a matter of equalizing the pressures of two bodies of air.

THE MECHANISM OF RESPIRATION

Breathing, the driving force of speech, is hardly a matter of glass bells and rubber balloons. It takes place, however, in a context of equalizing air pressures, and the mechanism that accommodates it includes, as in the analogy, (a) an airtight cage, (b) a pipe that leads into the cage, (c) a pliable sack attached to the pipe, and (d) mechanisms for changing the periphery of the airtight cage and thereby its size.

The Airtight Cage

Twelve pairs of ribs attach terminally to the backbone and seven of these to the sternum; three of the remaining pairs attach to the ends of the adjacent superior ribs instead of to the sternum. Two pairs of ribs are not firmly attached anteriorly. Adjacent ribs are joined to each other throughout their length by two sets of muscles, the interior and external intercostals. The sides of the ribcage, tapering at the top, are laced to the collarbone, the shoulder bone, and the neck by numerous muscles (see Figure 8).

The floor of the chest cavity or ribcage is an irregularly dome-shaped muscle, the diaphragm. It is attached throughout its periphery to the lower edge of the rib cage. *Diaphragm* comes from the Greek words meaning dividing wall. In Anglo-Saxon it is the *midriff* (midhrife or mid-belly). It is a striped muscle—subject to voluntary control—and peculiar to mammals. The frontal attachments are somewhat higher than the ones in the back. The center or apex of the horizontally elliptical muscle is tendonous and accommodates three tubes: the main artery and vein to and from the lower part of the body, and the esophagus. This is the floor of the airtight cage and is somewhat comparable to the rubber sheet of the analogy.

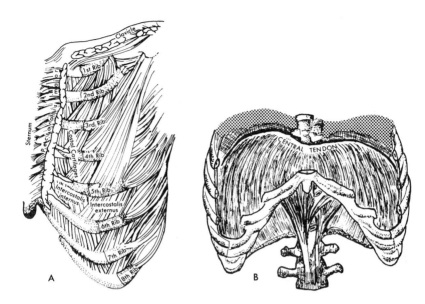

Figure 8. Representations of (A) the ribs, the sternum, clavicle, interconnecting musculatures and (B) the diaphragm.

The Pipe That Enters the Airtight Cage

Although two pipes come into the ribcage through the neck, one (the esophagus) does not concern you here, for it enters at the throat and exits through the central tendon of the diaphragm without affecting the chest. The pipe of interest in the present context is the trachea. It is about 4½ inches in length and is comprised of a succession of 16–20 cartilaginous C-shaped rings. It originates in the throat, at the larynx, and terminates within the cage.

The Pliable Sack

The trachea leads into the lungs, the exterior surface of which is red, moist, and slippery (pleura). The lungs are somewhat elastic and are airtight. The interior is a seemingly endless series of dividing pathways that terminate in microscopic areas, the alveoli (see Figure 9). Here the air of the ventilating process and the blood of the circulatory system are so intermixed that a measure of the oxygen and carbon dioxide contents of the one is a good index of these contents of the other. The general

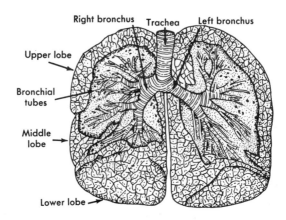

Figure 9. A representation of the lungs which fill the bony cavity (for a view such as this the diaphragm would be abnormally contracted.)

effect of the interior of the lungs to the casual onlooker might be a red spongy mass! Importantly, the lungs are not muscular, and are incapable of either drawing in air or expelling it. They are passive in the sense that the toy balloon in the mechanical analogy was passive.

Mechanisms for Changing the Size of the Airtight Cage

In your imagined play with the glass bell you pulled the rubber sheet at the bottom of the bell and then allowed it to return to its position of rest. There is no handle on the base of the central tendon and no external operator to pull it down. Yet it does fall and rise vertically. Recall, please, that the diaphragm is an irregularly dome-shaped muscle, affixed at its periphery. A muscle can both contract and relax, but it cannot push. This muscle, enervated by the phrenic nerves from the third and fourth cervical nerves, contracts as it tightens or becomes tense. When it does so, it tends to become flat. The central tendon, however, moves less than do the minor domes to the right and left of it. This movement increases the size of the thoracic cavity and creates a condition that requires air to rush into the lungs through the trachea. This is the major action of inhalation. There are minor ones, too. Unlike the glass jar, almost the whole of the ribcage can be moved away from the center of the cage. The ribs are socketed at their terminals and when the muscles that elevate them are relaxed, the mid-point of each rib is below the straight line that might be drawn between the two ends. The possibility for expanding the sides of the cavity is almost apparent.

But, to convince yourself, place the ends of your thumbs together, press the ends of your index fingers against the edge of a table with the two fingers as far apart as possible. Now, starting with your wrists two or three inches below the level of the table, raise them to the table level and observe how your thumbs move away from the edge of the table. The ribs, too, when pulled upward describe an arc that increases the horizontal dimension of the thoracic cavity. This movement provides an additional need for air to enter the lungs to balance the partial vacuum that is created by the lateral expansion of the rib cage. Additionally, the ribcage as a whole can be lifted. This movement, if it increases the distance between the top and bottom of the cage, again increases the flow of air into the lungs (refer to Figure 10).

The second movement you made with the sheet of rubber of the fictitious analogy was to release it and allow it to return to its position of rest. This, too, is accommodated by the mechanism of respiration. Inhalation involved contracting or tensing the diaphragm; exhalation includes relaxing it and allowing it to be pushed upward to a position of rest. The pressure that pushes the relaxed diaphragm upward comes from the viscera and organs of the abdomen. They have been put under pressure by the contraction of the gross muscles of the abdomen, ones that run horizontally and diagonally across the front of the body. The volume of the chest cavity is further reduced by relaxing the external intercostal muscles. Gravity tends to move the ribs downward (and inward). This compression can be hastened, and this change of speed may be important in speaking, by tensing the internal intercostal muscles.

The Muscles of Inhalation

The preceding discussion leads to some generalizations about the mechanism of respiration and should help you avoid some false reasoning about the processes that it supports. First, the diaphragm is a principal muscle of inhalation (not exhalation). Second, the lungs are not muscles. Third, the expansion of the airtight cavity is the requisite for inhalation. Fourth, this expansion can occur only through muscular action. And, fifth, control of the muscles that enlarge the rib cage is tantamount to controlling inhalation.

You can discover some of the muscles of inhalation as you sit at your desk and practice vigorous breathing. The ribs expand at your sides. The muscles that attach to adjacent ribs and serve as lifters are the external intercostals. The whole chest moves upward. This action is effected in part by muscles that extend downward from the neck over

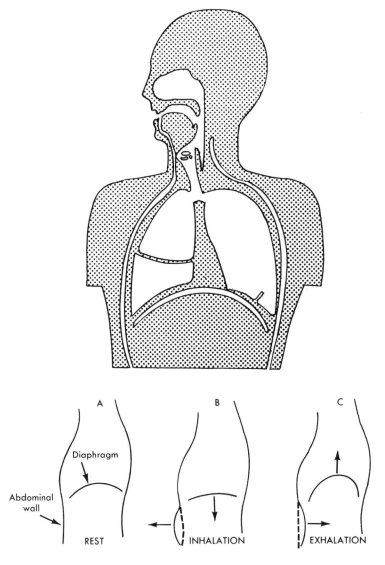

Figure 10. A schematic representation of the mechanism of respiration (frontal view) and of lateral views (A) rest, (B) inhalation, and (C) exhalation.

both the chest and the back. With more forceful inhalation, the pectoral muscles, along with others, come into action. These arise at the shoulder bones and fan out over the upper part of the chest.

MODES OF EXHALATION

The outward airflow that attends the reduction of the ribcage can be either relatively fast or slow. This rate depends upon the speed with which the gross muscles of exhalation are contracted, for example, the rectus abdominis, the transversus abdominis, the oblique externus abdominis, and the obliquus internus abdominis. These muscles of the abdomen set the general level of your speech. As they are contracted rapidly, the rate of flow of the air from the lungs to the external environment is relatively fast; as they are contracted slowly, this flow is relatively slow. In turn, the intensity of your voice is directly proportional to the rate of flow of the outgoing air. The flow of the outgoing airstream and the accompanying level of voice can be heightened somewhat by forceful contraction of the ribcage, accelerating the pull of gravity.

Stetson (see References at end of chapter) added a controversial topic to speculations about the relationship between exhalation and speech. He proposed that while the muscles of the abdomen set the general level or loudness of speech, the internal intercostals pulse this rate of flow somewhat. These modulations, superimposed upon the modal rate of flow, correspond acoustically to stressed and unstressed syllables. Whether this explanation can be verified experimentally or not, the observation is pertinent that the flow of outward breath is not even during speech. Indeed, there are many kinds of interruptions of the exhalations. Unusual ones occur in coughing and sneezing. More routine ones include the arresting of breathing, and the concomitant pause in speech that signals an afterthought, uncertainty, or loss of memory. Although these meaningful behaviors may be somewhat generalized within a culture, they also vary from speaker to speaker. Also, there are acoustic pauses that do not represent interruptions in the breath stream, simply absences of speech sounds.

In general, some speech is smooth and even-flowing; and, at another extreme, some is jerky and interrupted. These aural effects are accompanied by either relatively smooth exhalations or jerky interrupted exhalations. These different stresses have been referred to as degrees of force: effusive, expulsive, and explosive. Gray and his students, particularly Constans, attempted to relate these degrees of force, ranging from virtual singsong evenness (effusive) to dramatic super-staccato barks (explosive), to modes of exhalation (see References at end of chapter). The researchers were unable to establish any valid relationships.

THE AIR SUPPLY

The capacity of the lungs varies from individual to individual (vital capacity). Some air always remains in the lungs, is never expelled (residual air). The flow in and out with breathing is *tidal air*. Usually, the volume of the tidal air is determined by physiological requirements, and the time devoted to inhalation is roughly the same as the time devoted to exhalation. This is changed drastically in speaking. Inhalation occurs quickly, perhaps as a gulp. Exhalation, suited to the word, the phrase, and the sentence, is stretched out. A cumulative effect, however, is that more air is taken in and exhaled during speech than during normal respiration. This is probably related to many of the subjective feelings that speakers report, for example, lightheadedness. It may even relate to on-the-spur-of-the-moment textual changes that speakers make. In extreme circumstances, for example, ones involving sustained loud talking, the symptoms of hyperventilation have been observed. Principally, these include a reduction of the carbon dioxide supply in the lungs, a supply that is necessary in order to control automatically the respiratory processes.

APPLICATION

Inhalation is an essential adjunct to speaking, nothing more. Voice comes with exhalation. Inhalation, however, provides the air that is used by the wind systems that produce the sound of speaking. Most evaluations of what constitutes good inhalation for speech are subjective and arise from logical inference. A few facts have experimental verification.

Your loud voice requires more air than your soft voice. Also, there are lengthy passages in plays, poems, and songs that are more effectively read or are necessarily sung as single sweeps although the number of syllables far exceeds the usual number for one exhalation. These require deep inhalations. For the special purposes of speaking, the control of inhalation is largely directed toward providing an adequate reservoir of air in the wind system of the speaker. With some people this air supply appears to relate primarily to movements of the chest; for others, to movements of the abdomen; and for some to uniformly distributed muscular activity. Conventionally, the clavicular or "chest breathing" is least preferred and the distributed activity most preferred, although this advantage has not been established experimentally.

Respiration ranks high among the topics that would be expected to distinguish good and poor voices. Experimentally, this relationship has not been established. However, the adage seems appropriate, "Negative results are but a challenge to the methodology." It is too early to take a view that "respiration has nothing whatsoever to do with speaking except to be indispensable thereto." You have had experiences in which you ran out of air before the phrase was finished. You have heard faint voices among aging and ill people for whom breathing appeared to be labored. These experiences suggest that until much additional evidence has been collected, you should heed common sense. More than half a century ago, Vorhees as cited by Russell admonished a Music Teachers Association that perfect control of the breath means:

(a) ability to fill the lungs to their capacity either quickly or slowly;
(b) ability to breathe out as quickly or as slowly as occasion demands;
(c) ability to suspend inspiration . . . and to resume the process at will without having lost any of the already inspired breath;
(d) ability to exhale under the same restriction;
(e) ability to sing and to sustain the voice on an ordinary breath;
(f) ability to breathe quietly as often as text and phrase permit;
(g) ability to breathe so that the fullest inspiration brings no fatigue;
(h) ability so to economize the breath that the reserve is never exhausted;
(i) ability to breathe so naturally, so unobtrusively, that neither breath nor lack of breath is ever suggested to the listener.

About 16 years later, Russell wrote,

We can do no better than cite the following [the principles advocated by Vorhees] . . . and perhaps one other, at least, can be added:

(j) ability so to breathe as not to interfere with the muscular processes involved in artistic phonation, but on the contrary, so as to aid these processes where possible.

The span from the Vorhees statement to the Russell statement was about 16 years, from Russell to the present is more than twice as much.

SUMMARY

The driving force for speech is the airflow of exhalation. This force results from the contraction of muscles of exhalation and the relaxing of the muscles of inhalation. The action is to reduce the size of the rib cage. This action comes principally from the gross muscles of the abdomen. Thus, they are the ones that account for the speed of the outward airflow and the loudness of the voice.

One common misconception about respiration attributes active participation of the lungs in respiration in a manner implied by the word *squeeze*. Another gives to the diaphragm a major role in exhalation. This is implied by the word *push*.

The relationship between an outgoing airflow and voice is sufficiently immediate that speakers and singers are urged to attend to a good supply of air and to control the intake and outgo in ways that support the art of singing and speaking, not distract from it.

Exercises

1. The relationship of exhalation to vocal intensity has been stressed throughout this chapter. Fairbanks also emphasized this through entitling a chapter "Loudness in Breathing." The first sentence of the chapter is, "Adequate loudness is in part a matter of adequate breathing." Also, reference was made in the present chapter to effusive, expulsive, and explosive forms of force. Merry used these same terms in referring to "types of exhalation." Constans, in preparation for a kymographic study of the respiratory movements attending the "three forms of force," selected illustrative passages from speech textbooks. These passages follow. Read them aloud several times as meaningfully as possible. Decide for yourself whether or not the respiratory experiences are similar when reading the three groups of passages. Stand erect as you read. Experience the different kinds of feedback that accompany the following activities: (a) place one hand firmly upon your abdomen and feel the effects of respiration, (b) observe the respiratory movements as you read in front of a mirror, and (c) note during the playback of recorded material whether the audible aspects of respiration are the same from one group of selections to another. How do you suggest that the relevance of different "types of exhalation" might be tested?

Effusive

a. Jean Valjean listened but there was no sound; he pushed the door with the tip of his finger lightly. . . . He heard from the end of the room the calm and regular breathing of the sleeping bishop.

Lés Miserables
Victor Hugo

b. It was many and many a year ago,
In a kingdom by the sea,
That a maiden lived, whom you may know
By the name of Annabel Lee.

> *Annabel Lee*
> Edgar Allan Poe

c. Roll on, thou deep and dark blue ocean, roll!
Ten thousand fleets sweep over thee in vain;
Man marks the earth with ruin—his control
Stops with the shore. . . .

> *Childe Harold*
> Lord Byron

d. The day is cold, and dark, and dreary;
It rains, and the wind is never weary;
The vine still clings to the mouldering wall
But at every gust the dead leaves fall
And the day is dark and dreary.

> *The Rainy Day*
> Henry W. Longfellow

Expulsive

a. What ho! my jovial mates! Come on! We'll frolic it
Like fairies frisking in the merry moonshine.

> Anonymous

b. I impeach him in the name of the Commons of Great Britain
in Parliament assembled, whose parliamentary trust he has
abused.

> *Impeachment of*
> *Warren Hastings*
> Edmund Burke

c. It is a fearful thing to lead this great peaceful people into war,
into the most terrible and disastrous of all wars, civilization
itself seeming to be in the balance.

> *For a Declaration of War*
> *Against Germany*
> Woodrow Wilson

d. Oh, young Lochinvar is come out of the west,
Through all the wide border his steed was the best;
And, save his good broadsword, he weapons had none.
He rode all unarmed, and he rode all alone.

> *Lochinvar*
> Sir Walter Scott

Explosive

a. Halt—the dust brown ranks stood fast;
Fire—out blazed the rifle blast.

> *Barbara Frietchie*
> John Greenleaf Whittier

   b. Hath a dog money? Is it possible
      A cur can lend three thousand ducats?

The Merchant of Venice
William Shakespeare

   c. Strike till the last armed foe expires!
      Strike for your altars and your fires!
      Strike for the green graves of your sires,
      God, and your native land.

Marco Bozzaris
Fitz-Greene Halleck

   d. . . . 'This to me!' he said,
      'An 'twere not for thy hoary beards,
      Such hand as Marmion's had not spared
      To cleave the Douglas' head!

Marmion
Sir Walter Scott

2. The exercises of other chapters contain many selections from prose and poetry. Choose examples from them that seem to require one of the forms of force or types of exhalation.

3. If a spirometer is available, make several measurements of your vital capacity. If possible, collect these measures for all of the members of your class and plot them graphically as a frequency distribution with volume as the abscissa and number of cases as the ordinate. This should yield a curve similar to the one of Chapter 1.

4. Turn to page 273. Read aloud as much as you can on one breath. Count the number of words that you read (syllables would be a more exact unit). Repeat the exercise at a higher level of loudness. Repeat the exercise whispering. Now repeat the exercise as many times as you wish, speaking aloud and trying to get farther and farther into the material on one breath. It is not expected that in this brief exercise you will increase your flow of tidal air; rather you may quickly find some ways of conserving air and others of expending air rapidly through altering your manner of speaking.

5. Say aloud ten letters of the alphabet at one-second intervals. Consider the ten vocalizations as one unit. Place your hands firmly at different locations on the bony cavity and abdomen, keeping the hands in a single position throughout one unit. Indicate the extent of the muscular activity at each site. Let 1 stand for minimal activity (you should get this at the top of the sternum) and 9 maximum activity. Plot the values on a freehand drawing of the abdomen and thorax.

6. Holding the palm of one hand four inches in front of your mouth, say ten letters of the alphabet at a constant intensity and at one-second intervals as in the preceding exercise. Record, letter by letter, the amount of air

pressure that you feel, assigning 1 to minimum pressure and 4 to maximum pressure.

7. Make a free-hand drawing of the mechanisms involved in respiration and suggest the movements that occur in inhalation and exhalation.

References

Black, John W. and Walter B. Tomlinson, "Loud Voice: Immediate Effects upon the Speaker," *Speech Monographs*, 19 (1952), 299-302.

Constans, H. Philip, "An Objective Analysis of the 'Three Forms of Force' in Speech," *Studies in Experimental Phonetics*, Giles Wilkeson Gray, ed. University Studies No. 27. Baton Rouge: Louisiana State University Press, 1936.

Fairbanks, Grant, *Practical Voice Practice*. New York: Harper & Row, Publishers, 1944.

Judson, Lyman S. V. and Andrew Thomas Weaver, *Voice Science* (2nd ed.). New York: Appleton-Century-Crofts, 1965.

Kaplan, Harold M., *Anatomy and Physiology of Speech*. New York: McGraw-Hill Book Company, 1960.

Ladefoged, Peter, "Sub-glottal Activity During Speech," in *Proceedings of the Fourth International Congress of Phonetic Sciences*, Antti Sovijarvi and Pentii Aalto (eds.). The Hague: Mouton & Co., 1962.

Ladefoged, Peter, *Three Areas of Experimental Phonetics*. London: Oxford University Press, 1967.

Russell, G. Oscar, *Speech and Voice*. New York: The Macmillan Company, 1931.

Stetson, Robert, *Motor Phonetics*. Amsterdam: North-Holland Publishing Company, 1951.

Van Riper, Charles and John V. Irwin, *Voice and Articulation*. Englewood Cliffs, N.J.: Prentice-Hall, Inc., 1958.

5

Sound Production: The Modulation

The preceding chapter emphasized the importance of exhalation to speaking. Yet the exhaled airstream that flows from the lungs through the trachea and the mouth or nose is not in itself a stream of speech sounds. It only has latent possibilities for stimulating the production of voice. This outgoing stream is sometimes compared to the direct current of a battery. This steady current, if pulsed, becomes alternating. In similar manner, the airstream can be pulsed or modulated, converted to positive-negative phenomena with the oscillations occurring either regularly or irregularly. The modulations arise at points where the moving stream is obstructed. Thus, the moving airstream becomes the agitator for the production of sound when obstacles are put in its path to interrupt it. After the processes of modulation, there remains a gross movement of the airstream. It is somewhat irregular, a series of puffs. Traveling through this irregular stream of air is another type of movement, sound waves. They are the consequence of the modulation.

At whatever point the airstream is interrupted or modulated some of the latent energy of the flow is converted into sound energy and some, an infinitesimal part, into heat. The principal part remains with the air flow. It is relatively strong, still capable of moving most of the objects that it could have moved before it lost a part of its energy at the point of interruption. It remains sufficiently forceful to cause a candle that lies in its path to flicker. The ideal sound-producing system would be one that transforms the maximum amount of the energy of the airstream, indeed all of it, into sound energy. The speech mechanism does not do this. Yet the mechanism is far more than minimally efficient. It utilizes the airstream more than one time and at more than one place of interruption. This should bring to your mind the reference in Chapter 4 to the multiple sound-producing systems that contribute to speech.

The purpose of the present chapter is to indicate the structures of the neck and head that permit human beings to modulate the airstream of exhalation in order to produce speech. Once more, please remember the plural word *systems,* the sound systems of speech. One sound-generating system cannot account for speech; a person does not use the same structures in producing all of his speech. Also, it is helpful to keep in mind a fact mentioned in Chapter 1 as one strives to manage the mechanisms of speech: speech is an overlaid function. The production of speech relies upon structures and systems of muscles and processes that are physiologically vital to living. Speech gives to them a unique and important social role.

THE LARYNX

The larynx is an irregular cylinder that rests on top of the trachea and extends the path of the respiratory system upward to the lower level or root of the tongue. The entire length of the trachea and larynx is immediately in front of the esophagus. The two pipes, one for breathing and one for eating and drinking, cross immediately above the larynx. They form an X at the point of crossing. The air pipe must be open for every breath and closed for every swallow of food. This closure is made reflexively by contracting musculatures at the top of the larynx and by an effective closing action of the epiglottis, pulled upward—and at the midpoint, backward—from the main body of the larynx.

The larynx is one organ that modulates the airstream of exhalation. The sequential interruptions occur with only some segments of the breath stream, not with all of it. Consequently, these interruptions characterize only segments of the stream of speech. For example, the larynx is inactive, only an air passage, in the production of all of the speech sounds except the three vowels in *six fish stops.* In saying these words the larynx modulates the airstream only in the production of the three vowels, one-fourth of the speech sounds of the three words.

Students of singing and speaking often view the larynx as a somewhat isolated structure, "the organ of speech," and as one that is limited in usefulness to their interests. These students and performers seem to hold some proprietary rights to the house of the vocal folds. No, this organ functions importantly in normal breathing, swallowing, and the expending of sudden effort. It provides a defense against objects that slip by the epiglottis and are falling toward the lungs. It is a valve that regulates the flow of tidal air in quiet inhalation and exhalation. It is also a source of strength, as in lifting. Even as part of a sound-producing system the larynx is not an isolated entity; it is intimately coupled with cavities and structures of the mouth and nose, and its contribution to speech cannot be fully described apart from them. Only in order to understand the larynx and the muscles that control it as a modulator of the airstream is there any justification in viewing it apart from the over-all sound-producing systems.

The Structure of the Larynx

The top ring of the trachea is the base of the larynx. This ring resembles a signet ring and hence carries the name *cricoid* cartilage. The word has a Greek derivation. The descriptive names of natural phe-nomena often have an important imaginative component that is ex-pressed as an analogy. The signet portion of the ring lies at the back, an inch behind the projection of the Adam's apple. On top of the upper sloping surfaces of the signet are pivoted a pair of tiny "pyramids." With adjacent and extending structures, these resemble ladles; hence, they are called *arytenoids*. The "imaginative component" in this case has led to two analogies, *ladle* for the early dissectionist and *pyramid* for current ones. Hinged to the sides of the signet, extending forward along the ring, and covering the entire lateral and frontal surface is a "shield." Because of this apearance, it is named *thyroid*. This is a gross cartilage. The two sides or wings (alae) converge in the front of the neck at the Adam's apple. You can feel this protrusion in your neck. You can push it laterally from side to side, and you may note its rise and fall as you swallow. These are the principal structures of the larynx. You may see them schematically in Figure 11.

Muscles of the Larynx

The structures of the larynx are bound together by a system of liga-ments and several groups of muscles. Typically these are named for their terminal attachments, that is their origin and insertion, and their position,

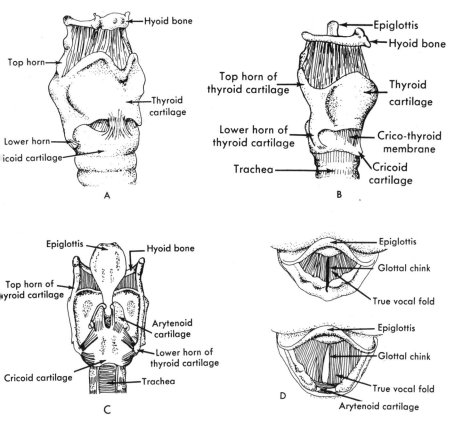

Figure 11. Representations of the larynx: (A) an anterior view that emphasizes the thyroid cartilage and its attachment to the cricoid cartilage; (B) a lateral view that emphasizes the attachments of the epiglottis and the shape of the cricoid cartilage; (C) a posterior view that emphasizes the signet portion of the cricoid cartilage and the attached arytenoid cartilages; (D) a top view that shows the thyroarytenoid muscles and the vocal ligaments and emphasizes the size of the glottal chink.

as *interior* or *exterior*. As noted in Chapter 4, a muscle can only contract and partially relax. It cannot push! The muscles of the larynx are central to the production of voice, that is to vocalization. It is important to understand this musculature, for the skillful use of it is essential to any personal program of speech improvement. A pair of crucial muscles run horizontally from the two arytenoids, attach along the interior walls of the alae of the thyroid cartilage, and terminate at the protrusion of the thyroid, the Adam's apple. These muscles, almost three-fourths inch long in an adult male, may cover, with their adjacent cartilaginous liga-

ments, the entire opening of the mid-larynx. They can shut off the outward air flow. They do so when the interior surfaces of the two arytenoid
cartilages are drawn together. These, the thyro-arytenoidius muscles, are
edged medially by a pair of ligaments (bundles of elastic fibers) and
these facing "whitish" edges are the *vocal folds, bands,* or *cords.* They
bound the glottal chink.

The thyro-arytenoidius muscles are under tension and exert a pull
from the thyroid to the arytenoids, sometimes minimal and at other
times considerable. The cartilages need not be displaced by this force,
for other muscles may exert pulls in another—indeed in the opposite—
direction. These "pulls" are important:

(a) the crico-thyroid muscles pull the thyroid forward,
(b) the posterior crico-arytenoids pull the arytenoids apart,
(c) the lateral crico-arytenoids pull the arytenoids forward and
    downward, and
(d) the arytenoid muscles may pull the two arytenoid cartilages
    together.

These five pairs of muscles "give and take" to produce tension or relative
laxness in the region of the vocal folds and to bring them together and to
separate them.

The drawing together of the two pivotal arytenoid cartilages has been
accounted for muscularly. With this movement, there is a lateral approximation of the vocal folds. This activity, learned by each human
being, occurs three times as you say *six fish stops.* The movement signals
the production of a speech sound that utilizes modulation of the airstream at the vocal folds. The separating of the arytenoids and the vocal
folds signals the production of speech sounds that do not utilize modulation in the larynx. This pair of behaviors also distinguishes whispering
and normal speaking.

Innervation.   The framework of movable cartilages of the larynx and
the network of paired muscles that activates them are normally innervated
for life-sustaining functions in reflex actions by the medulla. However,
tasks that fall to the larynx in connection with artistic performance in
singing and speaking are directed from the cortex. These include the
control of respiration and the tautness of the vocal folds to yield particular vocal pitches. Here the highest order of the nervous system is involved, the pyramidal tract.

There is yet another level of control between the reflex actions that
arise from the medulla and the voluntary ones that come from the cortex.
These are the learned habitual controls that accompany adequate speaking. They relate to normal intonation, approximating the vocal folds for
the production of some sounds and separating them for others, and the

singular control of the folds for whispering as apart from reading silently while moving the articulators. In Chapter 1 the hypothetical instance was proposed that your developmental years might have led to your learning Mandarin instead of English. You would have learned a language in which the literal meaning of words changes with the degree of tautness of the vocal folds. The control, in turn, would be in this mid-level habitual system. Antagonistic tensions of opposing sets of muscles also derive from the pyramidal or corticobular pathway, but at sub-cortical levels (see Figure 12). With prolonged practice, habitual controls are estab-

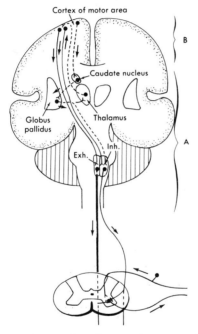

Figure 12. Suggested neural pathways that enter into the production of speech, both habitual speech (A) and deliberate speech (B).

lished that operate in a manner indistinguishable from reflexive ones. Much of the learning of the new habits of improved speech and of the learning to use a second language involve tedious exercises in establishing different sets of habitual responses.

Vocal-Fold Action

The vocal folds, under a certain tension (extrapyramidal pathways) and drawn together (pyramidal pathways), lie in the path of the outgoing breath stream. This is the case in producing a vowel and in humming. The folds hold up the free flow of air momentarily until sufficient pressure builds up below them to blow them apart. The pressure spent, the tension of the folds draws them to their blocking position again.

The tension of the folds and the amount of exertion that accompanies the process of exhalation interact to determine the rapidity of interruptions of the breath stream, perhaps one, two, or three hundred times each second. The outgoing breath stream is cut into microscopic pulses. With each interruption or modulation of the breath stream, a pulse of sound occurs and heat is generated (an infinitesimal amount). These are the dual results of a source of energy meeting a resistance and accomplishing work.

The gross puffs of air and the pulses of sound might seem to be synonymous. This is not true. The gross puffs of air move relatively slowly and persist only inches in front of the speaker's mouth. The pulses of sound, described in more detail in a later chapter, are minute, fast, and relatively far-reaching. The results of vocal-fold action make up the aspect of speech called *phonation.** This is voice. At this point segments of the breath stream have been modulated one time. A tonal aspect with pitch has been added to what would otherwise be whispered speech.

THE CAVITIES

What do the acoustic pulses that originate with the modulation at the vocal folds sound like? Any answer would be a conjecture, for the sound cannot exist, cannot be made independent of a laryngeal, pharyngeal, buccal, and skeletal environment. These surroundings are important, crucial, in determining the nature of the sound, even at the source. They provide resistance and thus load the vocal folds and affect their response to the airstream. The consequence of this is dramatically demonstrated in contemporary experiences with speech produced by individuals who are breathing a gas consisting of a high percentage of helium. These people are living deep in the ocean. Their speech as heard at sea level is high in pitch and unnatural. The cause lies in the unique loading of the vocal folds that is provided by helium. Similar vocal distortions are present with speech that is generated by hydrogen.

---

* There is another theoretical explanation of the process of phonation, one that postulates that each opening of the vocal folds is activated by a cortical command. Proponents of the aerodynamic view, the one suggested here, note the lack of experimental evidence to show that the folds can be driven more than 90 times per second through direct neural stimulation. However, there is also evidence that some muscle fibers insert into the vocal ligaments. These, of course, would be accompanied by neural fibers.

Each modulation at the vocal cords occurs midway in a pipe that terminates at the lips, and the pipe has peculiar properties. It is moist, warm, varies in surface texture from relatively soft to relatively hard, is curved and irregular in shape, and has a substantial hump at one place or another along its forward reaching axis. The hump is made by the tongue. The importance of this hump is illustrated by the fact that one engineer, while trying to generate vowels electronically, found it convenient to view the pipe as two abutting ones, resembling miniature automobile mufflers placed end to end. A bunching of the tongue divides the cavities, sometimes near the teeth, sometimes at the back of the mouth. Thus, one or another of the cavities may be the larger; also, the connecting pipe may be relatively long or short, and large or small in diameter.

The modulations of the airstream at the vocal folds are drastically affected by the physiological surroundings. These can be viewed equally well as the conducting pipe, the resonating system, or the vocal cavities. Importantly, the generated sound assumes some of the acoustic properties of this environment. For example, the mouth cavity, as with any mass or enclosure, has important acoustic characteristics. It is resonant to some frequencies. The particular ones change with each size of the mouth. If you tense your cheek muscles and snap a finger against the cheek, you hear a buccal tone. The tone changes as the mouth is more or less open. If there are two pipes instead of one, or three instead of two, there are two or three natural frequencies—and perhaps more—in the surfaces and enclosures that are coupled to the point of modulation.

Unusual arrangements of the pipe above the larynx occur with the saying of /m, n, ŋ (ng)/. In these instances the pipe extends upward from the larynx, through the pharynx and nasal passages, and terminates with the nostrils. Also, tangential to this principal pipe, through the nose, is one that extends forward into the mouth. This latter one is closed by the lips in the formation of /m/ and closed by a bunching of the tongue, differentially placed, in the saying of the other two sounds. A dead-end pipe is descriptively called *cul-de-sac*. The present section emphasizes the role of the cavities of the speech mechanism on the loading of the vocal folds. In a subsequent chapter the function of the same cavities as resonators will be treated (for clarification of phonetic symbols see Chapter 8).

THE BLOCKING STRUCTURES

It should be clear that the vocal folds interrupt the airstream periodically in the production of some sounds or phonemes of speech, but not all of them. Please turn your attention to the production of sound by other mechanisms within the speech-producing systems. If one merely puffs or exhales rapidly through the open mouth, he produces a sound that is audible. Try it. Reduce the size of your mouth opening and the character of the sound changes. Pucker your lips and you may produce a whistle. These are oral sound-producing systems, driven by the airstream of exhalation, with no vocal fold action. The breath is interrupted near the orifice of the mouth, considerably above the vocal folds. The interruption involves some of the same principles discussed with regard to modulation at the vocal folds. There is inevitably the aspect of pressure below the vocal cords. There is not, however, in the production of the sounds of English another set of elastic taut structures that, blown from their position, return to form another stoppage. The production of the trilled /r/, not used in American English, does meet these conditions. Also, a sound that is frequently made to suggest "I am cold!," and spelled *brrrr,* meets them.

Complete stoppages of the airstream occur at the palate with the production of /k/, at the dental ridge with /t/, and at the lips with /p/. In the first two instances the tongue is raised to make the closure. With the making of these sounds the ongoing airstream is halted while air pressure builds up. There is a sudden release of the pent-up breath and some of the latent energy of the air under pressure is converted to sound. The effect resembles an explosion. The acoustic differences of the three sounds /p, t, k/ may result from differences in the three pressures, differences in the suddenness of release, and the resonance and damping characteristics of the proximate cavities and surfaces. This latter is the usual explanation and is included within the term *place of articulation,* a term that will be used importantly in a later discussion of consonant sounds.

Partial stoppages of the breath stream always occur at or behind the teeth. The lower lip meets the upper teeth in the production of /f/. The tongue directs a steady jet of air at the edge of the upper front teeth with /s/. The air escapes through a broad valley between the tongue and roof of the mouth /ʃ/. The back of the tongue only slightly narrows the escape-opening within the mouth in the production of /ʍ, w, h/. The production of these sounds seems more similar to the modulations at the vocal folds than to the explosions and nonrepetitive positive pressures of the sounds of the preceding paragraph, and surely the production of /s, f, ʃ/ involves recurrent releases of air. In these partial blockings, pressure is built up; a segment of the pressure is released; more is built up; and again some is released. This recurs over the duration of a phoneme. The amount of change in the static pressure from instant to instant is small. First, there is more pressure and then with each escape there is less pressure, never an absence of pressure. The instant of the next release is not predictable and there is no assurance that the next release will closely resemble the preceding one in amount. The aural effect of the released air under pressure is somewhat like hissing. However, there is never certainty that the differing amounts of released pressure will be closely similar in acoustic character. The releases occur with varying amounts of turbulence, and in some instances, for example, /s/, a second partial obstructer, the teeth, modifies the output of an earlier one which occurs near the upper dental ridge. With this implied amount of variability within a single production of one of the partially stopped or fricative sounds of speech, considerable variability is to be expected among different renditions of the sound by the same speaker and considerably more among different speakers.

Multiple Modulation

You have read about two categories of sounds, distinguishable by the manner in which they are produced. In one the airstream is partially converted to acoustic energy at the vocal folds and in the other the stream is stopped either partially or completely at a particular place, for example at the lips. These places are termed points of articulation. There is also an important system of generating speech sounds that involves both of these sources in the production of a single sound. The airstream that is first interrupted at the vocal folds is further modified along the course of the coupled pipe, and sound is generated in both instances. These second interruptions, again, may be either partial or complete blockages. They are complete in the instances of /d, g, b/ and partial with /z, v, ʒ/.

INNERVATION

The fact that much of the reflex action of the larynx and pharynx is innervated by the medulla oblongata is clear. It is equally clear that to the talker the learned habits of speech are almost as automatic as the reflex movements. Speech is also affected by certain disturbances in the cerebellum. The effect here among persons with cerebellar impairment is a slurring of speech, an imprecision at the point of articulation. Evidently in normal speech some of the musculatures involved in tongue, lip, jaw, and pharyngeal movement derive some control from this sub-cortical region.

APPLICATION

This is a hurried explanation of voice and diction. It is also applied voice and diction, intended to lead to changes in your manners of talk-ing. Fortunately, the muscles of speech are innervated by the motor cortex and in particular by centers in Broca's area, close to the cortical region that represents the face. One can contract and relax these muscles and thus deliberately control the movements of speaking. At the cortical level the paired muscles of the systems that produce speech have uni-lateral control, usually from the left side of the brain. Single commands, then, direct the sets of muscles. You can control them.

If you wish to use your voice increasingly effectively you need to under-stand the mechanics of its production. You need to systematize your knowledge about the production and need to test your orderly arrange-ment against both experience and documented data. There is an evident willingness among uninformed laymen to give complete accounts for be-haviors of speech. Many of these are based on no more than "old wives' tales." You, an informed student, will be more exact.

The enumeration of muscles in this chapter is incomplete. It includes only those that are most frequently named in a description of speech production. They are sufficient to illustrate the mechanics involved in voice production and pronunciation: a muscle pulls, a muscle can be controlled, and—very importantly—all speech production is "muscle business." You must train particular muscles to act as you want them to act.

You will discover in making one speech sound after another that you are hearing one pitch after another and one loudness after another. These can be changed, but to produce the changes requires physiological changes. As a motivated student you will try to put the parts of your sound-producing systems into predetermined relationships and anticipate the acoustic results. This "play speech," this pantomime speech, this conscious speech may have significance beyond the immediate improve-ment of a single phoneme or the correcting of a single restricting habit. This single instance of consciously controlled speech may result in an insightful personal program. It may affect all of your speech, your evalua-tion of your speech, and that of others, and, in the light of some theories, the perception of speech. An incidental outcome of these private exercises is an increased regard for the exhaled breath stream.

SUMMARY

Some of the latent energy of the outgoing airstream is turned into sound. This is voice and speech sounds. This transfer may occur at the vocal folds or at the places of stoppage and of constrictions of the breath stream above the vocal folds. Together these places are the speech-producing systems.

The vocal folds are encased in the larynx and are momentarily open or closed, taut or lax, and long or short as a result of one degree or another of muscular contractions. The muscles control and alter the relative positions of the thyroid, cricoid, and arytenoid cartilages. These relationships set the vocal folds in a momentary condition that accommodates a momentary vocal output. The action of the vocal folds is further affected by the loadings put on them by the nearby cavities.

Control and use of the speech mechanism is learned behavior and subject to cortical control. With practice this control becomes habitual and apparently reflexive. To alter this behavior requires systematic and conscious mastery of the ordinarily unconscious activity of talking.

Exercises

1. (a) Read aloud passages from "20,000 Cycles Under the Sea" (Appendix A) and illustrate some of the unusual sounds that are suggested by Christopher Rand and Rabelais. (b) Explain to your class ten of the allusions in "20,000 Cycles Under the Sea," for example, the title, Daedalus, *The Sea Around Us*, Rabelais, and *Brave New World*.

2. Explain some of the efforts that have been made to produce speech artificially.

3. Blow across the tops of a pint and a quart bottle noting the tones that you produce. Pour some water into the bottles and repeat the blowing. How do you account for the change in the bottle tone? Can you make the tones indistinguishable?

4. Hum /m/ vigorously. As you do so, open and close the jaw, keeping the lips pressed against each other. Explain any difference in tonal quality. Record this hum. Do the apparent changes in quality appear in the recording?

5. As you have read Chapter 5 you have articulated many sounds. The following short selections merit reading frequently. Some of them are particularly "loaded" with particular sounds. Study your modulation of the breath stream, sound by sound, as you read these passages.

a. /u/ She left the web, she left the loom,
She made three paces thro' the room,
She saw the water-lily bloom,
She saw the helmet and the plume,
She look'd down to Camelot.

The Lady of Shalott
Alfred Tennyson

b. /b/ Beat an empty barrel with the handle of a broom,
Boom, boom, boom!

The Congo
Vachel Lindsay

c. /b/ Double, double, toil and trouble;
Fire burn, and cauldron bubble.

Macbeth
William Shakespeare

d. /p/ Speak the speech, I pray you, as I pronounced it
to you, trippingly on the tongue.

Hamlet
William Shakespeare

e. /m/ And the muttering grew to a grumbling;
And the grumbling grew to a mighty rumbling;
And out of the houses the rats came tumbling.

*The Pied Piper of
Hamelin*
Robert Browning

f. /w/ It's a warm wind, the west wind, full of bird cries,
I never hear the west wind but tears are in my eyes.

The West Wind
John Masefield

g. /w/ Sweet and low, sweet and low,
Wind of the western sea.

The Princess
Alfred Tennyson

h. /w/ Wind away.
Begone, I say.
I will not to wedding with thee.

As You Like It
William Shakespeare

i. /f/ Fair is foul, and foul is fair,
Hover through the fog and filthy air.

Macbeth
William Shakespeare

j. /f/ A fool, a fool! I met a fool i' the forest,
A motley fool; a miserable world!
As I do live by food, I met a fool,
Who laid him down and basked him in the sun,
And railed on Lady Fortune in good terms,

In good set terms and yet a motley fool.
"Good morrow, fool," quoth I. "No sir," quoth he,
"Call me not fool till Heaven hath sent me fortune."

As You Like It
William Shakespeare

k. /v/   Gloucester: But shall I live in hope?
Anne: All men, I hope, live so.
Gloucester: Vouchsafe to wear this ring.
Anne: To take is not to give.

Richard the Third
William Shakespeare

l. /l/   Alone, alone, all, all alone,
Alone on a wide, wide sea!

*The Rime of the Ancient
Mariner*
Samuel Coleridge

m. /l/   Elaine the fair, Elaine the lovable,
Elaine, the lily maid of Astolat,
High in her chamber up a tower to the east,
Guarded the sacred shield of Launcelot.

Idylls of the King
Alfred Tennyson

n. /l/   Come down to Kew in lilac time, in lilac time,
in lilac time;
Come down to Kew in lilac time (it isn't far
from London!)

The Barrel Organ
Alfred Noyes

o. /l/   The splendor falls on castle walls
And snowy summits old in story:
The long light shakes across the lakes,
And the wild cataract leaps in glory.
Blow, bugle, blow, set the wild echoes flying,
Blow, bugle; answer, echoes, dying, dying, dying.

The Princess
Alfred Tennyson

p. /l/   Consider the lilies of the field, how they grow; they toil
not, neither do they spin; and yet I say unto you that
even Solomon in all his glory was not arrayed like one
of these.

Matthew 6:28-29

q. /r/   Great rats, small rats, lean rats, brawny rats,
Brown rats, black rats, gray rats, tawny rats,
Grave old plodders, gay young friskers.

*The Pied Piper of
Hamelin*
Robert Browning

r. /r/   The road was a ribbon of moonlight over the
          purple moor,
          And the highwayman came riding . . .

> *The Highwayman*
> Alfred Noyes

s. /z/   The year's at the spring,
          And day's at the morn;
          Morning's at seven;
          The hillside's dew-pearled;
          The lark's on the wing;
          The snail's on the thorn;
          God's in his heaven, . . .
          All's right with the world!

> *Pippa Passes*
> Robert Browing

t. /dʒ/ Judge not, that ye be not judged. For with what judg-
          ment ye judge, ye shall be judged: and with what
          measure ye mete, it shall be measured to you again.

> Matthew 7:1-2

u. /k/   And the wheel's kick, and the wind's song, and
          the white sail's shaking . . .

> *Sea Fever*
> John Masefield

v. /k/   Hark, hark, the lark at heaven's gate sings.

> *Cymbeline*
> William Shakespeare

7. Make freehand drawings of the mechanisms that generate fundamental frequency (this chapter) and vocal intensity (Chapter 4).

8. The succession of unstable governments in France during the 1940-1950's led John Steinbeck to write *The Short Reign of Pippin IV*.* Passages that follow the fall of one government and that precede the coronation of King Pippin follow. Analyze them for their allusions to voice.

a. It will be remembered that when President Sonnet called on the Christian Atheists to form a government they could not agree even within their own ranks. Likewise the Socialists failed to draw support. The Christian Communists, with the support of The Non-Tay-Payers' League, failed to quality. Only then did M. Sonnet call the historic conference of leaders of all parties at the Eylsée Palace. . . .

b. For three days the struggle raged. The leaders slept on the brocade couches of the Grand Ballroom and subsisted on the bread and cheese and Algerian wine furnished by M. le Presi-dent. It was a scene of activity and turmoil. The Elysée Ball-

---

room is not only wainscoted with mirrors but also has mirrors on its ceiling, which created the impresson that instead of forty-two party chiefs there were literally thousands. Every raised fist became fifty fists, while the echo from the hard mirror surfaces threw back the sounds of a multitude. . . .

c. The seriousness of the impasse at last began to be reflected in the Paris press. The humorous periodical *Alligator* suggested that the situation should be made permanent, since no national crisis had arisen since the party leaders were taken out of circulation.

Great historic decisions often result from small and even flippant causes. Well into the second week, the leaders of the larger political parties found that their voices, which had gone from loud to harsh to hoarse, were finally disappearing completely.

It was at this time that the compact group of the leaders of the Royalist party took the floor. Having had no hope of being included in any new government, they had abstained from making speeches, and thus had kept their voices. After the confusion of eight days of meetings, the calm of the Royalists was by contrast explosive.

d. The Comte de Terrefranque advanced to the rostrum and took the floor in spite of an impassioned but whispered address by M. Triflet, the Radical Conservative.

M. le Comte in a clear, loud voice announced that the Royalist group had joined forces. . . . He therefore introduced the Duc des Troisfronts, whose proposal would have the backing not only of the other Royalist parties but also of the noble and intelligent people of France.

The Duc des Troisfronts, who under ordinary circumstances was shielded from public appearances, because of the split palate which has been his family's chief characteristic for many generations, now took the stand and was able to make himself not only heard but even understood. . . .

e. M. le Duc was so surprised that he had been able to say all of this that he sat down and had to be reminded that he had not arrived at the point. Once reminded, however, he graciously arose again. He suggested, even commanded, that the monarchy be restored so that France might rise again like the phoenix out of the ashes of the Republic to cast her light over the world. He ended his address in tears and immediately left the room, crying to the Gardes Republicans at the gates of the palace, "I have failed! I have failed!" But, indeed, as everyone knows, he had not failed. . . .

f. The Bourbons walked like emperors and smiled little Bourbon smiles when the king's health was drunk. But when they named their Pretender, the Comte de Paris—all hell broke loose. . . .

g. For a day and a night the battle raged while noble voices grew hoarse and noble hearts pounded. Of all the aristocratic partisans, only the Merovingians sat back, quiet, listless, content, and faint.

h. On 10:37 A.M., February 21, the elderly Childeric de Saone stood gradually up and spoke softly in his dusty Merovingian voice, which nevertheless was one of the few voices left. . . .

i. Burgundy leaped up, intending to shout, "Who? You?" but the bleat his tortured throat emitted sounded more like, "Whee? Yee?"

"No," said Childeric, "I am content to live as my latter kinds lived and to solve the problem as they did. I suggest for the throne of France the holy blood of Charlemagne."

Bourbon exploded in a thunderous whisper. "Are you insane? The line has disappeared."

"Not so," said Childeric quietly.

9. In the development of the human embryo, what is the order in which parts of the speech mechanism are formed? Has Roberta Teale Swartz taken undue liberty in the order of development in her poem?

> Embryo*
>
> Out of distortion, out of shapelessness
> A face waking in flesh,
> Dumb in the dark—no outcry—
> Only a stir,
> Till ugliness, hidden, dissolves,
> Leaves the forehead in place:
> Till congruous the slow mouth comes.
> Woven dust,
> What speech, what smile will you quicken,
> What unknown light?

References

DuBrul, E. Lloyd, *Evolution of the Speech Apparatus.* Springfield, Illinois: Charles C Thomas, 1958.

Dudley, H. and T. H. Tarnoczy, "The Speaking Machine of Wolfgang von Kempelen," *Journal of the Acoustical Society of America,* 22 (1950), 151-66.

Dunn, H. K., "The Calculation of Vowel Resonances and an Electrical Vocal Tract," *Journal of the Acoustical Society of America,* 22 (1950), 740-53.

Fulton, J. F., *Physiology of the Nervous System.* New York: Oxford University Press, Inc., 1938.

---

* From *Lilliput* by Roberta Teale Swartz, copyright © 1926 by Harcourt, Brace & World, Inc.; renewed 1954 by Roberta Teale Swartz (Chalmers). Reprinted by permission of the publishers.

Hast, Malcolm H., "Subglottic Air Pressure and Neural Stimulation in Phonation," *Journal of Applied Physiology,* 16 (1951), 1142-46.

Hoops, Richard A., *Speech Science: Acoustics in Speech.* Springfield, Illinois: Charles C Thomas, 1960.

Ladefoged, Peter, *Elements of Acoustic Phonetics.* Chicago: University of Chicago Press, 1962.

Lenneberg, Eric, *Biological Foundations of Language.* New York: John Wiley & Sons, Inc., 1967.

Meader, Clarence L. and John H. Muyskens, *Handbook of Biolinguistics, Part I.* Toledo, Ohio: Herbert C. Weller, (rev. ed., 1962).

Moses, Elbert R., Jr., *Phonetics: History and Interpretation.* Englewood Cliffs, N.J.: Prentice-Hall, Inc., 1964.

Negus, V. E., *The Comparative Anatomy and Physiology of the Larynx.* London: William Heinemann Medical Books, Ltd., 1949.

Richardson, E. G. and E. Myer, *Technical Aspects of Sound.* Amsterdam, N.Y.: Elsevier Publishing Co., Inc., 1962.

Wise, Claude M., *Applied Phonetics.* Englewood Cliffs, N.J.: Prentice-Hall, Inc., 1957.

6

The Vocal Sound Waves

In both Chapters 4 and 5 the puffs of air that attend speaking were noted. These and the pulses of sound that arise at a point of obstruction or constriction are separate disturbances. The sound travels at the rate of all sound. This is a predictable rate, usually quoted as 1120 feet per second in air at a reference temperature and pressure. The breath stream up to the point of modulation moves in keeping with the rate the speaker contracts his muscles of exhalation. At the place of energy transfer the rate is altered by the restricting blockage and the subsequent release of the air. These puffs of air have been termed *macroscopic* aspects of speech. Conventionally they have held limited interest for students of speech production. However, they are important. They impinge upon cavities and surfaces of the mouth and excite them at their natural frequencies. The puff of spent air with the release of /k/, for example, agitates the large cavity of the forepart of the mouth. This provides the unique property of the consonant, setting it apart from /t/ and /p/. The gross macroscopic puffs generate the *microscopic* features of speech. These are carried on the sound wave.

THE PHYSICAL BASIS OF SOUND

Since speech is sound and is audible you should understand the properties of sound if you are to understand speech. Physically, sound exists in waves, sound waves. These are hardly analogous to the somewhat regular swellings of water of a sea or to the ripples that spread outward after a pebble is dropped in a pool. Sound is a succession of pressure variations in the transmitting medium. There is a surge of positive pressure. This is followed by a pressure that is negative to the pressure of the surge. Said another way, there is a compression, a bunching up, of adjacent molecules and this is followed by a rarefaction, a spreading out, of the molecules. These two events occur at successive times. These alternations are highly regular in the sound waves of a musical tone and almost regular in the sound waves of a sustained vowel. There is hardly any regularity in the sound waves of the noises that result from the interruptions, partial or complete, of the breath stream at the lips, teeth, or palate. Yet even with these turbulences there is a succession of positive and negative pressures.

The Movement of Sound

What is the form of a pressure wave? Fortunately the molecules of the transmitting medium do not flow with the wave to which they contribute pressure. Should they do so, there would be a wind of the speed of a jet airplane at the moment it breaks the sound barrier and sets up a sonic boom. However, there is displacement of the molecules of the medium. The molecules do move in space. With the origin of sound, at the point of modulation, the most proximate molecules move slightly away from the point of origin, a minute fraction of a millimeter. Each moving molecule bumps the molecule (or molecules) adjacent to it and in its direction of swing and then rebounds. It is given another bump by the modulator, surges forward again, to rebound, to go forward, to rebound, and so on. If you were to observe the action somewhat removed from the modulator you would see the molecules surge forward, bump others, rebound beyond their original positions, bump molecules that are behind them and rebound forward, and so forth. Thus, the pressure wave exists in space and in time and includes these features:

a. each particular molecule moves only back and forth about its mean position, or, figuratively, its point of rest (this distance is but a fraction of the diameter of the molecule);

b. the effect of sound extends in all directions from a point of origin and the forward-backward moving molecules describe a globe about the point of origin;

c. the effect of the expanding-contracting globe is outward, creating larger globes;

d. in transmission, the original relative pattern of *more* and *less* pressure is maintained in the successive pushings of molecules (a great initial impact displaces a molecule *farther* than a small impact and this difference is maintained throughout the jostling globe);

e. the succession of relative pressures, be they regular or irregular, travels at approximately 1120 feet per second in air.*

The Dimensions of the Pressure Fluctuations

You have in mind that moving molecules carry a pattern of sound pressures along all radii that might be drawn from the center of a sphere. Implicitly, the forward and backward swings of a molecule are in a straight line and the minute distance that each traverses is proportional to the magnitude of the sound. What distinguishes the molecular excursions that arise from one sound source from those that arise from another? Surely the sway of a molecule would not be the same when transmitting a pattern of sound pressure set up

by a girl's voice and a man's
by a weak and a strong voice
by a resonant voice and a thin one
by a slow talker and a fast one
by crisp and slurred articulation
by *ee* and *ah*
by the words *mother* and *madre* or *mama* and *papa*
by a pipe organ and a violin
by stamping feet and a cuckoo clock

There is an infinite number of different sounds that can impinge on the ear. Of these, every identifying aspect is uniquely represented in the patterns of movement of the molecules and the sequences of sound pressure that they transmit. Moreover, listeners learn to identify aurally the sources of many of the sounds. The movements of molecules and sequences of pressure have four dimensions. In the instance of speech,

---

* The globular movement of the sound wave accounts for the rate of diminution of sound with increases in distance. If you will envisage the area of an expanding sphere you will appreciate that the area of a segment of the surface that is described by the same four radii increases more rapidly than the lengths of the radii increase. The area increases in proportion to the square of the distance. Consequently, the movement of the molecules that convey sound have less and less effect as the wave front progresses spherically. This leads to the rule that sound level diminishes inversely with the square of the distance from the source. This is an important rule in the classroom or auditorium, as well as outdoors.

all four are controlled by the talker's muscles. However, it is easier to understand the four dimensions if non-speech waves are examined first.

The succession of sound pressures is most easily explained in the instance of a sound source that generates a pure tone. The tuning fork, for example, sets up a series of repetitive identical events in the transmitting medium, such as air. Each of many molecules is pushed rhythmically once every time the prongs of the fork move outward. Successive pushes are of the same amount, and the distance that is retraced in the backward swing of the prong and the molecule is the same time after time. If the movements of the prongs of the tuning fork are restricted a bit, the prongs, and hence the molecules, move with the same regularity but less far. This distance is *Dimension 1* of the sound pressure pattern. It reflects the amount of sound pressure that is transmitted. Other factors held constant, as in this example, the amount of sound pressure is proportional to the distance the individual molecules are displaced (actually proportional to the square of the displacement).

Another aspect of the tuning-fork waves can be readily illustrated by sounding two forks in succession, one an octave higher than the other. The prongs of one may move in and out 256 times each second and the other 128 times. The distance of the excursions of the two sets of prongs might be equal. Imagine the action of one isolated molecule as it plays its part in propagating each pattern of sound pressure. It swings rhythmically, as before, back and forth, repetitively. Now with a fictitious and super-fast stop watch in your super-human hand and with your super-human eyes that are capable of clocking any speed accurately, please count the swings of the molecule. There are 256 swings per second in one instance and 128 in the other. *Dimension 2* of the pattern of sound pressures is the *frequency* of occurrence of the oscillation. This is often stated in cycles per second (cps) or Hertz (Hz). Before you lay down your watch, please time a single cycle: 1/256 and 1/128 second, respectively. This is the *period* of the wave. This measurement was not necessary. You could have computed it, for period is the reciprocal of frequency.

While you have your stop watch in hand, please try to find how long the tuning forks, once struck, will remain in oscillation. This would provide *Dimension 3,* the aspect of *time* or of *duration* of the succession of sound waves. The analogue in speech might be the duration of a vowel.*

---

* This conventional set of dimensions of the sound wave is imperfect. The dimensions are presented as being discrete; but you observe that *period* in the preceding paragraph is also a *duration*. In practice, *duration* is reserved for linguistic units, not single sound waves.

The sound pressures of speech are not simple alternating ones, as those generated by a tuning fork. But they are amenable to the same kinds of descriptions. The major difference between the sound waves of a tuning fork and the ones of speech is that there are successive pressures within each sound wave in speech and these are highly irregular. Instead of swinging forward and backward in a rhythmical fashion, always covering the same number of units of space (extremely minute distances), the molecule goes forward and backward irregularly within a single sound wave, as illustrated in the fictitious data of Table 1. The molecule in

Table 1. A fictitious example in arbitrary units of the alternate forward and backward movements of a molecule of air during one complex sound wave (read "forward 8, backward 1, forward ½ . . .").

Forward	Backward
8	1
½	13
1	½
12	1
½	10
1	½
6	3

Table 1 terminally arrives at its mean position, having gone a total of 29 units forward and an equal number backward. It is now thrust into motion again to retrace approximately the same pattern. The word *approximately* is important, for in speech an identical sequence of sound pressures seldom, if ever, recurs. There is some slight difference in the minor forward-backward swings of molecules in successive sound waves.

The topic under discussion is *Dimension 4* of the sound wave. This is the course traced by the molecules during a single sound wave. This course leads to a somewhat figurative term, *the shape of the wave*. This shape can be photographed, as in Figure 13, and is amenable to quantitative description. The description is labeled *the acoustic spectrum* of the sound. In effect, the irregular set of movements that constitutes a complex sound wave is described in terms of several sets of regular, periodic, or tuning-fork movements that, if occurring simultaneously, would produce in summation the singular irregular sound wave that is under examination. The sound wave described here arises at the vocal folds. They account for its frequency. The wave gets its shape from the

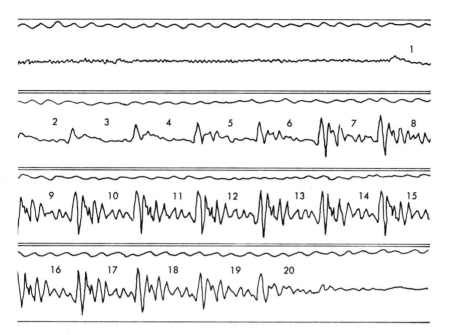

Figure 13. A representation of an oscillographic recording of the sound waves produced during a single rendition of /ɑ/ in the word *top*. The waves are numbered from 1 to 20. The time line above the waves is 440 Hz.

resonating cavities. A highly similar wave can be expected to follow it. A series of 10–14 of them might comprise the vowel of a rapidly spoken monosyllable, and 30–40, a slowly spoken one.

Resonance

The tone that arises at the vocal folds, frequently called the cord tone, is a theoretical sound. It does not exist in a listener's experience. The tone that is heard is the cord tone modified by the cavities and structures that serve as resonators. You read earlier that each cavity has its natural frequency. It is easy to imagine, then, that a tone comprised of many, many frequencies arises at the vocal folds. Immediately the waves of the tone pass through a resonator, the throat. The intensity of the frequencies to which the throat is resonant is increased. Then comes the similar action on the part of the resonator behind-the-bunch-of-the-tongue. This action affects different frequencies from those enhanced by the throat. There follows the action of the cavity in-front-of-the-bunch-of-the-tongue. It affects a singular band of frequencies. The periodic sound waves may also set the roof of the mouth in vibration and thus activate the nasal cavity at its natural resonance. The summation of these effects is a sound wave that is markedly different in shape from the cord wave. This shape or this acoustic spectrum is the direct result of resonators most of which are given their size by muscular control.

Aperiodic Pressures

The preceding paragraphs related particularly to those aspects of speech that recur with considerable regularity, essentially successive sound waves. Much speech, as you read in Chapter 5, is a series of irregular modulations, arising from blockages, partial or complete, in the pipe above the vocal folds. In a context other than speech, these nonrecurring bursts and hisses would be noise. As this portion of speech travels through a conducting medium, the molecules that are being jostled about might be envisaged as moving forward and backward in an almost random fashion. There would be no periodicity and slight probability that successive positive sound pressures would be similar. There are some predictable features of this motion:

a. no single displacement of a molecule is nearly as large as the displacement of the molecules in the periodic waves;

b. the molecule is displaced more frequently in the almost-random jerky movements than in periodic waves;

c. there are common features in the jostling of the molecules in successive productions of one phoneme and there are obvious dissimilarities in these patterns from one speech sound to another.

Thus, if one were to treat each movement of a molecule as the period of a wave it would be short and the corresponding frequency, high.*

The Medium of Transmission

Although most of your listening experience is with airborne sound, you are aware that any molecular substance transmits sound. The rate at which sound waves are propagated differs from one medium to another. The more tightly compressed the molecules, the faster sound travels. Thus, your ear when placed at a railroad track detects an oncoming train through iron earlier than through air. The sound that moves through water in "20,000 Cycles Under the Sea" (Appendix A) travels at a

---

* Essentially this is the treatment that pertains when sounds such as /f, k, t, p/ are fed through filters that do not pass high frequencies. The random fluctuations of short duration, that is of short periods, are filtered out. When speech is treated in this manner, it becomes badly distorted and unintelligible.

faster rate than it would in air. For reasons of practicality you may expect your classmates to be much interested in the transmission of voice in air and less interested in the esoteric matters of a substitute for air in space travel or of transmission of sound in underwater living. Yet this apparent truth ignores one of our most frequent listening experiences in verbal communication: hearing oneself. True, the globular transmission of sound reaches the speaker's ear airborne, perhaps 12 inches from the most distant point of modulation, the vocal folds. The time for the sound to travel this distance is about one millisecond. This same modulation at the vocal folds sets up sound waves in the moist tissue-bone route from the larynx to the middle and inner ear. This is the shorter route by one-half and the rate of sound transmission is faster than in air! Moreover, the loudness of the two sounds, airborne and "bone conducted," is estimated to be the same. Thus, you have good reason to be interested in sound transmission in media other than air. Your sidetone or acoustic feedback utilizes several media: flesh, bone, and ligaments, as well as air.

Reverberation. The imagined view in this chapter of spech in transit from a talker to a listener by air transmission has presumed a single one-way transmission channel. In reality speech usually occurs in the presence of reflecting surfaces—walls, floors, ceilings—and the sound waves that hit these surfaces are partially absorbed, that is, converted to heat. Also, partially, they are reflected much as light is reflected by a mirror. In a room that has highly reflecting surfaces, such as the Elysée Ballroom of Exercise 8-b of Chapter 5, the path of a sound wave may go from wall to wall several times. Ultimately the wave dissipates or wears out as the energy diminishes. Meanwhile, sound waves interfere with other waves. Sometimes reflected sound masks or makes unintelligible subsequently generated sound. The total effect is that a vastly different acoustic condition is set up in the room than would exist if the sound were not susceptible to reflection, for example, if the sound originated in free space. A convenient measure for the acoustic conditions of a room in this regard is *reverberation time*. This is the time required for a sound to subside in the amount of 60 decibels.* This is frequently

---

* The decibel (db) is used in stating relative sound pressure level. The unit is, technically,

$$db = 20 \log_{10} \frac{\text{Pressure 1}}{\text{Pressure 2}}$$

This is easier than it looks, for *Pressure 2* is often an arbitrary base level, 0.0002 microbar. Standard measuring equipment is available to show levels relative to this base. On such a "meter," conversation occurs at about 60 db (six inches from the mouth). The ear should not be exposed momentarily to sound in excess of 130 db nor continuously in excess of 90 db. The ear can detect about 100 gradations of level with a 1000 Hz tone. These are approximately 1 db apart.

several seconds. In a room in which the reverberation time exceeds one second, speech is somewhat garbled and hard to hear. However, the time may reach seven seconds in some locations that are used for public speeches.

NONACOUSTIC TRANSMISSION

The approximate speed of sound in air has been stated. Much speech is transmitted electronically by telephone, radio, television, and a hearing aid. Here speech is conveyed at the approximate speed of light, not the cumbersome slow one of sound. At the latter rate, speech would require four hours to travel across the United States; really, it goes electronically in milliseconds. Different rates of receiving one's own speech were mentioned above. Fastest of all would be a contact microphone pickup at the larynx and an electronic coupling to the ear or temporal bone.

STORED SPEECH

Much speech is recorded and reproduced. In fact, for many students the word *sound wave* has meant the glistening irregular tiny indentations on a phonograph record. For others, it means a vertical display on an oscilloscope, possibly an inch long. Not at all! A male voice might generate 112 sound waves a second. Each wave, then, in air would be ten feet long. It is stored in a fraction of an inch on the phonograph recording. Yet when it is replayed it again consumes ten feet in air. The correspondence of the original and reproduced waves in "shape" relates to the fidelity of the system.

APPLICATIONS

Every distinguishing element of a sound is carried by the four dimensions of the sound wave. This includes the aperiodic pressures. A single perceptible succession of these pressure fluctuations is your voice on the way to a listener. If he fails to hear the message, the sound pressure was inadequate. If he fails to hear correctly, you made the series of waves poorly in one or more of its four dimensions. If he hears either correctly or incorrectly and finds the sound unpleasant, the fault lies in your handling of your speech musculatures.

The frequency of the periodic waves is set by the vocal folds. If you are the talker, then with each burst of the folds that you hold under some tenson, one nearly periodic sound wave is set up. The period of the wave is the interval between successive bursts. If, as you engage in the fantasy of wave counting, you find that the periods of all your sound waves are essentially the same, it follows that your vocal folds are not varying the time between these microscopic bursts. You may say that the periods of the successive waves are the same or that the frequency is constant. It doesn't matter which you say, your listener will call you *monotone*. To change this, you contract or relax one or more sets of muscles affecting the tension of the vocal folds.

The amount of sound pressure transmitted, usually called the amplitude of the sound wave, is set by the rate with which the air is expelled from your lungs. This, as you learned in Chapter 4, is solely a function of the rate of muscular contraction in exhalation. Possibly you and a friend use the same rate of muscular contraction; yet the magnitudes of the sound pressures that you transmit are not the same. One person's sound-producing systems are more efficient than another's at the points of modulation. With your sound-producing systems, the way to achieve a greater sound pressure is to exert more effort during exhalation.

The complexity or the shape of the sound wave of your speech is also set by you. Through learned behavior you give the pipe above the larynx one configuration rather than another. You make enormous changes in that configuration as you speak, one set of shapes for *ee,* another for *ah.* These changes that accompany different vowels are similar to ones that account for the differences betwen sound-wave configurations that distinguish poor voices from good voices. All of them are qualitative changes or ones in *timbre.*

Finally, the duration of spoken phrases may seem shorter than "real" as you listen to a recording of your speech. The fault does not lie in the recorder. You either halted your exhalation or you turned off the crucial modulating system and the pause began. Silent exhalation instead of a modulated airstream ensued.

A telephone transmitter or a microphone picks up speech to carry it to remote listeners, to record and preserve it for a time, and to permit either the speaker or his teacher to hear it for critical examination. The microphone picks up the successive pressure variations that are in transit in the air and takes them to the recording head. The microphone that is sufficiently sensitive to react to the molecular displacements—the microphonic aspects of speech—also reacts to any other such pressures that impinge upon it, for example the macrophonic elements. It behooves the speaker, then, not to talk directly into a microphone that is close to his mouth. He will "blast" the microphone. At the same time, the power of the sound wave diminishes rapidly as the distance from the sound source is increased. Here is the inverse square law. Thus, you transmit or record a stronger signal rather than a weaker one if the distance between the microphone and the mouth is short.

Although amplifiers can compensate for distance, the supersensitive system often picks up many unwanted ambient noises. A frequent excuse is, "The noise level of the system is high." For related reasons, recordings should not be made in highly reverberant rooms. The reproduced message is then heard as being more garbled than it really was. The recording is faithful; the difference lies in the fact that an on-the-spot observer is able to ignore some acoustic events and attend only to the selected ones he wishes to follow. This phenomenon is termed *the cocktail party effect.* It has been subjected to many quantitative investigations.

SUMMARY

The relationship between one's performance and the sound wave that he generates follows:

The speaker produces:	The sound wave exhibits:
a. Rate of vocal fold openings	Frequency (Hz)
b. Rates of muscular contraction in exhalation	Relative sound pressure levels
c. Shaping of the cavities of voice production	Sound waves of singular shapes (acoustic spectrum)
d. Duration of muscular contraction in exhalation	Durational features of the units of language

The microphone-reproducer system yields a faithful rendition of the frequency and durational characteristics of the sound waves in transit; with current engineering the systems are capable of preserving the features of sound pressure level and acoustic spectrum to the satisfaction of hi-fi connoisseurs.

Exercises

1. Show a phonograph record to the class and explain what you *see* on the disk.

   a. Relate what you see to the four dimensions of the acoustic events that were recorded.

b. Present some of the material of the disk from memory and then play what you have read. The class will search for similarities and differences between the two renditions.

2. The following passage has been used as material that can be read with the speaker intending to convey any of several emotions: grief, indifference, anger, fear, contempt, hate. Groups of listeners were highly successful in identifying the intended emotions from recordings of the sentences. The readers were given contexts for the materials that made the different emotions appropriate. These sentences were then extracted from the recordings and reproduced out of context. The readings were clearly differentiated in rate and frequency, two of the four dimensions of voice. The other two were not studied. Try to express the several meanings as you read the lines.

There is no other answer. You've asked me that question a thousand times and my reply has always been the same. It always will be the same.

3. The four dimensions of sound are not completely independent. For example, frequency usually rises as the speaker adds to his sound pressure level. This is easily illustrated. Simply sustain the vowel *ah* at several loudness levels, giving no thought to frequency. The frequency rises with added sound pressure. Also note how both frequency and loudness typically drop at the end of a sentence. Observe further examples of this relationship as members of the class give two-minute speeches on one of these topics:

a. Religion and the state
b. The influence of Rome on American life
c. Indoctrination is not brainwashing
d. Leonardo da Vinci and Robert Fulton, a comparison
e. What elocution means to me (with examples).

4. Convert the values of Table 1 into a sound wave that resembles a wave of Figure 13. Use graph paper. Assume that the frequency of the wave you are drawing is 200 Hz.

5. a. Describe the least reverberant room you have visited, perhaps an anechoic chamber.
b. Describe the most reverberant room you have visited.

6. The difference between pronunciations of *nitrate* and *night rate* is a difference in *juncture,* an aspect of duration. Prepare a list of ten contrasts in juncture.

7. Through voice control, convey the sense of selected lines of the following passage to a listener and ask him to tell you the meaning of what you read. This requires special attention to matters of frequency, duration, and sound pressure.

a. Esau Wood sawed wood. Esau Wood would saw wood.
b. All the wood Esau Wood saw Esau Wood would saw. In

c. other words, all the wood Esau saw to saw Esau sought
d. to saw. Oh, the wood Wood would saw! And oh, the
e. wood-saw with which Wood would saw wood. But one
f. day Wood's wood-saw would saw no wood, and thus the
g. wood Wood sawed was not the wood Wood would saw if
h. Wood's wood-saw would saw wood. Now, Wood would saw
i. if Wood's wood-saw would saw wood. Now, Wood would
j. saw wood with a wood-saw that would saw wood, so
k. Esau sought a saw that would saw wood. One day Esau
l. saw a saw saw wood as no other wood-saw Wood saw
m. would saw wood. In fact, of all the wood-saws Wood
n. ever saw saw wood Wood never saw a wood-saw that would
o. saw wood as the wood-saw Wood saw saw wood would saw
p. wood, and I never saw a wood-saw that would saw as
q. the wood-saw Wood saw would saw until I saw Esau saw
r. wood with the wood-saw Wood saw saw wood. Now Wood
s. saws wood with the wood-saw Wood saw saw wood.

8. In class, two students will read alternately, each reading any five of the following phrases. The listeners on one side of the room will respond to one speaker and the remaining listeners to the other speaker. Listeners will be provided with pads of paper, one sheet for each speaker. Listeners will write nothing after hearing Phrase 1. They will write either *fast* or *slow* after hearing Phrase 2; write either *loud* or *soft* after hearing Phrase 3; write one descriptive word about the speaker's vocal quality after hearing Phrase 4; and draw a line that suggests the vocal inflection of the phrase after hearing Phrase 5. (This could be an upward slope, downward slope, both, or a straight line.) Each speaker collects the descriptions that relate to him.

to keep a margin	angle of the wing
into the landing	out from the circle
before the other	only then can we
on the other hand	and start a spiral
starting to break	under the wing tip
if we were coming	is of the rudder
power to help you with	is flying downwind
if there is little	trimming of the plane
they should be given	hold the glide longer
vary your pattern	don't pick up too much
in for the landing	that it won't drop back
in order to keep	first check the traffic
we level the wings	use forward pressure
the same as the one	first lower the nose
show you what I mean	wings are kept level
worse than a good one	results in a skid
as we get higher	check the gas supply

the plane is level   how strong the wind is
ahead of the plane   to wing toward the road
in a shallow dive   slip close to the ground

9. The following paragraphs from "European Scientific Notes" (USN, Office of Naval Research), July, 1966, seem to stretch the boundaries of voice and diction. Read the paragraphs thoughtfully and try to suggest new realistic dimensions to be anticipated in this field.

Deeper Voices From the Deep

The Speech Transmission Laboratory is one of the world's leading centers for research in general voice communication. It is a part of the Swedish Royal Institute of Technology, which is located near the center of Stockholm—just on the northern edge of the shopping and business area.

The Laboratory employs about 30 scientists, who are roughly divided into three groups: electronics-oriented engineers, physiologists and psychologists, and linguistic experts. The latter group includes both classic linguistic analysts and mathematicians who are employing the modern techniques of communications theory and information theory.

The research conducted at the laboratory covers the entire field of speech and hearing: speech communication research on a broad basis, speech analysis, speech synthesis, speech and hearing research of medical interest, and speech analysis and restoration in high ambient air pressures.

The latter topic is of particular interest to deep-sea divers—particularly in a "sea lab" situation. But all of the other studies also support this highly specialized research.

The problems of speech in sea lab conditions are twofold. The first problem is the distortion caused by pressure. This is an interesting phenomenon, as sound itself is not distorted by differences in pressure—rather the speech track, principally the soft tissues in the throat and back of the mouth, is distorted and rendered less resonant. This problem has already been studied for several years.

The second problem is the distribution of speech in a helium-oxygen atmosphere. . . .

10. Relate the discussion in the section *Reverberation* to Steinbeck's description of Elysée Palace (Exercise 8, Chapter 5).

References

Fairbanks, Grant, "Recent Experimental Investigations of Vocal Pitch in Speech," *Journal of the Acoustical Society of America,* 11 (1940), 457-66.
————, *Voice and Articulation Drillbook,* 2nd ed. New York: Harper & Row, Publishers, 1960.

Flanagan, J. L., *Speech Analysis, Synthesis, and Perception*. New York: Academic Press, Inc., 1965.

Harbold, George J., "Pitch Ratings of Voiced and Whispered Vowels," *Journal of the Acoustical Society of America*, 30 (1958), 600-01.

Peters, Robert, *Research on Psychological Parameters of Sound*. Wright Air Development Division, Wright-Patterson Air Force Base (Technical Report 60-249), 1960.

————, "Dimension of Quality of the Vowel [æ], *Journal of Speech and Hearing Research*, 6 (1963), 239-48.

Peterson, G. E. and H. L. Barney, "Control Methods Used in the Study of Vowels," *Journal of the Acoustical Society of America*, 24 (1952), 175-84.

Pierce, John R. and Edward E. David, Jr., *Man's World of Sound*. Garden City: Doubleday & Company, Inc., 1958.

7

Your Voice With Your Listeners

You have learned that the exhaled breath stream may activate the vocal folds, may be arrested and released by blocking structures, and may be impeded by a constriction. Thereby, the airstream is modulated one or more times. A system of cavities is coupled to the modulator, and the outcome is a series of acoustic events that includes the speaker's voice and the making of a series of sounds. Both the voice and the sounds are conveyed on the same sequence of sound waves, a singular series of varied pressures, propagated globally. The process usually is purposeful and occurs in a social environment. There is at least one listener. He is intended to hear the voice and to decode the series of speech sounds. He may also evaluate the voice, judge the merit of the formation of the speech sounds, and test the validity of the decoded message. This chapter focuses on the first of these, the voice. You and your fellow students are evaluating each other's voices. Inevitably, then, you are listening to each other. You are using your sense of hearing.

Speaking and listening are closely interdependent. As Karl U. Smith says, "Man's sensitivity to sound is closely correlated with the physical characteristics of the sounds he produces in speech. Comparable examples could be multiplied to show that the nature and efficiency of hearing in animal species reflect the development of sound-controlled behavior by processes of natural selection." The following paragraphs treat the ear in a manner parallel to earlier treatments of the speech mechanism.

THE EAR

Hearing is an active behavior that involves a set of neural fibers that run from the inner ear to the cortex and another set from the cortex to the inner ear. Much remains to be learned about this behavior. Therefore, as you read about hearing, imagine that most sentences begin, "According to so-and-so's theory of hearing . . ." The sensory receptors of your ear respond to variations in air pressure when these variations fall within a particular band of frequencies. This band covers about ten octaves from approximately 16 Hz to 16,000 or 20,000 Hz. The end organs of hearing lie firmly imbedded in the mastoid portions of the right and left temporal bones. Each is connected with the exterior air-transmission channel by a pair of abutting canals, the middle ear and the auditory meatus (*meatus* is canal, natural passage, or the opening to such a passage).

The auditory meatus lies within the anterior base of the pinna or external ear. This canal is slightly crooked and about one inch long. At its inner end it is covered by a delicate membrane, the eardrum. This drum or *tympanic membrane* is slightly conical and lies across the ear canal at an angle, and pointing inward. Its axis when your head is erect makes nearly a 45-degree angle with the floor. Fibers run concentrically from the middle of the drum to the periphery. This delicate membrane, under tension, gives and rebounds in keeping with the succession of varying air pressures or displacements of adjacent air molecules that impinge upon it, coming through the ear canal.

The Middle Ear

Lying behind the eardrum is an air-filled cavity, scarcely larger than one cubic centimeter. This is the middle ear. The static air pressure within the middle ear corresponds to that of the outside air. This balance is maintained by opening your eustachian tube from time to time while swallowing or yawning. This tube extends from the roof of the nose to the middle ear, a little more than one inch. It is the only opening to the middle ear.

The movements of the eardrum reach the end organ of hearing (the inner ear) through the mechanical action of a series of three minute bones, the *ossicles*. They are named descriptively and imaginatively. The malleus or the hammer attaches to the eardrum and moves back and forth with it, in keeping with the positive and negative pressure fluctuations of the medium, usually air. The stapes or stirrup fastens to a membrane that covers the entry to the inner ear, the oval window. Between these two extreme bones and connected to both is the leverlike incus or anvil. It reduces the minute movements of the eardrum to accom-

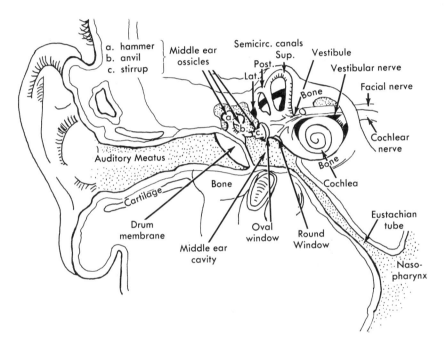

Figure 14. A representation of the outer, middle, and inner ear and associated structures and canals, for example, the vestibular organs and the eustachian tube (after Brodël).

modate (a) the resistance offered by the oval window, behind which lie fluids that are set in motion by the movements of the window, and (b) the delicate structures of the cochlea. The ossicles are fascinating objects to view, similar in size to the parts that a watchmaker handles with tweezers and a magnifying glass.

The Inner Ear

The cochlea (or snail) houses the mechanism that converts relative air pressures into nerve impulses, that is, changes a physical stimulus to neural actions. Here is a spiraling tube of two and three-quarters turns that is relatively broad at the base and narrow at the apex. It is divided horizontally throughout its length by a bony shelf and a lateral extension from the shelf—the basilar membrane. This is about 31 mm long. This division terminates near the apex, leaving a small connecting space between the two halves, the helicotrema. One side of the divided chamber is closed by the membranous oval window attached to the footplate of the stapes; the other is closed by the round window which merely faces back into the middle ear. Thus, as the hammer-anvil-stirrup chain pushes the oval window inward, either the fluid or a turbulence within the fluid is moved slightly along the basilar membrane. With sounds of great level, this movement extends through the helicotrema at the apex of the coil, down the other side of the membrane, and finally distends the round window outwardly.

With the preceding gross description of the ear in mind you may proceed to a more microscopic examination of the cochlea. Figure 15 shows the cochlear canal in cross section. From the shelf a second membrane in addition to the basilar membrane arises to run outward and upward at a 40- or 45-degree angle relative to the basilar membrane,

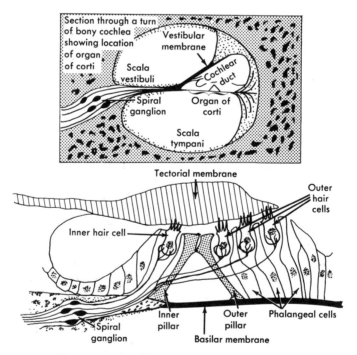

Figure 15. A cross-sectional view of the cochlea.

and, like it, to terminate at the outer wall of the cochlea. This is Reisner's membrane and it, too, runs almost the full length of the cochlea. This means that there are three small canals instead of two and the plunger action of the stapes is against the end of this canal bounded by the two membranes.

Between the two membranes, Reisner's and the basilar, is a series of minute arches and many hair cells that connect directly to the auditory nerve. The cells fall in orderly rows, two on one side of the arches and three on the other. The three hair cells shown near the center of Figure 15, arising from the basilar membrane, are possibly in contact with the tectorial membrane much, is not all, of the time. The manner in which the pressures of the liquids, one inside the Reisner-cochlear canal and the other in the basilar-Reisner canal, and the organ of Corti (the arches and the hair cells) interact is a topic for argument and the basis for many theories of hearing. At the organ of Corti, however, the successive pressure variations of the air-link between the speaker and the listener are converted into neural pulses that go to the listener's cortex by way of the eighth cranial nerve.

In general, the apical end of the basilar membrane is responsive to relatively slow pressure fluctuations, frequencies as low as 16 Hz, and the basal end to pressure fluctuations that occur as often as 16,000 or 20,000 times per second. More exactly, a considerable portion of the membrane, at least the upper half, is somewhat sensitive to low frequencies, ones no higher than 1550 Hz. The upper part of the frequency range of the ear is particularly susceptible to damage that arises with certain illnesses, and as a normal part of the aging process is likely to be considerably and progressively reduced in sensitivity.

Actions of the Cochlea

Two important distinctions are made by the end organ of hearing and projected to the cerebral cortex: frequency differentiation and amount-of-sound-pressure differentiation. The listener can tell one frequency from another and one intensity from another when the differences exceed quantifiable minima. Fortunately, the on-off response of hearing is almost as rapid as any on-off action of a sound source. This allows you to follow rapid fluctuations between voice and alternations of pauses and speech sounds.

In combination, the capacities to experience and differentiate frequencies and to experience and distinguish magnitudes of sound account for the ear's ability to respond uniquely to the four dimensions of the sound wave that were discussed in Chapter 6: frequency, sound pressure, wave form, and the presence or absence of sound (duration).

Threshold. The phrase *exceed quantifiable minima* in the preceding section suggests an important limitation of the capability of the ear to receive and differentiate both frequencies and magnitudes. Any minimum in either regard is called *threshold.* There is a minimum sound pressure level at each frequency that distinguishes hearing something from hearing nothing, experience from no experience. This is a crucial threshold of hearing. It is revealed in an audiogram, illustrated in Figure 16. This shows the minimum pressure to which a particular ear is sensitive at each of several frequencies.

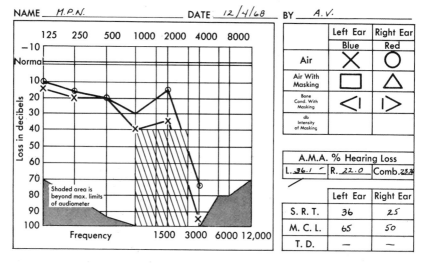

Figure 16. A reproduction of an audiogram. Normal or perfect hearing would be represented by a line coinciding with 0 from one side of the audiogram to the other. The central shaded area of the audiogram indicates frequencies and intensities of these frequencies that are deemed essential for the reception of speech.

There is also a minimum difference that can be distinguished between frequencies. For example, 256 Hz sounds different from 200 Hz, but probably 255 and 256 Hz sound the same. The difference threshold at 1000 Hz is 3 Hz and this proportion, 0.003, holds over a considerable band of frequencies. The difference threshold, whether applied to frequency or some other physical attribute of sound, gives rise to a useful phrase *just noticeable difference* (j.n.d.). Thresholds, then, relate to any minimal difference that gives rise to a change in auditory experience. This can be a minimal time that a tone needs to exist to give rise to an experience of tone or a minimal change in wave form to be recognized as a different acoustic event. You can easily extend the list. These many thresholds are minutely different from one set of normal ears to another. The artist, speaker, and critic, then, may expect diversity rather than agreement in auditory and affective responses to speaking and singing.

THE DESCRIPTION OF VOICE

In the transmitting medium the sound wave or series of waves of speech has four dimensions, as explained in Chapter 6. In the receptive organ of the ear and in its cortical projection the four properties of the sound wave yield sensations or experiences. The four interpretations that the listener makes from speech waves are loudness, pitch, quality (timbre), and rate. Each listener has learned to like and to dislike some vocal behaviors associated with each of these. Perhaps you wish to think of these affective responses as biases or prejudices. At least, there is a singular meaning that attends the sensation *for the listener.* In the association areas of his cortex, the sound becomes linked with experience, for example, with faces, prejudices, words, and all of the personal significances of his private life. These four aspects of voice will be treated here and reviewed in Chapter 12.

Pitch

The frequency of sound waves is linked to the subjective experience of pitch. This is not only a single momentary experience, as would accompany a rapidly spoken monosyllable, but is also a succession of these responses. There is a long-term experience of pitch as speech continues through a sentence, a paragraph, a poem, or a public address. True, the listener tends to assign an average pitch to what he is hearing, whatever its length. His sophistication, specialization, motivation, and keenness of perception come to bear on his interpretation of it. This average pitch or *key* is *high, low,* or *medium* and he assigns this description to this one dimension of the voice. The description fits or fails to fit the age and sex of the speaker. Please notice that this is another judgmental rating. If the listener is a student of music he may unconsciously differentiate between middle C and C sharp. Whatever the key, the listener is probably prejudiced against hearing it constantly throughout a sentence and beyond. The descriptive word is *monopitch* or *monotone* for the voice that lingers overly long on the same or nearly the same pitch.

A listener expects variety in the pitch of a voice. He usually calls the changes in pitch *inflection* and sometimes *intonation*. Also, he expects to find variety among the upward and downward changes in pitch. A particular inflection is not expected a second and third time with repeated syntactic structures. What matter if the oral reader varies his monopitch if the effect is *sing-song?* This distracting behavior is often present in the memorized recitations of children's poetry.

Figure 17 shows a *melody curve.* This is the pitch of a speaker plotted on a musical scale. The speaker is Kenneth MacKenna and the passage that he is speaking is from a Broadway play of the early 1930's by Kaufman and Hart:*

> Not in the classroom or on the field, but in those small chosen hours, those all-revealing hours when we sat and talked about ourselves and each other—talked with a warmth and a richness that never can be recaptured. Those were the hours when we discovered and embraced that greatest of all glories, friendship. Of all the things that I take away from here, the one that I most treasure and for which I am most humbly grateful, is a friendship that I have found. I hope he will always be by my side all through my life. And lastly, this I've learned: I've learned to value ideals above everything else. Let them ever be our heritage, our guiding force. As we go out into the world, as we take up our chosen professions, we are clad, as it were, in shining armor.

Time is shown on the abscissa of Figure 17 with each vertical bar indicating one second and with the intervening marks showing one-tenths of a second. Frequency is represented on the ordinate. Between the words of the script and the melody curve is a record that depicts intensity or sound pressure level. This does not concern you at the moment. You are interested here in the fundamental frequency and pitch. This figure does not show MacKenna's fundamental frequency wave by wave, but is a plot of average pitch over successive 1/24's of a second. Obviously the speaker was not monopitch. How often did he use one pitch? How often another? What was the range of pitches that he used? These are shown in the frequency distribution in Figure 18. Here the fundamental frequency or pitch of the voice is shown on the abscissa and the number of instants (an instant here is 1/24 second) during which the actor used a particular pitch is shown on the ordinate.

Paradoxically, the listener who is labeling a speaker monotone—an effect that often seems to justify a nap—may hold an expensive ticket for a show in which the comedian demonstrates his forte, *deadpan* and *monopitch.* This imagined situation suggests that *appropriateness* must be included in a list of criteria for good pitch control. Under this label the listener reflects many marks of his culture. To name a few, the woman's

---

* From *Merrily We Roll Along* by George S. Kaufman and Moss Hart. Copyright 1934 and renewed 1962 by Anne Kaufman Schneider and Catherine Carlisle Hart. Reprinted by permission of Random House, Inc.

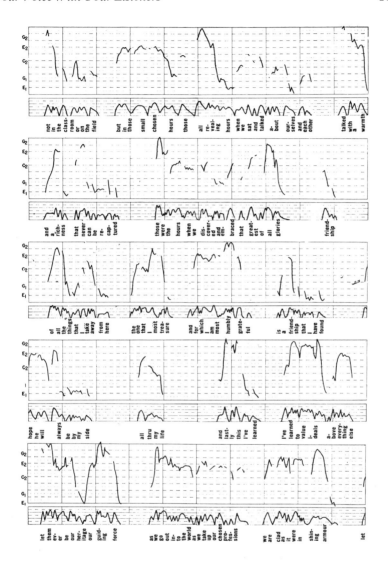

Figure 17. A melody curve. This is a plot of the average frequency with which Kenneth MacKenna spoke in successive 1/24's of a second in "Merrily We Roll Along," by Kaufman and Hart (from Milton Cowan, "Pitch and Intensity Characteristics of Speech," *Archives of Speech*, I [Supplement] Plate 25, 1936).

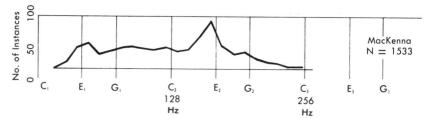

Figure 18. A frequency distribution of the measures plotted in Figure 17. The pitch is plotted on the abscissa and the number of times that each pitch occurs may be read from the ordinate. Each measure is an average over 1/24 of a second.

voice is higher than the man's; the child's voice is higher than the adult's; the pitch of oral reading is higher than the pitch of classroom speaking; the pitch of anger is higher than the pitch of indifference; the terminal downward inflection may denote finality, indifference, grief; and the terminal upward inflection may suggest inquiry or sarcasm. These are learned interpretations and there are many that are similar to these examples.

Loudness

The magnitude of the molecular disturbance in the propagation of the sound wave is determined by the relative rate with which exhalation occurs. This you learned earlier. In turn, this magnitude of excursion of the molecules accounts for the listener's experience of loudness. Implicitly the sound exceeds the threshold of hearing; hopefully, it comes up to the threshold of comfortable listening, whether the listener is in a quiet or a noisy environment. It is lamentable to hear listeners complain of having to strain to hear a speaker. This is a figurative remark; nothing in the ear can be voluntarily tensed or strained in the same manner that one is able to flex the muscles of his arm. However, the listener may lean forward a few inches and thereby receive a bit more sound pressure by taking advantage of the inverse square law. But the complaint is real. The posture is real. It exemplifies a geometric principle in sensory perception. Listeners seek a comfortable listening level! Practically, a threshold of comfortable listening should be determined by the most distant listener, never by one near the speaker.

A level of talking that is above a "natural level" is difficult for a speaker to maintain. Many listeners have reacted with satisfaction to a speaker's promise to talk louder so that everyone can hear him, only to find that the new and, for him, unnatural level lasts through only a few phrases or sentences. The student whose natural level of talking, self-appraised, consistently draws from listeners the criticism of being too soft has some serious practice ahead and should start at once. He should practice in as large a room as he can find.

As with pitch, the listener finds that variety in loudness adds interest to his listening experience. Of course, both the general level of the speaking and the variations from the average must be in keeping with the content of the utterance and with the occasion. This, again, is a matter of appropriateness. As a potentially interesting speaker you will do well to devote time to practicing selections that seem to require different levels of loudness. The selections that you use for practice are not designated by a musician's *fff* or *ppp*; the novice must try different levels and various ways of modifying the level, such as suddenly, slowly, and the like. Some guidance comes from Exercise 1 of Chapter 4. These selections will provide practice for suiting the voice to the word and will give you confidence. Seek evidence from your listening peers and teachers that your judgment in matching the word and voice is good. When you have gained confidence and know your vocal potentialities, the off-the-cuff and conversational speech is all the more likely to have an accompaniment of good vocal level.

Turn again to Figure 17. In the traces of physical intensity (the lines between the text and the melody curve) the solid horizontal lines indicate 10-db graduations. Thus, in the first line there is a range of 25 db.* Obviously, MacKenna was not reading at a single intensity and we are sure that his listeners were not hearing him at a single loudness. A study of the text alongside the two curves, the one for pitch and the one for intensity, reveals two interesting relationships:

a. the peaks in intensity coincide with stressed syllables, and

b. the peaks in intensity accompany rises in the melody curve.

The first of these relationships has been noted for a long time, for example, by Scripture (1906) and Panconcelli-Calzia (1957), and contributed to Stetson's view that the syllable, not the speech sound, is the basic unit in language. The second relationship, the interaction between intensity and fundamental frequency, has been referred to earlier, especially in Exercise 3, Chapter 6. This correlation is of first-order relevance to the student who would inject variety into either his intensity or fundamental frequency. Changes in one probably induce changes in the other.

---

* As noted in Chapter 6, the decibel is a logarithmic unit indicating power or sound pressure level relevant to some convenient standard. The difference between the softest vocalized tone and the loudest shouting, with the microphone of a sound level meter approximately six inches from the mouth, is about 40 db.

Duration

The speaker's exhalation stops; the succession of molecular disturbances stops; and the listener notes a pause. This is one of his responses
to the time dimension of talking. The speaker's exhalation continues;
the molecular disturbances change from one pattern of bumping to
another, and still to another in short intervals of time. The speaker's
articulators are scarcely in one position before they are withdrawn to
another. The listener interprets what he hears as *fast talking*. This is
another of his responses to the time dimension of talking. A different
behavior by the speaker would have led to an interpretation of *slow talking*. Together, pauses, the rate with which sounds succeed each other,
and the length of the total speaking performance—and its segments, such
as the individual lines of a play—comprise the durational aspect of the
listener's experience.

Turn again to Figure 17. Notice that the first nine syllables consume
1.5 seconds. They are followed by a pause of one-half second. The next
nine syllables take up 2.5 seconds. Several of the pauses are of an order
of one second each. Simply from observing the spacing of the words of
the text, it is obvious that MacKenna was using variety in his gait of
speaking!

There is more to duration than is implied by the phrase *rate of talking*.
Every event in speech exists in time. For example, earlier in the discussions of the listener's experiences of pitch and loudness the word *sustained* was used. This designated speaking that spans considerable time.
Although a sustained vowel might last throughout only a single breath,
sustained speaking is more. It is on-going. The earlier emphasis on variety in both loudness and pitch pertains to on-going speech. The listener
scarcely notes the monopitch of a brief announcement, and cannot reli-
ably isolate the persons with monopitch voices on the basis of a one-word
test. Such judgments are based on sustained speech. Yet the single word
also has an important aspect of duration. Indeed, at a microscopic extreme, the single sound wave has duration. This was referred to earlier as
period. The auditory experience generated by a single wave is a click
with timbre; the experience of five or six waves is pitch and timbre. With
a longer sample, *monotony* might be appropriate. Importantly, the dimension of duration includes an affective response of *like-dislike*.

The pause is an important part of the durational dimension of speech.
The listener expects a pause to separate thought units or emphasize an
idea. Both the speaker and listener grasp verbal material in "thought
units." These are usually linguistically unified segments of sentences. The
listener, in turn, accepts the speaker's divisions of sentences—if they

make sense. These divisions are set off by pauses. The difference between their making sense and not making sense is whether words that are closely coupled in syntax and meaning are grouped between the pauses. If the sensitive speaker and listener were to exchange places, reading the same material and rendering it satisfactorily, one might use more pauses than the other, but probably the reader with the more pauses would include among his many pauses those that the other speaker would use among his sparse pauses. Both would sense the relationships among the words, one designating more subunits of context or syntax than the other. This grouping of words is *phrasing* and in this context pauses are figuratively referred to as *punctuation*. The pause that occurs as an interruption within a brief syntactic and meaningful unit, for example, one that separates the preposition from its object or the article from its noun, is not acceptable to the listener.

Words-(or syllables) per-minute (or second) is frequently used as a unit of rate of talking. Above, you noted that MacKenna spoke nine syllables in 1.5 seconds and another nine in 2.5 seconds. This is stage speech! If living room conversation were transplanted to the stage it would drag. As an opposite extreme, if the speech of the radio newscaster were transplanted to the public address system of the football stadium it would be inappropriately fast. These are matters of "the rate that the system will accommodate." Subject matter also affects rate of talking. The newscaster slows down as he recites a brief eulogy of a dead colleague. A good or proper number of linguistic units per minute is as meaningless as a proper number of steps per minute in a dance. This depends on the music. With words, the rate depends on the circumstances. And, in both instances, variety is the rule.

Few sentences are unintelligible because of fast utterance. The listener can repeat the words he has heard, within the limits of his memory span, whether he has heard them spoken rapidly or slowly. This is not to say that the *meaning* is extracted as readily from a fast sentence as a slow one. However, there may be nothing that the listener misses in fast sentences that improved composition and articulation would not remedy. Principally, the listener objects to being led from the outset of a composition to the end at a steady fast pace. He prefers variety. This you can prepare to give him through deliberate practice and speaking fast and slow in selections, in sentences, and in phrases within sentences.

Quality

The shape or the acoustic spectrum of the sound wave was determined by the configuration of the pipes that coupled the vocal-fold modulator to the point of egress at the lips. The shape of the sound wave gives the listener a summative experience of quality or timbre. It is summative in a very real sense. The ear reacts to the constituent frequencies of the complex wave, singling them out as expertly as the mathematician might have isolated them through applying Fourier analysis. Yet when all of the frequencies of the wave are heard simultaneosuly—the high frequencies at the base of the cochlea and the low ones at the apex—the listener experiences vocal quality or timbre.

Probably every conceivable vocal quality is a preferred one with some listener. The qualitative experience is highly subjective and the like-dislike responses arise from associations and from one's culture. A pleasing voice quality, then, in the last analysis, is one that accompanies pleasant associations, although another listener might call the same quality displeasing, even defective. This response may be modified by perscriptive advice, provided there is good rapport between the adviser and advisee. As a rule, American listeners object to characteristically nasal voices and to strident, harsh, and breathy ones. The adjectives *resonant, vibrant, full,* and *rich* express approval of a voice. The words *thin, metallic,* and *muffled* denote disapproval. In this dimension descriptive words are poorly defined and inexactly used. The meanings are difficult to communicate. You became aware of this as you worked with Exercise 8, Chapter 6.

You can produce a multitude of vocal qualities readily. The mimic does as he suggests the voice of his associates, teachers, and actors; the reader does as he reads animal stories to children and "makes voices" that seem to convey the animals' dialogues. These variations of qualities, easily attained, only point the way to the possibility for achieving the less nasal, less harsh, or less breathy, and the more resonant voice; in short, toward improving muscular control of the resonators of the speech mechanism.

Relaxation of the throat frequently comes into the improvement of quality. Rigid musculatures in the pharynx may constrict the cavity that is coupled to the vocal folds.

THE PROXIMATE LISTENER

Although we noted sidetone earlier, your attention is called to it again here because of its significance in your appraisal of your own timbre. As you know, you are the first auditor of your speech. Yet with this triumph your primacy ends. You are not your best judge of loudness. The talker's ineptitude in this area has led to such instructions as "double effort" and "half effort" instead of "twice as loud" or "half as loud." You are not your best judge of pitch. The singer is often called *flat* although he is confident that he is on key. You are not a good judge of your rate, either. The composite experience of your own voice is far from a true version if the voice that the listener "out front" hears is accepted as the one that matters. It follows that the description which "the other listener" gives is the reference point from which change (improvement) occurs. This other listener may be a classmate, a teacher, or simply a person with whom you are engaged in a conversation. His query, "What did you say?" may be a criticism of your loudness level.

APPLICATIONS

The end product of voice is a listener's reaction. You can do little to alter the likes and dislikes that he has developed. In fact, he has never verbalized many of these. He holds them unconsciously. He is, however, applying his criteria of *good*, of *acceptable,* and of *substandard* to your voice and to those of your common acquaintances. The properties of sound that your listener finds in your voice, not his reactions to them, are entirely in your control. You can change the pitch that he hears, the loudness, duration, and the quality. Your listeners' criticisms and suggestions may well become your guides.

Listeners expect—yes, demand—speakers to show flexibility in pitch and both fast and slow inflections. The speaker, knowing this, should practice to achieve this flexibility in reading set pieces as a student pianist practices the scale, and should expect this variety to manifest itself appropriately in impromptu speech. Pitch is but an example. A drill in any of the dimensions of voice today is for an application tomorrow. You must practice deliberately and often in order to achieve variety in the four dimensions of voice that are appraised by listeners. There is no single right way to say a sentence, tell a story, or read a poem. As you practice different renditions of the same material your judgment and the evaluations given you by listeners will lead to an assurance that what you thought was an improvement really was one. This improvement, self-gained, is yours always. Do not draw the implication that the fruit of practice lies in saying the lines of someone else; not at all. The object of your improvement has to do with your everyday speech as well as your speech for special occasions.

SUMMARY

The listener evaluates the oral product of the speaker. He hears it through a mechanism that is peculiarly fitted to the four dimensions of sound. He is limited by a series of thresholds. As these are exceeded he experiences four psychological dimensions: pitch, loudness, quality, and rate. The relationship of these to causal factors follows. Chapters 4 and 5 contributed the information in the left-hand column; Chapter 6 added that of the middle column; and the present chapter, that of the right-hand column.

The speaker produces:	*The sound wave exhibits:*	*The listener hears:*
a. A rate of vocal-fold openings	Frequency (Hz)	Pitch
b. A rate of muscular contraction in exhalation	Sound pressure level	Loudness
c. A shaping of the cavities of voice production	A singular shape (spectrum)	Voice quality (timbre)
d. A duration of muscular contraction in exhalation	Durational features of the linguistic units	Aspects of rate

Throughout the subjective experience of listening the listener is placing evaluations on the merit of the signal he hears. These are learned affective responses and frequently reflect associations with previous liked and disliked experiences.

Exercises

1. Read aloud the ballad "Curfew Must Not Ring Tonight" (Appendix A). Who are listeners in the poem? Explain the Sexton's state of hearing. Does this affect the way you read the lines?

2. What description is given of the listeners in Goodrich's letter to Choate? (Appendix A).

3. From a kernel sentence, several transformations are easily formed, for example, queries, negatives, passives, negative-queries, negative-passives, and negative-query-passives. What generalizations can you make with respect to voice as you say these kernel sentences and their transformations?

    a. Kernel: The truck has hit the car.
       Transformations: Has the truck hit the car?
                           The truck has not hit the car.
                           The car was hit by the truck.
                           The car has not been hit by the truck.
                           Has not the truck hit the car?
    b. Kernel: The girl has worn the pin.
    c. Kernel: The boy has saved the woman.
    d. Kernel: The student has written the paper.
    e. Kernel: The teacher has bought the book.
    f. Kernel: The repairman has fixed the furnace.

4. Read these lines aloud and generate a similar set for reading to the class. On which of the four dimensions of voice are you depending especially?
    Jack climbed a beanstalk; Jill went after water.
    Jack didn't go after water; Jill went after water.
    The beanstalk has nothing to do with water; Jack climbed the beanstalk.
    Jack didn't climb the beanstalk for water; Jill went after water.

5. Rework the plan for improvement of your voice production that you prepared earlier. Include within your thinking a notion of "voice stretching," that is extending the dimensions of your voice beyond their usual limits. Insofar as possible, use the present tense instead of the future and tie your proposals to a definite time schedule. Some of the following suggestions may be provocative: imitate a "good voice"; develop a 20-foot volume; engage in vocal play while babysitting; develop a specialty of reading animal stories aloud to children; call someone's attention to a paragraph in the daily newspaper and read it to him, preferably from an adjoining room; at a fixed hour daily practice one or two vowels in isolation and in at least ten words; memorize a passage and say it aloud frequently; memorize a passage in a foreign language and say it to people for whom the language is vernacular; work with a foreign student trying to improve his English; volunteer to read for a blind student; engage in negative practice, deliberately

making some of your typical errors; become conscious of the raised versus the lowered uvula; work with scout troops and engage the members in a speech game; create opportunities to talk such as making social calls and showing your college to prospective students and their parents; imitate English vowels using an electric razor or the busy signal of a telephone as the sound source and your own resonating cavities; blow out candles while making fricative or plosive consonants; practice making vocal sound effects; be a motivating listener; using a phonograph playback, listen to yourself saying a phrase, listen to the phrase again . . . continue through 10 or 12 listenings (then turn to another phrase); tally the times daily that you are asked to repeat what you said.

6. The same word or sentence can be said in manners to suggest many different meanings. You have practiced this in Exercise 2, Chapter 6. Here are more opportunities. If possible, practice these with a classmate and try to describe the dominant vocal dimensions that you use with each.

   a. Say *yes* in manners that imply certainty, doubt, indecision, and sarcasm.
   b. Say *no* to imply "Definitely not," "Well, maybe," "I'm surprised to learn that," "I'm annoyed to learn that."
   c. Say "I shall come" to imply determination, pleasant agreement, surprise, annoyance.
   d. Say "He's a fine fellow" to imply you admire the person about whom you're talking; you dislike the person; you are surprised at the newly discovered qualities of the person.
   e. Say "I like Bill" to imply the opposite, irritation and surprise that anyone could conceivably accuse you of liking Bill, indecision about your feelings, specific indication that your liking is for Bill and not for anyone else who may be present, your answer to the question "Who likes Bill?," and an aggressive, emphatic answer to the question, "Who could possibly care for Bill?"

7. Extend the following ambiguities in which the listener's meaning of the the sentence depends upon the speaker's voice control. Provide at least five additional examples.

   a. There is an orange tree.
   b. The Greeks were idol worshipers.
   c. She's feeding the horse chestnuts.

8. Read the following selection and be prepared to discuss how it relates to the material of this chapter and how it extends the material about the ear.

Dinosaur Ears*

A dinosaur's stapes—the singular form is the same as the plural—is a thin, cordlike bone in the middle ear. It's tiny—only the size of a match—and, doubtless for this reason, tends to get lost. Stapes,

---

* "The Talk of the Town," *The New Yorker*, November 2, 1957.

which had never before been found in a dinosaur, are proof that
dinosaurs could hear, but we had already guessed that.

9. The following passage is a line from a play *Dr. Knock* (Jules Romains).
Early in the play, Dr. Knock purchased the medical practice of Dr. Parpalaid,
an elderly and honest general practitioner. Dr. Parpalaid has returned to pay
his successor a visit. The speech has many emotional overtones and provides
opportunity for much vocal variety.

> Come here, Dr. Parpalaid. Look. Oh . . . you'll have glanced out
> often enough between the strokes of those good games of billiards
> you used to play. Over there Mont Aligre marks us off from the
> rest of the world. We can see Mesclat and Trebures on the left . . .
> if it weren't for the way the town rises up just in front of us I be-
> lieve we could see every village in the valley. But all you ever saw
> was the scenery. You've a taste for scenery, as I remember. A
> rough countryside, barely scratched by civilization! But I show it
> you today teeming, pulsating beneath the life-giving touch of the
> noble science of medicine. The first time I stood here looking out . . .
> the morning after I came . . . I wasn't over confident, I can tell you.
> It didn't seem to make much odds whether I stood here or not. The
> whole place turned its back on me. But now . . . like an organist
> at his keyboard . . . I pull a stop, I touch a note . . . and from far
> off the sounds respond! In two hundred and fifty of those houses
> . . . we can't see them all for the distance and the trees . . . there
> are two hundred and fifty rooms, and in each one at this very
> moment somebody is testifying to the might of medical science.
> Upon two hundred and fifty beds those prostrate forms bear wit-
> ness to life's meaning . . . and through me they are all made one
> with the great cause I serve. And at night it's more wonderful
> still. For the lights are lit . . . and they're of my lighting. People
> with nothing the matter with them go to sleep in the dark . . .
> blotted out of existence. But the sick man has his night-light or
> his lamp. Yes, then everything untouched by the healing art fades
> away and is forgotten. The villages vanish . . . and those lights as
> I look at them are like a starlit sky in which I reign almighty.
> And, remember, when those men and women wake their thoughts
> turn first to me and my prescriptions. In a minute or two now
> you'll hear the clock strike ten. At ten o'clock my patients, every
> one, take their temperatures for the second time. Picture it, my
> deaf Parpalaid! Two hundred and fifty clinical thermometers lifted
> in unison and gently placed and held beneath two hundred and
> fifty silent tongues!

10. The following poem was written by Phineas Fletcher in *The Purple
Island* (1633). On the basis of your reading, prepare to report the ways
in which this is an inexact description of the ear.

> The entrance winding . . . Where stands a braced drum, whose
> sounding head—obliquely placed—struck by the circling air, Gives
> instant warning of each sounds repair. . . . The drum is made of
> substance hard and thin. . . . This drum divides the first and second

part, In which three hearing instruments reside. . . . The first an hammer called, whose outgrown sides Lie on the drum; but with his swelling end first in the hollow stithe, there fast abides: The stithe's short foot doth on the drum depend, His longer in the stirrup surely placed; The stirrup's sharp side by the stithe embraced But his broad base tied to a little window fast . . . .The little windows ever open lie. . . . The cave's third part in twenty by-ways bending, Is called the labyrinth, in hundred crooks ascending . . . As when a stone, troubling the quiet waters, Prints in the angry steam a wrinkle round, Whither soon another and another scatters, Till all the lake with circles now is crowned, All so the air struck with some violence nigh Begets a world of circles in the sky; All which infected move with sounding quality. These at Auditus' palace soon arriving, Enter the gate and strike the warning drum; To these three instruments fit motion giving, Which every voice discern: then that third room Sharpens each sound, and quick conveys it thence; Till by the flying poast 'tis hurried hence, And in an instant brought into the judging sense.

11. A few examples of thresholds were listed in the chapter. Extend these, taking into account all four dimensions of the voice.

12. Writers have in mind that at least poetry and plays will be spoken and that the meanings of the lines will be enhanced by the speaker's voice, its pitch, loudness, timbre, and rate. There are no satisfactory substitutes for this voice. However, as one looks at attempts that have been made either to provide substitutes or to guide the voice, he cannot help but be impressed by what is expected from the oral reader. Many writers have attempted to express visually the substance that they wish to be conveyed by the voice. An example of this is the intonemes developed by Ernest and Marion Robson. One line of this follows. Can you decipher the code? Can you make your voice follow it?

References

Cowan, J. Milton, "Pitch and Intensity Characteristics of Stage Speech," *Archives of Speech*, Vol. I [supplement], 1936.

Gray, Giles W., "Phonemic Microtomy: the Minimum Duration of Perceptible Speech Sounds," *Speech Monographs,* 9 (1942), 75-90.

Hirsh, Ira J., *The Measurement of Hearing.* New York: McGraw-Hill Book Company, 1952.

Jerger, James, ed., *Modern Developments in Audiology.* New York: Academic Press, Inc., 1963.

Panconcelli-Calzia, G., "Early History of Phonetics," in L. Kaiser, *Manual of Phonetics*. Amsterdam: North-Holland Publishing Company, 1957.

Robson, Ernest M. and Marion M., *Intonations of English in Print*. Parker Ford, Pa., 1963.

Scripture, E. W., *Researches in Experimental Phonetics*. Washington D. C.: Carnegie Institution of Washington, 1906.

Smith, K. U. *Delayed Sensory Feedback and Behavior*. Philadelphia: W. B. Saunders Co., 1962.

Stetson, R. H., *Bases of Phonology*. Oberlin, Ohio: Oberlin College, 1945.

Wever, Ernest Glen, *Theory of Hearing*. New York: John Wiley & Sons, Inc., 1949.

8

Perceiving Your Speech

In Chapter 7 you were asked to face up to your listener's evaluations of your voice. In this chapter you are asked to come to grips with the necessity for the listener to identify what you say. The perception of speech is a human accomplishment to which you have given little thought, but simply taken for granted. It is, however, a remarkable achievement that is far from perfectly understood. It seems to occur in the left temporal lobe of the cortex and may involve different centers than, for example, the perception of music. The perception of speech is given separate treatment in this chapter because it is apparently closely allied to the production of speech.

The term *perception of speech* is used here with a special and limited meaning. Basically, it is the recognition of the meaningful linguistic units, the words that you hear. In your study of foreign languages the teacher often dictated passages for you to write. The problem was in being able to identify the words. This view of speech perception does not belittle the importance of your understanding the semantic meaning of a passage. This is an implicit topic in Chapter 12. The present emphasis, however, is on aural recognition of words.

There are three cues to speech perception. This generalization is based on the assumption that each of three theories of speech perception is somewhat right. There are *acoustic* clues, which are the ones typically emphasized and for which you prepared by studying Chapter 7. There are also clues of *probability* and *utterance* of speech sounds and words, both of which will be discussed in this chapter.

Obviously, the perception of a word is phenomenal behavior. It exists such a short time! However, in the view of the preceding paragraph, it exists in three places or in three modes. It is an acoustic event generated by a speaker to you, a listener. It is a probable event in terms of your stored-up experience with your language. It is a set of neural experiences that you have programmed over and over again as you have said the word.

THE ACOUSTIC CLUES

Intermediate between the brief period of a single sound wave and the span of an exhalation is a series of similar sound waves that represent a single speech sound. The central five or six waves of the series illustrated in Figure 13, Chapter 6, might be taken as representative of the series. The waves that precede these increase in level from one to the next and change in shape to approximate the representative ones. The few waves following the central ones diminish in level and lose the typical pattern of the central ones, yet the listener hears the series as a single sound of speech. It is distinguishable from other sounds of his language. The single sound may be an entire syllable, but more often than not the vowel is only the nucleus of a syllable and precedes or follows one or more consonants or lies between them.

On the average, the listener may expect to hear from five to nine English syllables a second, and since the most typical English syllable is comprised of three sounds he may expect to hear 15–27 sounds a second. The reduction of this set of rapid experiences and the identification of the words does not *seem* difficult to people for whom the language is vernacular, provided the sounds are well made; yet it is really more difficult than it seems. A stranger to the language hears a stream of gibberish. A young child may hear no more. Students' notes from a lecture often disagree, and in tests expert stenographers have been found to give different transcriptions to the same aural material.

The words *auditory, aural, listening, hearing,* and their synonyms emphasize the importance of a person's responses to acoustic clues in the perception of speech. Likewise, almost by definition, these responses are associated with the individual phonemes or sounds of speech. The next two sections of this chapter describe these sounds and the third section relates this description to the acoustic properties of the sounds. The focus throughout is on perceiving or understanding speech through audition.

THE SOUNDS THAT YOU HEAR IN SPEECH: PHONETICS

Phonetics is a systematic classification of the sounds of speech and is often called *the science of speech sounds*. For some workers phonetics is a generic term that includes the voice, articulation, and pronunciation. From this view all of the observations of the preceding chapters have been about phonetics. The present discussion is more limited. It treats the sounds of English and emphasizes your reception of these sounds. As a child you learned to preceive language before you learned to speak it. In your study of languages you have noted the aural emphasis. Now, as you try to improve your speaking you are emphasizing improved perception. Most of the sounds that you hear in standard American English are represented by the symbols below, extracted from the alphabet of the International Phonetic Association. Chapters 9 and 10 will emphasize your producing these sounds well. Somewhat arbitrarily the sounds are placed in three divisions.

Vowels

[i] *eat;* [ɪ] *it;* [e] *fame;* [ɛ] *wet*; [æ] *at;* [ɑ] *father;* [a] the first sound of *eye;* [ɔ] *caught;* [ɒ] *calm* (in case this vowel is differentiated from [ɑ]); [o] *ro*tate; [ʊ] *pull;* [u] *troop;* [ʌ] *cup;* [ə] *a*bove (this vowel is called *schwa*); [ɝ] or [ɜ] *bird*.

The vowels are the sounds that you hear as similar to sung sounds with quality, pitch, loudness, and rate clearly evident. This is not enough to delimit them, however. The vowels and diphthongs are the nuclei of syllables, for example, the central sounds in *but, cat, seem, find*. When you are describing or naming them as though they were words they are preceded by the article *an*, not *a;* also, in this circumstance you use a formal version of *the*, not the colloquial form.

Diphthongs

[oʊ] *woe;* [eɪ] *mate;* [aɪ] *aye;* [aʊ] *house;* [ɔɪ] *boy;* [ɪu] or [ju] *cute* or *you*.

The diphthongs are the glides that you hear as a speaker progresses from one vowel to another within a single syllable. Thus, a diphthong is a closely joined pair of vowels. Listen attentively to *eye* or *I,* spoken slowly. Do you hear a pair of vowel sounds in rapid succession, or a glide from one to another?

Consonants

[p] *pat;* [t] *take;* [k] *key;* [s] *see;* [f] *fly;* [θ] *thin;* [ʃ] *shake;* [b] *bad;* [d] *done;* [g] *good;* [z] *zip;* [v] *vise;* [ð] *they;* [ʒ] *vision;* [m] *mike;* [n] *no;* [ŋ] *ring;* [l] *line;* [r] *trip;* [h] *how;* [w] *won;* [ʍ] *when;* [j] *young,* [dʒ] *judge;* [tʃ] *church.*

The consonants are sounds that usually have a popping sound or more or less swishlike noise, friction, or aspiration accompanying them, as /s/ or /t/. You talk about them as *a* /t/, not *an* /t/.

PHONEMES

Another word for speech sound is *phoneme.* There are three definitions of a phoneme, overlapping but differing in emphasis.

   a. Daniel Jones, the author of an important dictionary of British pronunciation, wrote that a phoneme is a family of speech sounds. Thus, the /i/ in *freeze* and the one in *keel* are of the same family of sounds. Are you hearing the difference between the sounds?

   b. For many linguists and anthropologists who have followed the lead of Leonard Bloomfield, the phoneme is a sound that *makes a difference.* The initial and terminal /l/ in *little* are usually different sounds, designated "light" and "dark" *l* and symbolized /l/ and /ł/. Since either might be used for any /l/ in the English language, the "light" and "dark" *l*'s are not phonemic.

   c. Morris Halle designates a phoneme as a bundle of distinctive features. Thus, the place of articulation, the presence or absence of nasality, the presence or absence of aspiration, the presence or absence of voicing and the like summate to make a singular linguistic experience.

There have been a host of alphabets to denote how people hear their language. Benjamin Franklin (1768) originated diacritical markings. Thomas Sheridan (1780) hoped "to establish a *standard.*" Henry Sweet developed the "broad Romic" with particular reference to the sounds of Old English. George Bernard Shaw, through his will, contributed a continuing effect on phonetics and the English language and other phonetic alphabets. Each system of shorthand is, of course, a way of noting in writing what one hears. Nearly a thousand years ago, Orm, working in England with religious writings, used double consonants after short vowels and single consonants after long vowels in a unique method of describing what he heard. Ellis, frustrated in his efforts to explain his listening experiences with English sounds, turned to Helmholtz and as a result of his quest translated *The Sensation of Tone* from German.

Close Listening

Do you begin to sense that your view of speech perception was relatively gross? If so, you are ready to note some aural modifiers to the symbols that you studied above. These are called *diacritical* modifiers. p^h is an aspirated or exploded /p/. The first sound in *pop* is always exploded; the last one may be or not.

ꞁ means that the vowel sounds as though it was made higher in the mouth than would be expected. Perhaps you hear *ten* as *tin*.

uᴛ means that the vowel is made lower in the mouth than would be expected. Note two ways of saying *roof*.

iꞁ means that the vowel is made farther back in the mouth than would be expected. This may remind you of *freeze*.

oꞁ means that the vowel is made farther forward in the mouth than would be expected.

ɑː means that the vowel is prolonged.

ɑːːː means that the vowel is sustained.

ʔo means that the sound is initiated with an audible burst at the vocal folds, "the glottal stop."

ĩ means that the vowel—in this case /i/ is nasalized.

ˈ when placed as an apostrophe means that the subsequent syllable is given primary stress.

ˌ when placed near the bottom of a syllable and preceding it indicates that the succeeding syllable has secondary stress.

You will need several more combinations of vowels than are listed above if you try to record accurately the speech you hear about you. You will need triphthongs, for much speech includes glides that encompass more than two vowels. You can, of course, indicate the triphthongs and unusual diphthongs by combinations of vowels beyond those listed earlier. The regional *off-glide,* for example, is common in American speech; it may begin with any vowel and terminates in schwa or at least a vowel that approaches schwa.

You will also need more than one /r/ to describe the speech you hear. You have known for a long time that speakers vary widely in the way they say this sound. As you become more expert in hearing sounds you will find that even a single speaker is not consistent in his production of /r/. A more complete listing of the IPA symbols or a standard dictionary may help as you attempt to distinguish sounds. If the brief description in the dictionary leaves you puzzled, ask your teacher or someone else who is versed in phonetics to say the different *r*-sounds for you.

Stress is deceptively difficult to perceive. As noted earlier there are special marks to indicate primary and secondary levels. The lowest level is implied when neither of the others is marked. The three levels are evident in ['sɛkən͵dɛrɪ].

A convenient short cut in your noting of pronunciation to indicate a consonant that seems to serve as a syllable, especially /l, m, n/ as in *fiddle, solemn, soften,* is to put a dot under the terminal symbol: ['fɪdl̩], ['salm̩], ['sɔfn̩]. Another one that is convenient in noting American pronunciations is the *hooked schwa* /ɚ/. If you hear *river* in New England you might describe it ['rɪvə]. In the Midwest you would conveniently add the /r/ by noting ['rɪvɚ].

FORMANTS AND LOCUS

Each target phoneme is a singular distribution of acoustic energy among frequencies below 7000 Hz. This is the basis for the acoustic clues to speech perception. In vowels the energy is concentrated in two or three bands of frequencies, termed *formants*. These frequencies are present in the cord tone resonated by the cavities described in Chapter 5. Each formant stimulates the basilar membrane at a particular place and in a certain amount. Synthetic vowels have been generated electronically by the blending of two synthesized formants. However, they have been made increasingly intelligible by the addition of a third formant, approximately 600 Hz above the second and of the same intensity as the second formant. This is especially true of the front vowels, the ones of *seat, sit, met, mate,* and *sat.*

The formant concept is applicable to some consonants as well as to vowels: for example, the four consonants of the word *unrolling.* But *locus* is a more useful concept in describing the crucial concentrations of energy of a consonant than is formant. *Locus* is a "fixed frequency position" that becomes associated aurally with a consonant and provides the important clue for the perception of individual consonants when spoken in context with vowels. The energy of the consonant that precedes or follows a vowel seems to arise from a singular band peculiar to that consonant. This is the locus of the consonant. The acoustic event is very transitory, for the consonant blends into the vowel, which yields another helpful descriptive term, *transition*. This is the gradual shift from the locus to the quasi steady state of the vowel in a syllabic environment. Both of these characteristics provide important clues for identifying a consonant, which is characterized by rapid acoustic change. Both are so powerful or suggestive that in the production of an isolated spoken vowel from which the consonant has been deleted there may be sufficient clues for listeners to identify the unheard consonant that was spoken preceding the vowel.

Further evidence of the important interaction between a consonant and adjacent vowel comes from segmenting the phonemes of a stream of recorded speech. These may be extracted and set aside as "building blocks." They may then be reassembled to form new words. As a listener, you would find that some consonants retain their intelligibility and that others (as *pig, five, make*, and *thrash*) are very frequently misunderstood in the new phonetic environment. In order to achieve highly intelligible monosyllables nearly a thousand building blocks are needed!

A common procedure in studies of the physical cues to recognizable speech is to introduce either distortion or attenuation into a line that is conveying speech to a listener. This procedure led to establishing 20 bands of frequencies that contribute equally to the intelligibility of speech. The frequencies above and below 1650–1900 Hz contribute equally to intelligibility. This procedure also permits the ranking of different phonemes in terms of their intelligibility.

Obviously, acoustic clues contribute to your perception of the words of speech. These clues come from audible frequencies below 7000 Hz. The relative amounts of acoustic energy momentarily associated with singular bands of frequencies distinguish one phoneme from another.

CLUES OF PROBABILITY

Word Probability

The more probable an event of oral language, the more readily it is perceived. This principle certainly applies in the perception of words. There have been a number of tabulations of English words yielding "the most frequently used 1000 words," "the second thousand most frequently used words," and so forth. This establishes an order of probability. In a testing circumstance in which listeners were required to write the individual words that they heard, they were 67 per cent correct when the words were among the 1000 most frequently used and were 59.5 per cent correct when the words were among the 10,000 most frequently used. The scores of the intervening categories decreased systematically from the most common to the less common word categories.

The familiar vocabulary itself may differ somewhat from person to person. For example, in an experiment in speech perception, listeners were divided according to their interests and their values as shown by the Allport-Vernon Scale. Thus, a listener was designated as primarily political or social or economic in his interests. Commonly used words were categorized similarly as political, social, or economic. Each group of listeners was most successful in identifying the words that matched its interest!

Tables 2 and 3 show two widely divergent categories of words. At first glance, all these short, one-syllable words look readily familiar. Yet the words of Table 2 are heard frequently in students' speaking and

*Table 2. Words you hear frequently in classrooms.**

the	is	are	there	with	not
and	it	was	one	has	war
of	you	be	or	go	were
to	they	he	will	at	had
a	this	for	but	our	from
in	we	on	as	which	his
that	have	I	all	by	very

* These words were heard more than 1000 times—the most frequently used words—in samples from a series of 600 speeches by 250 students, in a total of 300,000 words.

those of Table 3, rarely. These are only examples of hundreds of words

*Table 3. Words you hear infrequently in students' speeches.**

bawl	pal	chick	pint	clog	pot
calm	prone	dealt	quart	dip	reign
cuff	roam	fetch	shed	frame	skid
dukes	slim	gulf	spy	heap	sway
gift	tack	jack	tempt	jet	thread
hoist	tore	knot	twin	limb	vain
keg	vice	mask	wad	monk	whirl
lust	wren	nap	breeze	oar	yacht
mouse	belt				

* These are examples of words that were heard no more than two times in a series of 600 speeches by 250 students, in a total of 300,000 words. The examples are chosen to show short words.

that could be listed. It is readily apparent that the words of Table 2 are ones that are frequently expected and that the ones of Table 3 are less likely to be heard. The listener catches the frequently used words in context even though the speaker gives them minimal phonetic differentiation.

Closely akin to the probability that arises from disproportionate usage of a natural vocabulary is one that derives from routinized vocabularies of different sizes. The more limited the number of words of a vocabulary, the better your chance of understanding them. An experimenter asked listeners to identify words of special vocabularies of 2, 4, 8, 16, 32, and 256 words. These were heard under difficult noisy conditions of listening. Words of a 2-word vocabulary were 80 per cent intelligible in a condition under which words of the 32-word vocabulary were less than 40 per cent intelligible. This advantage of the small vocabulary accounts for the formal messages and small number of different messages used by flight crews, telephone operators, and military personnel.

Phonemic Probability

The speech sounds that you hear occur in very unequal numbers. Interestingly, each phoneme is about as likely to occur in one type of material as another. This is summarized in Table 4. Here the most probable upper half of the phonemes are more intelligible than the less likely lower half, particularly within a single type of sounds: for example, consonants.

A third aspect of probability that provides clues for speech perception comes from the *context* of the message. These clues probably relate both to meaning and the rules of syntax. Several experimenters have compared listeners' ability to identify the same words heard both in isolation and in sentences. The advantage provided by context is apparent. This advantage is even apparent in groups of words representing an approximation to context. A word of explanation: one might turn the successive pages of a book. He might begin with the word *the*. On page 2 what is the word that follows the first *the? Man*. On page 3 what is the word that follows the first use of *man? Charged*. On page 4 what is the word that follows the first use of *charged, charge, charges? Were*. On page 5, and so on. This approximation to context generated "Eat mushrooms please *speak* to drive there." *Speak* was more readily identified by listeners when heard in this context than when it was spoken alone, as were all items that were tested similarly.

Table 4. An arrangement of phonemes from relatively frequent ones to relatively infrequent ones in different types of written material.*

Phoneme	Labels on Household Boxes	Legends for Cartoons	Comics	Gettysburg Address	Old Testament	Newspaper Story	Sixth Grade Reader	Average
ɪ	7.0	9.0	6.0	5.0	7.0	8.0	6.0	6.9
n	8.0	7.0	8.0	8.0	9.0	7.0	7.0	7.8
t	8.0	7.0	8.0	7.0	7.0	9.0	7.0	7.6
ə	8.0	7.0	7.0	6.0	5.0	10.0	10.0	7.6
r	6.0	5.0	8.0	6.0	5.0	8.0	9.0	6.7
d	4.0	5.0	3.0	6.0	9.0	6.0	4.0	5.3
s	1.2	3.1	2.2	3.0	4.0	3.0	2.0	2.6
ɑ	5.7	5.0	5.4	3.5	4.3	5.3	5.5	5.0
l	1.1	1.6	1.5	4.8	7.0	1.7	3.3	3.0
ð	2.0	3.3	3.8	3.2	5.0	1.5	3.8	3.2
æ	2.5	3.1	2.4	4.4	4.3	3.6	2.4	3.2
ɛ	3.3	3.1	1.5	3.6	1.0	2.1	4.0	2.7
i	5.6	3.0	4.4	3.5	3.6	2.6	4.1	3.8
m	4.1	2.5	3.7	1.1	1.6	3.0	3.6	2.8
k	3.4	3.2	4.7	3.2	2.3	3.2	3.6	3.4
f	2.6	1.3	2.1	2.4	1.1	0.8	1.6	1.7
z	1.3	1.8	1.8	0.4	0.4	1.5	1.5	1.2
ɔ	2.9	1.9	2.0	1.6	2.3	2.3	5.8	2.7
e	2.2	1.1	1.1	3.5	2.4	1.7	1.2	1.9
ʊ	1.5	2.2	1.9	1.5	1.1	2.6	0.4	1.6
b	1.6	2.1	1.5	0.8	0.5	1.9	1.4	1.4

Table 4. (continued)

Phoneme	Labels on Household Boxes	Legends for Cartoons	Comics	Gettysburg Address	Old Testament	Newspaper Story	Sixth Grade Reader	Average
w	0.7	1.6	1.4	0.5	0.2	0.2	1.7	0.9
ʊ	1.5	1.9	1.3	1.9	2.4	1.1	1.4	1.6
h	0.6	2.2	2.2	0.5	1.5	1.1	3.3	1.6
v	1.9	2.0	1.6	2.5	1.9	1.7	2.0	1.9
p	3.2	2.0	1.5	1.9	1.0	1.2	3.8	2.1
j	0.5	1.8	1.9	0.3	0.0	0.0	0.3	0.7
g	0.6	1.1	2.0	1.2	2.9	0.0	0.9	1.2
o	0.7	0.7	0.9	1.9	0.2	0.4	0.0	0.7
ŋ	0.7	2.5	1.5	1.1	1.2	1.7	0.4	1.3
ʃ	2.6	1.8	1.8	0.9	0.4	1.5	2.0	1.6
θ	0.0	0.0	0.3	0.5	0.0	0.0	0.5	0.2
ʌ	0.0	1.3	1.6	1.6	3.2	0.8	1.0	1.4
ɝ	0.2	0.3	0.0	0.0	0.0	0.0	0.0	0.1
ʍ	0.3	1.8	0.8	0.3	1.5	0.1	0.7	0.8
aɪ	2.2	4.7	2.6	0.8	1.6	0.1	2.5	2.1
aʊ	0.4	1.5	1.2	0.5	1.2	0.4	0.7	8.4
ɔɪ	0.0	0.0	0.2	0.0	0.2	0.0	0.0	0.1
ju-ɪu	0.3	1.1	0.0	0.0	0.0	0.2	0.4	0.3
tʃ	0.5	0.0	0.3	0.0	0.0	0.2	0.7	0.2
dʒ	0.5	0.0	0.3	0.3	0.0	0.4	0.0	0.2
ʒ				(essentially zero)				

* The entries are average percentages from several transcribers and therefore do not summate to 100 percent in each column. The similarity of the frequency of occurrence of the different phonemes from one type of material to another is apparent.

130

CLUES FROM YOUR UTTERANCE

The motor theory relates to clues to speech perception that relate to the neurological and muscular accompaniments of one's own speech. Perhaps one hears other talkers speak (that is, pronounce words) as he speaks. The motor theory cannot or has not been proved. Most of the data that support it are also compatible with the data of the preceding section, cues of probability. There you reasoned that you had a vocabulary and you were recalling from storage at any moment the most likely word or sound. Here you reason that you are completely familiar with the muscular movements and neural activity that go with producing a word or a sound. These are contributing (mediating) to your perception of the word.

It is true that you at least tend to hear a word in the manner that you pronounce it. You may hear *Dorothy* or *diamond* said over and over with three syllables, but if you say the words with two syllables this is the way you perceive them. The speaker may say [tɛn], but if your pronunciation dialect calls for [tɪn] this is probably the way you hear it. This behavior is in keeping with the motor theory of speech perception.

MISCELLANEOUS CLUES TO SPEECH PERCEPTION

Speech perception has only recently been an area of investigation. We have discussed the three principal clues, but there are a few others which should be mentioned. Even these additional clues might be incorporated into one of the other three classes.

The phonetic complexity of a word relates to its perception. The comparison, cited earlier, of more and less familiar words showed also that one-syllable words of two sounds are identified correctly by 55.9 per cent of the listeners while those of three, four, five, and six sounds were recognized by 56.2, 58.3, 63.0, and 67.7 per cent, respectively. Similarly, two-syllable words are more readily heard than one-syllable words of the same number of sounds; four-sound words of one and two syllables are identified by 58.3 and 66.5 per cent of the listeners, and five-sound words by 63.0 and 68.9 per cent, respectively.

Some impediments to speech perception seem to relate to human frailty. If listeners are asked to identify the final three words of aural sentences ranging from short to long they are progressively less successful with the longer sentences. This detrimental effect of sentence length increases systematically as noise is introduced into the system.

Similarity in sound (rhyme) affects perception in a manner that can be either helpful or harmful. The letters of each of these sets sound somewhat alike: (b, c, t, d, v) and (f, m, n, s, x). The two sets also contrast in sound. As the letters are *viewed* in random order and then identified in writing, some errors quite naturally occur. These errors of identification are preponderantly *within* a set, not between sets. This type of mistake also characterizes listeners' errors in trying to recall these materials after hearing them.

An unfamiliar language has built-in interferences to speech perception. Foreign listeners are consistently less able to perceive English words than are American listeners, even when marking responses on a simple multiple-choice response form. Interestingly, the relative skill of these students in perceiving oral English words relates to other aspects of their orientation to English: for example, the amount of time they devote to pauses in their English speech. In turn, American students have difficulty identifying words spoken by foreign speakers. This topic could either relate to clues of probability or to the matter of utterance.

APPLICATIONS

You are making your first few notes in phonetic characters. Old habits of spelling and punctuation intrude. Worse than that, you are finding that you are not writing what you hear but what you would say if you were pronouncing the words (motor theory). A listener tends to supply the sounds that are absent when he hears a phrase made up of partial words that are elided. The discrepancy between what a person hears and what he thinks he hears may become apparent with the tenth or twelfth replaying of a sentence. Then he discovers that the final sound of one word is simultaneously the initial sound of the following word; that /n/ has been substituted for /ŋ/; that one-half of the vowels are really schwa /ə/; and so on.

In any event, you interpret the series of sounds that you hear. This code has been acquired by a lifetime of listening. The symbols of this chapter are only a convenience. Possibly you are questioning seriously your capacity as a listener for the first time. Proficiency in listening is a prerequisite to speech improvement.

Here, then, is good and sufficient reason for you to study literature. Study it orally, read operas and plays before attending them, participate in Shakespeare's plays, and others. Welcome the opportunity to hear repeat performances of programs a second and third time.

SUMMARY

Your capacity to hear a word varies with the acoustic properties of the spoken word. It also depends on your readiness to hear the word, that is, its probability to you. Your speech perception of a word also may vary with your skill in saying the word. The International Phonetic Association has provided a phonetic alphabet that permits one to transcribe aural English into visual symbols. Efficient use of the transcription system stimulates exact perception of speech.

Exercises

1. Indicate the number of phonemic changes that would be required to make the words of the following groups identical in sound.
  a. Examples:
    1. First, to make two words identical in sound:
       pear
       care
       Answer: 1 change (they would be identical except that /p/ is not the same as /k/).
    2. Three words:
       quaint
       saint (quaint and saint)
       faint (quaint and faint)
       (quaint and saint)
       Answer: 5 changes (/kw/ are two sounds and different from /s/; therefore, 2 changes for this pair, *quaint* and *saint; quaint* and *faint*, again two changes; *saint* and *faint*, one change).
    3. Four words (extend the principles of Examples 1 and 2):
       Grew Crew Groove

grew	—	—	—
crew	1	—	—
groove	1	2	—
drew	1	1	2

       Total, 8 changes.
  b. Twenty problems similar to the examples follow:

1. pass	2. fine	3. gold	4. swain
past	find	bowl	slain
cast	sign	cold	flame
task	kind	bold	plain

5. throw	6. bust	7. code	8. hulk
froze	fuss	told	halt
prose	but	cold	pulp
probe	bus	coal	fault
9. limp	10. wren	11. stove	12. stale
limb	went	sold	jail
lend	rent	stole	dale
lent	lent	soul	gale
13. barn	14. love	15. dog	16. lip
bark	lull	gone	lift
bought	low	don	lisp
spark	lag	darn	list
17. peg	18. wait	19. chaff	20. thumb
keg	which	shaft	from
egg	wake	chap	come
pay	wig	shack	sum

2. George Bernard Shaw once wrote *fish* as *ghoti*. He explained that he got the /f/ from *enough,* the /ɪ/ from *women,* and the /ʃ/ from *motion.* Provide five other original spellings of words, taking the examples and rationale from our common vocabulary.

3. As you attempt to explain the sounds you hear, English orthography keeps adding difficulties to your task. What constitutes a silent letter in spelling? Most dictionaries give some principles about how letters sound and how different phonemes may be spelled. The silent letter remains an enigma and, to some extent, a matter of definition. Since the difference in spelling between *can* and *cane* is the final *e,* one may infer that the pronunciation of the nucleus of the syllable is determined by the presence or the absence of the final *e* and that, consequently, it is not "silent"; it affects the phonetics of the word. No principle can explain the *c* in *czar, indict, victuals,* and *scene.* In spite of the inconsistency between English orthography and pronunciation, the detection of silent letters as distinguished from "ways of spelling a sound" is difficult. Determine to your satisfaction the silent letters in the following words. Start by transcribing them sound by sound.

a. autumn awe bead bough bought bouquet bowl bright calf
b. calm case catch caught climb colonel column comb come
c. condemn cough could czar diphthong doubt dough dumb
d. eight enough feign fight freight friend fright gnat
e. gnome gnu half hasten head heights heir island knack
f. knave knead knee knew knife knight knit knock
g. knot knew knowledge knuckle numb laugh leave light
h. listen love make martyr mean meat might mnemonic
i. neighbor neither night often ought pneumatic pneumonia
j. psalm pseudo pseudonym psychology ptomaine quick read
k. receive receipt reign rheumatism right righteous rough

l. salmon school show sign sight sleigh soften sought

m. subtle talk taught technique thorough though thought

n. throw thumb tomb tongue tough true two walk Wednesday

o. weight whistle whole would wreck wren wring wrist write

p. zylophone

4. Read the following passages in a formal manner. Most of the passages contain diphthongs. Identify them and pronounce them clearly.

    a. Words are like leaves; and where they most abound,
       Much fruit of sense beneath is rarely found.

> *Essay on Criticism*
> Alexander Pope

    b. Silently one by one, in the infinite meadows of heaven,
       Blossomed the lovely stars, the forget-me-nots of the angels.

> *Evangeline*
> Henry W. Longfellow

    c. Good night, sweet prince;
       And flights of angels sing thee to thy rest!

> *Hamlet*
> William Shakespeare

    d. Pale green-white, in a gallop across the sky,
       The clouds retreating from a perilous affray
       Carry the moon with them, a heavy sack of gold.

> *The Gale*
> John G. Fletcher

    e. And when even dies, the million-tinted,
       And when night has come, the planets glinted,
       Lo, the valley hollow
       Lamp-bestarred!

> *In the Highlands*
> Robert L. Stevenson

    f. Yea, though I walk through the valley of the shadow of death, I will fear no evil: for thou are with me; thy rod and thy staff they comfort me.

> Psalms 23:4

    g. I heard the trailing garments of the night
       Sweep through her marble halls!
       I saw her sable skirts all fringed with light
       From the celestial walls!

> *Hymn to the Night*
> Henry W. Longfellow

    h. Forty flags with their silver stars
       Forty flags with their crimson bars,
       Flapped in the morning wind.

> *Barbara Frietche*
> John Greenleaf Whittier

5. a. Transcribe the English alphabet phonetically. Which letters begin with a consonant and which with a vowel?
   b. Would one say "a *L*" or "an *L*," "a *n*" or "an *n*?" Why?

6. Read aloud and explain in detail the error in listening that is exemplified in the following account:*

> If you don't think psychiatrists can write their own ticket, latch on to this one, which comes to us from a member of the American Medical Association. "An architect commissioned to draw up plans for a new out-patient wing for a local hospital called the various department heads to ascertain the number and types of rooms they wanted. 'And for the child-psychiatry unit,' the head psychiatrist told him, after outlining several offices and staff rooms, 'a nice, big waiting room.' 'O.K.,' said the architect. He sent the sketches along several weeks later. Examining them, the head psychiatrist noted with astonishment provision for a large room with a circular depression in the middle, marked 'Pool, tiled, 1 ft. deep.' He got the architect on the phone and asked how come. 'Why, that's the wading room you people asked for,' the architect said."

7. Transcribe in phonetics 50 consecutive words from each of the following: *The Old Testament,* an elementary school reader, "directions" on household boxes, comic strips, a news story. Compare the proportions which you find with those of Table 4.

8. These are examples of short words that are used frequently in children's literature (*Thorndike,* first 10,000 words), but were never used in 600 classroom speeches. Does each word sound to you like a familiar one as you use it in a sentence or does it sound like a rare experience?

aloft amiss bower broth calf chink claw cull dame darn dirge drake elm fin floss fore gape gill glen hath heath jig kneel lark marsh maid moor muck nip pang paw prowl quaff rein romp shalt shew skein slew spade spun strew stun surf swore thy trance troll vane wont yawn zealous.

References

Berger, Kenneth, "The Most Common Words Used in Conversation," *Journal of Communication Disorders,* 1 (1967), 201-14.

Black, John W., "Accompaniments of Word Intelligibility," *Journal of Speech and Hearing Disorders,* 17 (1952), 409-18.

————, Sadanand Singh, Oscar Tosi, Yukio Takefuta, and Elizabeth G. Jancosek, "Speech and Aural Comprehension of Foreign Students," *Journal of Speech and Hearing Research,* 8 (1964), 43-48.

---

* *The New Yorker,* Vol. 30, No. 25 (July 31, 1954).

————— and Marian Ausherman, *Vocabulary of College Students in Classroom Speeches*. The Ohio State University: Bureau of Educational Research, 1955.

Fairbanks, Grant, "Experimental Studies of Time Compression of Speech," *Journal of the Acoustical Society of America*, 28 (1956), 591-92.

Harris, Cyril M., "A Study of the Building Blocks in Speech," *Journal of the Acoustical Society of America*, 25 (1953), 962-69.

Jones, Daniel, *Everyman's English Pronuncing Dictionary*, 12th ed. New York: E. P. Dutton & Company, Inc., 1963.

Miller, G. A., G. A. Heise, and W. Lichten. "The Intelligibility of Speech as a Function of the Context of the Test Material," *Journal of Experimental Psychology*, 41 (1951), 329-35.

The Principles of the International Phonetic Association, 1949 (reprinted 1963), the Secretary of the International Phonetic Association, Department of Phonetics, University College, London, W.C.I.

Shaw, George Bernard, *Androcles and the Lion*, with a parallel text in Shaw's Alphabet (*The Shaw Alphabet*). London: Penguin Books, Inc., 1962.

Wise, Claude Merton, *Introduction to Phonetics*. Englewood Cliffs, N.J.: Prentice-Hall, Inc., 1958.

9

English Vowels

In your reading of Chapter 3 you were asked to prepare a program for the improvement of your speech. In later chapters this took more definite form. Specifically, in Chapter 8 you became aware of some of the intricacies of speech perception. This always precedes speech production. Now you are reading about the sounds of English speech with a view to improving your production of these sounds. This chapter is devoted to your understanding and improved production of the vowels and diphthongs of English. The following chapter is devoted similarly to consonants.

In retrospect of the two consequences of modulated air stream, speech sounds and voice, your interest in the present chapter is with the former. These are experiences. The sounds arise as different sound pressures impinge upon your ear and are conveyed from the outer ear, through the middle, and to the inner ear. Here neural impulses are set up that arouse learned meanings in the cortex. The speaker sets up the sound pressures. As he modulates the airstream of exhalation, he produces the stimuli for phonemes, for words, and for sentences. Some of the phonemes, for example, /t, k, p/, are carried along bounded before and/or after by voice. Others occur concomitantly with voice and are indistinguishable from it. Vowels—and there are a dozen of them in English—are formed at one and the same time that voice is produced. The contour of the system of pipes or cavities, above and anterior to the vocal folds, determines which of the several possible vowels is spoken. The purpose of the present chapter is for you to study the vowels and diphthongs of your language from the viewpoint of the *speaker,* that is the production of vowels. This is very closely allied to your perception of the vowels, one aspect of the topic of the preceding chapter.

The vowels that you make are the differentiating acoustical elements among some words. For example, the vowel distinguishes the singular *man* from the plural *men* and the tenses of verbs, for example *sit, sat,* and *come, came.** The vowel also is tagged in the description of voice. Is your voice breathy? If so, it is during vowel production. Loud? Again, it is as you say a vowel. Is your key high? If so, it is during the saying of vowels.

THE PHYSIOLOGICAL VIEW OF THE VOWEL

Some dimensions of the contours of the pipe-resonating system can be changed readily, the boundaries shifted about. You will recall that the voice system from the vocal folds to the lips resembles two pipes abutted at a junction of reduced size, essentially a third pipe. This junction is at a hump in the tongue, a place at which the tongue is bunched or where it is brought close to the roof of the mouth. Your pipe-resonating system originates at the vocal folds and terminates at the lips. This appears to provide little leeway for altering the vowel-producing mechanism, perhaps hardly enough to account for the vast qualitative variability among the vowels. Nevertheless, the leeway is adequate if properly used.

One way to change the pipe-resonating system is to bunch the tongue at different places along the axis of the front portion of the system, that which lies in the mouth. This changes the lengths of both pipes, and, of course, their lengths relative to each other. If your tongue is bunched or humped near the front of the mouth, you make one of the *front* vowels /i, ɪ, e, ɛ, æ/. If you divide the buccal cavity (mouth) well back in the mouth, you are likely to produce a back vowel /u, ʊ, o, ɔ, ɒ/. For the

---

* This important and useful feature of vowels can easily be overstated. Try saying normal sentences while making a single vowel. You can say them and listeners can understand them. This is not the case if you use a single consonant. This observation conforms to the historical fact that many Egyptian monuments are inscribed only with consonants, no vowels.

English Vowels

central vowels /ɑ, ɝ, ɜ, ɚ, ʌ/, and a sound that is not said in isolation, schwa /ə/, the tongue is bunched "midway" along the length of the mouth. Obviously, the bunching of the tongue or the partitioning of the mouth occurs in a slightly different front-back location with the dozen vowels. This is only one differentiating physiological parameter of vowel production. The groupings of the vowels are apparent in Figure 19, front to back, that is front vowels, central vowels, and back vowels.

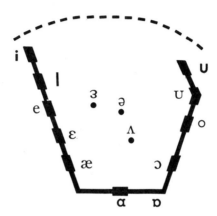

Figure 19. A representation of typical positions of the tongue during the production of vowels. The figure shows the places at which the tongue tends to be bunched, at the front of the mouth in the left of the diagram and at the back of the mouth in the right; near the roof of the mouth at the top of the diagram and some distance below the roof at the bottom of the chart.

A second way of altering the contours of the pipe-resonator system that generates vowels and voice simultaneously is in effect to increase the volume of one or both pipes by changing the vertical dimensions of the mouth. This, too, is shown in Figure 19. The change is made by the lower jaw. Some vowels are produced with the jaws almost closed. The upper jaw is rigid, but as the lower jaw (mandible) is opened degree by degree successive changes are made in the volume of the pipes and accompanying differences occur in the vowel sounds that are resonated. The differences may occur gradually, merely matters of degree, but if the sounds are recorded and played back to listeners they are heard as a succession of different and distinct vowel sounds. This is the second differentiating physiological parameter of vowel production and gives rise to a common classification of the vowel sounds as a function of jaw opening:

Closed (the word is also appropriately written *close*):
/i, ɪ, ʊ, u/
Half-closed and half-open: /ɛ, ɚ, ɜ, e, o, ə, ɚ/
Open: /æ, ɑ, ɒ, ɔ, ʌ/
This classification can also be read from Figure 19.

A third way of labeling the cavity-pipe system is to change the shape of the opening of the front orifice. Some vowels are made with the mouth rounded, even with the lips slightly puckered, as /u/; others, with a narrow slit between the lips and with the corners of the mound slightly drawn back, as /i/. It is probably inaccurate to use this symbol for the similar vowel that is formed with the lips somewhat rounded. Try exaggerating the lateral stretching movement associated with /i/. You may approximate this vowel as it is spoken in several languages, especially German. Now try to make this sound while rounding the lips for /u/. The vowel that you are now making is not used in English, but is phonemic (makes a difference) in many languages. Here, then, is the third differentiating physiological parameter of vowel production, the rounding of the lips.

There are subtle physiological conditions that attend the unique configurations of the vowel-producing mechanism, some of which may be typical of everyone's production of the vowels and others not. For example, some vowels are typically spoken with the tongue relatively relaxed and pliable, as /ɑ/; others with the tongue more rigid, as /i/. The difference that you feel in the surface of the pipe-resonators probably does not affect the acoustic properties of the system—its absorption and reflection; yet it may induce a systematic and important effect on the contour of the back section of the pipe-resonator system. If you will turn this statement around, the relative rigidity of the tongue may be a side effect of muscular contraction in the rear of the mouth and pharynx. Changes in the size of important resonators may occur there. The distinction between a *tense* and a *lax* vowel can be helpful in the teaching of English vowel production to students of English as a second language. This suggests that the relative rigidity of the tongue is a fourth differentiating physiological parameter of vowel production and one to which you can give attention, especially if you are trying to lose a distinctive pronunciation dialect.

How invariable is the length of your pipe-resonator system? You have noted that the lips tend to pucker and thus to lengthen the front section of the abutting pipes in the production of some vowels. Another variation occurs at the lower end of the system. The larynx rises and falls as you talk. This type of movement is outwardly visible in the bobbing up and down of the Adam's apple. An effect of this is to shorten and lengthen the pipe-resonating system. This relative length is a fifth differentiating physiological parameter of vowels.

This description of the physiological parameters of vowel production is, of course, generalized. Ever so many old sayings begin, "There is more than one way . . . ," and you may add, "to make a vowel." You can clench your jaws tightly, pucker your lips, and probably succeed in producing all of the English vowels recognizably. This is the ventriloquist's skill and depends upon compensatory movements within a fixed position of the visible mouth. He takes advantage of the means at his disposal for altering the contours and apertures of his vowel-making system. You can do it, too. But there is no prize for this contortion in oral behavior in normal talking. Instead, you clearly differentiate among the vowels according to the physiological uniqueness of each and thereby achieve acoustic uniqueness. Except for pedagogical reasons there is little ground for distinguishing between vowel production acoustically and physiologically, nor for differentiating between vowel and voice production. As a speaker illustrates one, he demonstrates them all.

MEASUREMENTS OF VOWELS

You already know that each vowel is associated with unique features of sound waves, particularly bands of frequencies or formants (Figure 20). You also associate these formants with equally singular contours of the pipe-resonator system. You know also that neither the vowel nor voice as it originates at the vocal folds can be examined in isolation. The vocal folds of an excised larynx simply cannot be blown apart rhythmically in a realistic fashion apart from the coupled pipe-resonating system. Theoretically, the tone at the vocal folds has the spectrum that is ever diminishing in intensity from low to high frequency and inclusive of all frequencies.

Some Physical Data About Vowels

The vowels have differentiating and interesting features apart from formants. You *can* manage your vocal folds and exhaled airstream to yield a wide variety in pitch, loudness, and duration of vowels. Try it. Now try again, exceeding the variety of the first trial. This is a skillful manipulation, but it is somewhat similar to the reference in the preceding section to the ventriloquist with clenched teeth. You force yourself to do this odd sort of talking; it is not the way the voice "happens." There are several relatively static dimensions. If you simply say the vowels factually

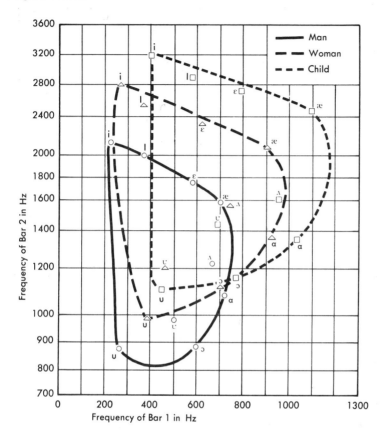

Figure 20. A graphical representation of the typical frequencies of the first and second formants of English vowels. The frequency of the first formant is plotted on the abscissa and of the second formant on the ordinate. Thus a single point on the graph represents both values (after Peterson and Barney).

as in the monosyllabic words *top, tap, tape,* and so forth, (1) the closed vowels are higher in pitch than the open ones, (2) the open vowels last longer than the closed ones, and (3) there are systematic differences in sound pressure level among the vowels of an order of four decibels. One set of measurements in these regards is summarized in Table 5.

A Statistical View of Vowels

There being but one vowel per syllable, there are fewer vowels than there are consonants in language. But since there are only one-half as

Table 5. Mean values of fundamental frequency, duration, and sound level measurements of 11 English vowels as spoken by 16 male speakers.

Vowel	Frequency in Hz	Duration in Milliseconds	Relative Intensity in db
i	146	159	0.0
ɪ	142	135	2.9
e	137	191	1.8
ɛ	138	153	3.1
æ	133	208	3.4
ɑ	133	192	3.7
ɔ	135	209	3.2
ʌ	141	154	2.2
o	137	197	3.7
ʊ	149	153	2.5
u	153	200	2.6

many vowels and diphthongs as consonants, each vowel might occur especially frequently without upsetting the balance. But the vowels do not occur equally often in speech. Table 6 anticipates Chapter 10 and will be referred to when you study the next chapter. In the table the percentages are presented with which each of 41 vowels (and diphthongs) and consonants is found in the initial, medial, and the final positions of a sample of somewhat more than 3500 common one- and two-syllable English words. Each column may be read apart from the others. The inclusion of the consonants (Chapter 10) permits a comparison of the relative occurrence of vowels and consonants. Less than 4 per cent of the one-syllable words begin with a vowel! The most-frequent vowels to begin two-syllable words are /ɪ/ and /ə/, and the most-frequent terminal vowel, /ɪ/.

THE INDIVIDUAL VOWELS

The objective of your study of this chapter lies in your improved production of the vowels that you came to recognize in Chapter 8. As you were hearing and transcribing the vowels you were also mouthing them, that is, saying them. But a tremendous inconsistency in this production persists in spite of one's best efforts. The following treatment of vowels and the lists of words associated with each are intended to reinforce the

Table 6. The percentages in which the different sounds appear in the initial, medial, and final positions of words of one- and two-syllable lengths (you may read as "chances in 100").

Phoneme	Initial Position One Syllable	Initial Position Two Syllable	Medial Position One Syllable	Medial Position Two Syllable	Final Position One Syllable	Final Position Two Syllable
i	0.2	0.4	4.1	2.1	0.6	0.1
ɪ	0.5	4.8	7.5	10.7		9.2
e-eɪ	0.3	0.4	4.6	2.5	1.3	1.9
ɛ	0.5	1.0	5.8	3.9		
æ	0.5	1.1	7.2	4.0	0.1	
ɑ	0.5	0.8	4.5	2.8	0.1	0.1
ɔ	0.1	0.8	3.9	1.8	0.5	0.1
o-oʊ	0.4	0.9	4.1	2.1	0.8	1.6
ə		4.0		5.2		0.5
ʌ	0.1	0.4	5.5	2.3		
ɝ·ɚ·r	4.7	6.6	15.3	10.1	3.6	16.9
u	0.1		3.2	1.5	0.8	0.4
ʊ			0.3	0.2		
ɔɪ	0.1	0.1	0.5	0.2	0.3	
a	0.1	0.5	1.9	0.6	0.3	0.1
aɪ	0.1	0.3	3.9	2.3	1.2	0.6
ju-ɪu	0.1	0.1	0.3	0.5	0.1	0.2
p	6.8	8.1	2.4	2.7	5.8	0.8
b	8.6	7.0		1.8	2.0	0.6
t	6.6	4.8	2.6	5.8	17.2	14.5
d	5.0	6.1	0.2	2.9	8.8	6.8
k	9.1	8.5	2.1	3.8	8.7	2.5
g	6.2	2.9	0.1	1.2	2.2	0.2
f	7.0	5.9	0.2	1.8	2.6	0.7
v	1.4	1.8	0.2	1.4	2.7	1.0
θ	1.8	0.8		0.3	2.6	0.6
ð	0.5	0.3		0.3	0.3	0.1
s	16.9	10.6	2.8	4.5	6.2	8.3
z	0.1	0.2	0.1	0.9	3.5	2.1
ʃ	3.0	0.7		0.8	1.9	1.2
ʒ				0.1		
h	4.7	4.1		0.3		
tʃ	1.7	0.9		0.4	3.9	0.3
dʒ	1.3	0.9		0.6	2.6	2.0
m-m̩	3.6	5.4	1.3	3.1	4.8	2.3
n-n̩	2.4	1.8	5.1	7.1	6.5	10.9
l-l̩	4.9	3.9	7.2	5.9	6.2	11.6
w	3.8	2.9	1.9	0.9		
ʍ	0.8	0.4		0.1		
j	0.6		2.0	0.2		
ŋ			1.2	0.7	1.9	2.0

145

materials of Chapter 8, that is, your *speech perception,* and to add dimensions that will lead to changes in production.*

A special aspect of the following descriptions of the sounds is the probable phonetic environment of the sound. You may readily concoct nonsense syllables that allow you to practice a sound in a realistic context.

/i/

The vowel of *eat, feet, see* is a closed, front, unrounded sound, /i/. It is frequently said without its full differentiating quality. But this slighting is insufficient to introduce many confusions in listening. The ones that arise in abnormal communication such as in a noisy environment are likely to involve /u/. *Three* often is heard as *two!*

In some languages /i/ and /ɪ/ are not phonemic. Either can be said with equal propriety. In English, however, *fit* and *feet* are very different words. The distinguishing of the two sounds is difficult if the speaker has not acquired them in his youth. When /i/ occurs in words of three to six sounds the chances are about one in ten that /tʃ/ or /ə/ precedes it. It is likely to be followed by /t/ or /d/.

Illustrative Words:

a. antique apiece appease asleep athlete beastly beaten
b. beetle bereave beseech besiege buckwheat ceaseless
c. cedar chiefly compete compute concede conceive
d. congeal deacon dealing deceit decent deepen defeat
e. demon depot disease eastward equal esteem even fatigue
f. feeling female fifteenth greeting heater impeach
g. leader measles oblique people pretext redeem regal
h. retail seaport secrete seedling sleeper sleepy species
i. steamer sweeper sweeten threefold threescore treatment

Illustrative Sentences:*

a. These three wheels will leave tracks in the wheat field.
b. He'd say that the Eastern teams will easily lead the league this year.
c. We teach our radio speakers again after they join the fleet and go to sea.

---

* Whatever lists of words that are used here or in later chapters are necessarily chosen arbitrarily. Please use your best judgment about whether or not the examples are applicable.

* Subsequently the word illustrative is omitted. The primary purpose of the listings, however, remains illustrative. This does not preclude their use as materials for practice.

/ɪ/

The vowel of *it* and *city* is a closed, front sound, one of the most frequent of English sounds, is often spoken as schwa and interchanged with /ɛ/. Spanish or Italian influences may contribute to confusion between /ɪ/ and /i/ among speakers of those languages, for neither language has both sounds. The sound is normally the terminal sound in *y*-nouns and *ly*-adverbs, although many speakers say /i/ instead. The sound is usually the final one in the names of the days of the week, but these are often spoken with /eɪ/ instead. The pre- and post-phonetic environment of the sound is highly variable, with /t, n, s/ most frequently following it and /ŋ, f, g, m, tʃ, n/ most frequently preceding it.

Words that contain this sound tend to be more intelligible than words that do not contain it. Possibly this is because it is so often a part of multisyllabic words.

Words:

a. fill fish hip midst rill steer since six tin acid
b. active any axis bandit beauty befit begot bishop
c. blissful bucket budget chiefly cynic deceit decree
d. defeat disease eddy effect eldest elect ending
e. endless fifteenth fleecy impeach impede impose
f. indulge infest infuse instance package painting
g. pansy pigeon pinion pivot placid precinct puppy
h. redeem savage secrete sicken signet sinful
i. sixteen sixty socket speedy stigma stoic summit

Sentences:

a. This money, taken in Monday, fills the till.
b. Little chills may indicate illness.
c. Fifty big fish filled a ring near the summit.

/e, eɪ/

The vowel of *ate* and *fade* is front and half closed. When sustained it is, of course, a pure vowel, not the closely related diphthong said in pronouncing the first letter of the English alphabet. American pronunciation does not make a rigid distinction between the two closely related sounds, the vowell and the diphthong. You will wish to study your pronunciation to find whether you discriminate between them consistently or by happenstance.

The vowel /e/, when not clearly differentiated as a singular vowel quality, may become an /ɛ/ or /æ/. The most-frequent pairs of sounds involving /e, eɪ/ include a preceding /z, v, dʒ/ and a subsequent /t, n, s/.

Words:

   a. ache age aim bake cake cape chain chase clay date
   b. flake freight grape graze haste hay jade jay ray
   c. scale shake slate stake stay taint vague wage abate
   d. able apron attain blockade bouquet craven create
   e. debase degrade domain efface eighty estate estrange
   f. fable fatal framework gaily gracious graven
   g. greyhound haven lately locate maple nameless nitrate
   h. obey paleness papal patience player playmate racial
   i. rainfall rainy subway surname trading unstained vacant wafer

Sentences:

   a. May I make potato salad today?
   b. Trains and airplanes take the sailors away.
   c. There were few complaints about the strained and humane behavior of the statesmen.

/ɛ/

The vowel of *Ed, sell,* and *fetch* is front and half closed. Some speakers substitute the vowel /ɪ/ for /ɛ/; others substitute the neutral /ə/. The sound is particularly likely to be followed by /r, l, n, s/ and to be preceded by one of the affricatives /dʒ, tʃ/. Words that contain this sound tend to be more intelligible than words that do not contain it.

Words:

   a. belt bend bent best bled blend bless breath care cleft
   b. crest desk drench edge egg fret friend guest hem hen
   c. hence knelt lair less mesh mess neck nest peck pen pest
   d. pledge quell quench quest scarce sketch sled spare sped
   e. stem sweat tell ten tenth text thread tread trees trend
   f. twelfth wear web well vest any bearer bevel contempt
   g. defect eddy eldest ending endless error pressure prestige
   h. rector render terror vengeance

Sentences:

   a. The word is *men,* not *min;* and *many,* not *Minnie.*
   b. After resting in western Tennessee, Betty went to Texas.
   c. Twelve elves of all lengths nestled and slept next to that shelf.

/æ/

The vowel of *add, badlands, "baa baa black . . ."* is a front, open vowel. Sometimes /ɛ/ is said in its stead. In General American speech the sound /æ/ is consistently used in words in which some other English-speaking groups would say /a/. The sound /æ/, particularly with a harsh and nasal quality, is often used by non-English-speaking peoples in their humorous ridicule of the sound of American English. Possibly one should infer that /æ/ affords special opportunity for a nerve-racking experience with the listener. The student who is described as having a harsh or strident voice may well devote special attention to achieving the quality of this vowel while relaxing the musculatures of the pharynx.

The vowel /æ/ frequently precedes /n, ŋ, m/; it often follows a friction-like consonant, a plosive, or a nasal—in short, almost any consonant. Words that contain this sound tend to be more intelligible than words that do not contain it.

Words:

a. askance attach bandit canal cascade channel climax
b. cash cramp rat slant swam thrash vast
c. collapse contact craftsman crafty cranny cravat
d. dabble dazzle demand distract enact encamp enchant
e. enhance expanse fallow fathom fragment gallop grandma
f. gravel hammock handsome jackal jangle landmark lava
g. nasty pansy placid plasma sadden salmon sample sanguine
h. savage scaffold shabby sparrow supplant tactics talent
i. topaz vanquish waxen

Sentences:

a. Winesap apples have a red cast that is not apparent in this picture because of the shadows.
b. Last Saturday we attached a latch and fastened the door.
c. An adder and an asp had a last stand.

/a, ɑ, ɒ/

The vowels in *what, calm, pappa,* and (with exceptions) *aunt* are closely related. All are open, central sounds, and the habits of pronunciations of people of many sections of the United States do not make the use of key words to illustrate the differences among the three sounds very effective. The vowel /a/ is readily illustrated as normally being the first of the two elements of the diphthong /aɪ/ of *eye*. The second is usually found in a pronunciation of *father*. The third is illustrated with the key words *calm, sorry,* and so forth. However, in General American speech these words probably fall in the /ɑ/ phoneme and the target vowel is neither heard nor spoken consistently. The most-frequent sounds to follow the /ɑ/-group are /r, l, k/ with /t, b, p/ also occurring much more often than would be expected by chance. The most likely sounds to precede the vowels are /j, h/ with the plosives also occurring more often than would be expected by chance.

Words:
  a. bark charge dark don golf jar large marsh rod shod tar
  b. want was yarn arbor archer ardor argue armchair armor
  c. balmy barker bonnet closet congress darken depart
  d. donkey embalm farmyard foggy guitar harbor hearty
  e. hedgehog hemlock holly honor involve landmark marine
  f. marvel novel olive optic pocket process robber
  g. scarlet somewhat spotless starch stocking target
  h. wanton workshop

Sentences:
  a. John's aunt gave him a lot of tops.
  b. The scholars of the province are allotted a bronze plaque to award to an artist.
  c. Proverbs and prophets are said to be the products of tropics.

/ɔ/

The back, open vowel /ɔ/ is not differentiated for many speakers from the preceding group of vowels. Failure to differentiate it, however, can hardly be glossed over in the manner of failure to distinguish among /ɑ, a, ɒ/. The confusion or collapsing of these vowels is one of the most frequent characteristics of severe pronunciation dialects and "substandard" speech. Some words depend upon the qualitative difference between /ɔ/ and the other vowels for intelligibility, for example, *calk* vs. *cock,* or *caught* vs. *cot,* or *taught* (taut) vs. *tot.* The most-frequent sounds to follow /ɔ/ are /l, r, s/ and the frequent sounds to precede it include /g/ and /f/. The presence of the vowel /ɔ/ in a word tends to reduce the intelligibility of the word.

Words:
  a. awe broad broth cause cloth corpse crawl cross
  b. fraught gauze gloss hall pawn quart song stalk staunch

c. sworn troth trough vault war accord aloft appall
d. austere borrow boss caution costly dogged drawer
e. falter faucet foster frosty glossy horrid lawyer
f. morsel northern orbit orchard organ orphan ostrich
g. palfrey quarrel sordid stormy swarthy thoughtful
h. throng wardrobe

Sentences:

a. Applause at football and baseball games abroad is sometimes abhored.
b. Many first-born children withdraw from asphalt.
c. The rainfall during the far-off autumnal storm almost caused the awnings to fall.

/o, oʊ/

The vowel /o/ and its related diphthong may come into your saying *solo, polo,* and *so-so.* The vowel and diphthong are interchanged in American pronunciation much like /e/ and /eɪ/. The formation of the diphthong entails only minor shifts in the pipe-resonator system for both /o/ and /ʊ/ are back, half-open vowels. The sounds frequently precede and follow /r, l/ and follow one of the friction-like consonants.

Words:

a. blow floor fold fort hold home load porch prone quote
b. slope soap sold stove swore vogue worn ago although
c. ashore awoke chauffeur devote doleful domain fallow
d. fellow follow forum frozen furrow glory going hallow
e. hello hollow homesick hopeful nomad obey omen omit
f. polar portal portend portrait postpone proclaim roller
g. seaport sofa solar stoic stony topmost total wardrobe

Sentences:

a. We hold our own vocal language in oral storage.
b. A score of old donors voted soberly and bemoaned the woeful revolt.
c. Is it a moment for boldness, for a social motion?

/ʊ/

The vowel /u/ is easily initiated in isolation; the vowel /ʊ/, however, is more difficult. The speaker frequently starts with a key word, for example, *pull,* and the mistakenly sustains /u/ instead of /ʊ/. Moreover, the vowel /ʊ/ is rare in English. This rarity may be in part attributable to the relative difficulty that speakers have in initiating it in isolation. The phonetic environments of the vowels /o/ and /ʊ/ are similar; both are quite frequently followed by /r, l, k/ and are preceded by a variety of consonants. The presence of the vowel /ʊ/ in a word tends to reduce the intelligibility of the word, perhaps because of the rarity of the vowel.

Words:
    a. book brook bull bush cook look pull push put allure
    b. assure barefoot booklet bullet bully bulwark bushel
    c. pulpit rural

Sentences:
    a. A push-pull tube was put in the circuit.
    b. The bushes by the brook are crooked.
    c. The good buff-colored book was put on the pulpit.

/ʌ, ə, ɜ/*

The back, half-open vowel /ʌ/ and the central vowel /ə/ are closely related, the former seeming to be a more full, stressed version of the latter. The schwa carries minimum stress and this is, of course, less than the stress of a syllable that contains /ʌ/ and is spoken in comparison. Hence, the rule "A schwa cannot be spoken in isolation." Both vowels /ə, ʌ/ are in *above*. It is inappropriately limiting to refer to /ʌ/, a stressed schwa. True, both sounds are unique in stress. True, also, as all vowels are spoken with minimum or little characteristic quality, they tend to become the schwa /ə/. To the extent that this substitution contributes to slovenly speaking, it is to be treated as faulty and substandard. To the extent that this substitution facilitates the lack of emphasis of the ever-so-frequent and redundant connectives, articles, and prepositions of oral language, it is to be accepted and encouraged. In other words, occasion, content, and context interact with the saying of the vowels to determine whether or not /ə/ is the appropriate vowel in *little* (*"L'il* Abner"), *and, the, an, of*.

The syllabic consonant, transcribed /l̩, m̩, n̩/ instead of /əl, əm, ən/, was explained in Chapter 8. This syllable seems to intrude itself into regional pronunciation dialects by analogy and changes some monosyllables into two-syllable words as with *flown, blown, school, rule, cone,* and *sown*.

The use of schwa with /r/ is closely related to the use of schwa with another central vowel, /ɜ/; this and the hooked schwa were treated in

---

* The apparent inconsistencies of pages 141, 142, and 152 are deliberate and reflect the approximations inherent in the descriptions of the vowels.

Chapter 8. As explained there, with r-coloring schwa becomes the final sound of a General American pronunciation of river ['rɪvɚ]. Importantly and not discussed earlier, the other one with r-coloring, /ɝ/, becomes the nucleus of *bird* [bɝd]. In some pronunciation dialects the r-coloring is absent and the words become ['rɪvə] and [bɜd].

The intrusion of a second syllable in words that are normally one-syllable words occurs also with schwa + /r/, as with *flour, sour*. One of this family of related vowels /ʌ, ə, ɜ/ occurs very frequently before /l, m, n/ and after /l, m/.

Words With Schwa /ə/:

   a. abridge afire ancient appraise arouse array ashore
   b. autumn balloon blissful bottom census cherub children
   c. citron deacon earldom entrails era extra famous
   d. fruitful grievous headland herald instance inward
   e. island jocund lament legion lengthen lion monstrous
   f. needful occur oral orphan parrot patrol pregnant quiet
   g. remnant royal serene sermon spiral spokesman strengthen
   h. stigma turnip vigil vowel warrant workman worship
   i. youthful zealous

Sentences:

   a. The parade of tradesmen caused business to be suspended.
   b. There is an urgent need for science to acquire thoughtful standards.
   c. Can we ascribe the estranged kinsmen of the matron to the agent's diet.

Words With the Hooked Schwa /ɚ/:

   a. acorn acre adder auburn author barter
   b. batter bluster cellar chapter clamber conjure cupboard
   c. digger doctor effort either falter fodder forgot
   d. fracture glimmer helper hither honor injure inner
   e. junior lower martyr northern offer other oyster
   f. partner peddler plunder power prosper quarter quiver
   g. rumor slumber solder splinter squander structure
   h. tempter thunder tractor tuber valor vesper waiter
   i. warbler

Sentences:

   a. The owner wondered which led to the greater error, the coward or the doer.
   b. Purportedly the pursuit was of the robbers by the archers.
   c. The odor of a tincture pervades the cloister.

Words with /ʌ/:

a. brush but come cut fund jug jump lung pluck
b. plumb plus rub rump shrub trump tug us young buckwheat
c. button druggist fumble funny grumble gutter hunger
d. justice luggage mushroom muskrat onion oven plunder
e. ruddy rustic scuffle slumber stubborn stumble
f. tonnage trouble trusty uncouth unused uproot vulture

Sentences:

a. After supper Mulder muttered about the nuts in the oven.
b. Though rebuffed he was unhurt by the blunder.
c. Ultimately the struggle against the locust will call for a higher budget.

Words with /ɝ/:

a. birch burr clerk first girl girth herb lurk
b. scourge swerve verse were work absurd affirm
c. bluebird burgess certain clergy convert curdle disturb
d. divert exert flourish furnish hermit inert infer insert
e. invert nourish outward pearly perverse proverb
f. purchase purpose rehearse reserve reverse revert
g. service subvert turban whirlwind worthless

Sentences:

a. Some myrtle curled above the ferns in front of the workshop.
b. Defer the search for the thirteenth earl.
c. The sermon urged that certain virtues be discerned early.

/u/

The closed, back vowel /u/ is a relatively rare vowel in English, but not so rare as /ʊ/. It usually is given a clear-cut quality that readily distinguishes it from others, although there are regional substitutions of /ʊ/, and probably no one would give a "preferred" pronunciation for *roof,* except his own habit. For example, in some regions /ʊ/ or /ʌ/ is substituted for /u/, especially after /r/ as in *room* or *broom.* More importantly, the vowel /u/ is interchanged indifferently with the diphthong /ɪu/ as in *rule* and *student.* The vowel is often preceded by /l/ and followed by /m, l/.

Words:

a. brew chew crew duke flute fruit groom hoot loom poor
b. proof soon spool spruce sue swoon allude balloon

   c. bedroom bridegroom brutal costume cuckoo deluge demure
   d. during elude gloomy include intrude junior jury loosen
   e. lucid manure pollute pursue resume ruby rumor scruple
   f. teaspoon truly tuber uncouth uproot

Sentences:

   a. The schoolroom truly proved to be strewn with huge costumes.
   b. Two clues thereto were found by noon.
   c. Reprove and reproof come from the same root.

THE DIPHTHONGS

The glide that you make in the production of a diphthong probably includes successively the stimuli for several vowels if brief isolated portions of the glide were excised and maintained sufficiently for their phonetic character to be apparent. Indeed, a vowel alone has been called *polyphthong!* The transient state of the total glide of a diphthong includes two clearly recognizable vowel qualities. In many words both qualities must be heard, for the diphthong is phonemic as *cootie* vs. *cutie.*

Two diphthongs have been treated lightly in these discussions. There is scarcely any distinction between them and their principal vowels. Neither /oʊ/ nor /eɪ/ is phonemic in American English! Whether the vowel or diphthong is made in words that contain the phoneme is determined by the speaker's pronunciation dialect, the formality of the occasion, the speaker's bent toward "elegance of diction," and a host of related influences. Four other diphthongs are distinctive components of American speech, all phonemic in some words.

/aɪ/

Use of the diphthong /aɪ/ and the study of the sound are convincing evidence that you use the vowel /a/ even though your use of it as a separate vowel may be foreign to your dialect and deemed "highfalutin." The most-frequent difficulty in the production of /aɪ/ is the omission or slighting of the second element, particularly before /r/ as in *tire* and *entire.* The sound is often followed by /l, n/ and preceded by /f, p/.

Words:

   a. blight bright brine crime dry fright gripe guile kind
   b. mire plight pride quite spire squire strife while
   c. abide aspire bequile comply confide consign conspire

    d. deny deprive design disguise divide dryer godlike
    e. grandsire highness imply inscribe knighthood lying
    f. malign meantime noontide outline revise rider sometime
    g. subscribe suffice tiger triumph viper wayside whereby

Sentences:
    a. Why not invite every fireman who resides on the island?
    b. Unseen by your eyes, a tiny idler guides those five strings.
    c. Magpies, black as graphite, reside on all the nearby islands.

/aʊ/

The diphthong /aʊ/ is a highly variable sound. Both elements are subject to regional variations of pronunciation, for example /æʊ, æu, ɑʊ, ɑu, ɛʊ/ as well as such "triphthongs" as /ɪæʊ/ and frequently the second element is omitted, *our* and *are* becoming indistinguishable. Words that contain /aʊ/ tend to be more intelligible than words that do not, irrespective of the "odd pronunciations." The sound is frequently followed by /t, n, d, r/ and preceded by /w, n, t/.

Words:
    a. bout brown clown crouch crowd crown doubt drown fount
    b. gout gown growl hound lounge mount mouth noun ounce
    c. pouch prowl round rouse shout shroud sour spout
    d. trout vouch abound aloud announce background bounty
    e. cloudless confound counter county coward farmhouse
    f. founder hourly outgo outspread outstretch outweigh
    g. power pronounce prowess resound surmount thousand vowel

Sentences:
    a. Countless devout scouts crowded down southward.
    b. Now we ourselves shout, "Outline the way to bountiful living."
    c. The house that towers over the fountain doubtless shades the
       ground.

/ɔɪ/

The diphthong /ɔɪ/ is an infrequent sound in English. Nonetheless, it is usually well said and words that contain it tend to be more intelligible than words that do not. Speakers who do not distinguish between /ɔ/ and /ɑ/ tend to substitute the latter vowel in the diphthong /ɔɪ/. There is also an interesting substitution of /r/ or /ɝ/ for /ɔɪ/ by some speakers in *boil, oysters, oil,* and *toilet.* The nucleus /ɔɪ/ is most frequently followed by /l, s, n/ and preceded by /n/.

Words:

a. boil boy broil coil coin foil hoist joy loin point
b. spoil toil toy troy void adjoin anoint appoint boiler
c. buoyant cloister exploit loiter moisture noiseless
d. oilcloth oyster royal toilet voyage

Sentences:

a. Coins are preserved in oil.
b. Soiled soybeans can be used for oilcloth.
c. Ralph Royster Doyster's mother was hardly coy.

/ɪu, ju/

The diphthong /ɪu/, the alternative glide /ju/ and the vowel /u/ are often used interchangeably. This exchange explains why George Bernard Shaw, in writing lines for an American character, sometimes spelled the American pronunciation as *dook* and *noo*. Perhaps in the same category of words, or possibly in a less obvious one, is the practice among American speakers to use /u/ rather than /ɪu/ after /r/ as in *rule* and *ruin*, and after /l/ as in *lute*. The diphthong is frequently followed and preceded by /r, t, m, s/.

Words:

a. few fume fuse mule muse mute news pew pure tune youth
b. accuse acute argue beauty bugle bureau endue endure
c. fury fusion futile future human humane impute infuse
d. juicy mucous nephew newborn nuisance produce pupil
e. rebuke reduce refuge refute renew repute review seduce
f. steward student tribute tumult tunic unique unused
g. yourselves youthful

Sentences:

a. The new unit, Azure, used few utensils.
b. The clues refuted the view that he failed to do his duty.
c. Lutes and flutes are unique among tuneful musical instruments.

MODIFICATIONS OF VOWELS

The vowels that have been enumerated are target sounds. These are the vowel sounds that teachers assume they are usually saying. These sounds are the nuclei of stressed syllables. On-going speech is often something else: *again* becomes /ə'gɪn/, *ten* becomes /tɪn/, *wrap* becomes

/rɛp/. If you will transcribe all of these instances and study the vowels in relation to Figure 19, you will notice that in each instance the target vowel has been changed to one that lies above it on the vowel diagram. This is a frequent occurrence in colloquial speech and is called "raising the vowel." You read of this from the auditor's viewpoint in Chapter 8 and noted it /ɪ/. Now you are the speaker and you are trying to manage your own production of sounds. Is the point clear? Obviously, you must check all of your vowels, as produced, and guard against raising, fronting, lowering, and backing. However, raising the vowel is the most prevalent of these.

In another context you read that the nucleus of the syllable is given one of three degrees of stress: primary, secondary, or minimal. These words illustrate all three: *advocate, celebrate, calculus, authorize, demagogue*. These words have only two degrees of stress, primary and minimal: fountain, country, commas, highly, little, Alice. These words have no minimal stress, only primary and secondary: *uptown, cowboy, egghead, bookshelf, windmill, earpiece, stairway, filet*. In the unstressed syllable, schwa and /ɪ/ become the target vowels. The speaker is unaware that he is using these and when called upon to transcribe polysyllabic words typically writes full-dress vowels, not the ordinary weak ones of colloquial usage. The point to keep in mind is that vowel quality varies with stress. There can be an improper formal rendition of a vowel and an improper unstressing. As in earlier chapters, you are advised to be intelligible and to use a voice appropriate to the occasion.

APPLICATION

This chapter has been a series of exercises. As you read the words and sentences that are included with each brief discussion of vowel and diphthong, many questions arose. One of these was, "Which is the correct way to say this word?" That question will be treated in Chapter 11. Meanwhile, in the language of earlier chapters, you are *stretching your voice* to new dimensions.

This chapter gives a physiological account of the vowels. In the preceding chapter you read of them from an aural point of view. Now, hopefully, you can adjust the pipes of the speech-producing system to create the vowel sounds. One way of turning Table 6 into action is illustrated in this monologue.

> My instructor suggests that I improve my vowel quality. Since I wish to make the most improvement possible and make it in the shortest time possible, I shall begin with the vowel that occurs in

the most words. That vowel, once mastered, will upgrade more different words of my speech than any other. Indeed, now that I think of it, I am practicing this vowel a lot anyway, simply as I talk; my present practice is apparently with poor habits. I must master the saying (physiological parameters) of the most-frequent vowel and practice it with good habits!

SUMMARY

There are approximately a dozen vowels in English. Physiologically these are differentiated by:
  a. the front-back placement of the bunch of the tongue
  b. the up-down opening of the jaw
  c. the tense-lax solidity of the tongue
  d. the circular-flatness of the lip glottis
  e. the length-shortness of the oral cavity.
These characteristics of the resonators, in turn, account for the formants that are specified to each vowel and relate to other differentiating physical features of vowels, their pitch and intensity.

The vowels distinguish some words from each other. More importantly, they convey the larger part of voice quality, of pitch, and of loudness. The vowels /ɪ, æ/ occur disproportionately often; /ɪu, ɔɪ, ʊ/, rarely. Illustrations of the target vowels, that is syllabic nuclei, in words and sentences are provided.

Exercises

1 a. The discussion of each vowel included three sentences that were loaded with the vowel. Read aloud and transcribe the vowels phonetically, leaving one blank space for each consonant sound.
  b. Construct three additional sentences that are loaded with each vowel.

2 a. Construct a sentence that contains at least five schwas. Underscore the related letters.
  b. Construct a sentence that contains at least five front vowels. Underscore the related letters.
  c. Construct a sentence that contains at least five back vowels. Underscore the related letters.
  d. Construct a sentence that contains at least five open vowels. Underscore the related letters.

3. Read the first three syllables of line 1 of this chapter that contain pure vowels and sustain for six seconds the nucleus of each syllable. Do this for every fifth line on the page. You are probably having difficulty, either in decision or in production, with two classes of sounds, schwa (it cannot be made in isolation) and diphthongs. You will be wise to choose the first three syllables that contain neither.

4. Illustrate the different manners of spelling the vowel sounds. (Some dictionaries list these in the introductory material.) Write, for example, all of the ways of spelling /ε/.

5. Compose lists of 12 words that contain one vowel sound, 12 words that contain two different vowel sounds, and 12 words that contain three different vowel sounds.

6. The following words have been picked by college students as containing "phonetic surprises." Transcribe the vowels of the words phonetically:

> acre aeolis agile amateur Amherst aphesis aye bade bathe beguile bologna bough bouquet calm ceiling chateau Cheyenne Chicago Chili choir cognac cologne colonel cough croquet dial diphtheria diphthong Dorothy education egg embalm exile Faust flaw fog forehead Friday fuel fungi fuselage gaol gauze gnat gnome goal guarantee hearth height hiccough hue hymn icicle incognito insoluble Iowa isle itinerary judge kernel knew knight know knowledge laboratory laugh layman lingerie lymph maelstrom mixture moccasin Myrtle mute naive nuisance nuptial ocean often operetta opossum papaya perforate Phoenix pleasure pneumonia precedence prescribe psalm psychology quay raspberry really roof rough sabre sandwich scythe Seine sleigh society sophomore Stephen subpoena succulent Swarthmore syncope talk Thames theatre Thomas Thursday tongue toward Tuesday victual virtual walked warrior Wednesday wheelbarrow whence white worship Yvonne

7. Transcribe the vowel in the final syllable of each line of "Curfew Must Not Ring Tonight" (Appendix A).

8. Prepare an oral report on the vowel shift in English.

9. Explain your understanding of the relationship between physiological phonetics and acoustic phonetics.

10. Extend the following lines with three words that illustrate the nuclei of the stressed syllables of the words that are listed:
   a. toy, Roy, broiler
   b. kite, Kaiser, aye
   c. lout, bower, cow
   d. mute, duke, ruler
   e. sail, say, phaeton
   f. so, dough, rower

11. A diphthong is said to be a rising diphthong if the second element is higher on the vowel diagram than the first element. Cite 12 words that contain rising diphthongs. Contrast these with 12 *off glides*.

12. Daniel Jones devised the concept of cardinal vowels. Basically, there were four of these: one made with the tongue as high and as far front as possible, one made with the tongue as low and as far front as possible, one with the tongue as low and as far back as possible, and one with the tongue as high and as far back as possible. What were the four cardinal vowels? Pronounce them both in your customary manner, sustaining them, and following the descriptions of this exercise.

13. Mark Twain reputedly spoke with a drawl. This would be a feature of his vowel production. How would his vowel production differ from yours? Read a paragraph aloud to demonstrate a drawl. Are you necessarily introducing diphthongs?

My Watch*

My beautiful new watch had run eighteen months without losing or gaining, and without breaking any part of its machinery or stopping. I had come to believe it infallible in its judgments about the time of day, and to consider its constitution and its anatomy imperishable. But at last, one night, I let it run down. I grieved about it as if it were a recognized messenger and forerunner of calamity. But by-and-by I cheered up, set the watch by guess, and commanded my bodings and superstitions to depart. Next day I stepped into the chief jeweler's to set it by the exact time, and the head of the establishment took it out of my hand and proceeded to set it for me. Then he said, "She is four minutes slow—regulator wants pushing up." I tried to stop him—tried to make him understand that the watch kept perfect time. But no; all this human cabbage could see was that the watch was four minutes slow, and the regulator must be pushed up a little; and so, while I danced around him in anguish, and implored him to let the watch alone, he calmly and cruelly did the shameful deed. My watch began to gain. It gained faster and faster day by day. Within the week it sickened to a raging fever, and its pulse went up to a hundred and fifty in the shade. At the end of two months it had left all the timepieces of the town far in the rear, and was a fraction over thirteen days ahead of the almanac. It was away into November enjoying the snow, while the October leaves were still turning. It hurried up house rent, bills payable, and such things, in such a ruinous way that I could not abide it. I took it to the watchmaker to be regulated. He asked me if I had ever had it repaired. I said no, it had never needed any repairing. He looked a look of vicious happiness and eagerly pried the watch open, and then put a small dice box into his eye and peered into its machinery. He said it wanted cleaning and oiling, besides regulating—come in a week. After being cleaned and oiled, and regulated, my watch slowed down to that degree that it ticked like a tolling bell. I began

---

* Mark Twain.

to be left by trains, I failed all appointments, I got to missing my
dinner; my watch strung out three days' grace to four and let me go
to protest; I gradually drifted back into yesterday, then day before,
then into last week, and by-and-by the comprehension came upon
me that all solitary and alone I was lingering along in week before
last, and the world was out of sight. I seemed to detect in myself a
sort of sneaking fellow-feeling for the mummy in the museum, and
a desire to swap news with him. I went to a watchmaker again. He
took the watch all to pieces while I waited, and then said the barrel
was "swelled." He said he could reduce it in three days. After this
the watch averaged well, but nothing more. For half a day it would
go like the very mischief, and keep up such a barking and wheezing,
and whooping and sneezing and snorting, that I could not hear myself think for the disturbance; and as long as it held out there was
not a watch in the land that stood any chance against it. But the rest
of the day it would keep on slowing down and fooling along until
all the clocks it had left behind caught up again. So at last, at the
end of twenty-four hours, it would trot up to the judges' stand and
just in time. It would show a fair and square average, and no man
could say it had done more or less than its duty. But a correct average is only a mild virtue in a watch, and I took this instrument to
another watchmaker. He said the kingbolt was broken. I said I was
glad it was nothing more serious. To tell the plain truth, I had no
idea what the kingbolt was, but I did not choose to appear ignorant
to a stranger. He repaired the kingbolt, but what the watch gained
in one way it lost in another. It would run awhile and then stop
awhile, and then run awhile again, and so on, using its own discretion about the intervals. And every time it went off it kicked back
like a musket. I padded my breast for a few days, but finally took
the watch to another watchmaker. He picked it all to pieces, and
turned the ruin over and over under his glass; and then he said there
appeared to be something the matter with the hair-trigger. He fixed
it, and gave it a fresh start. It did well now, except that always at
ten minutes to ten the hands would shut together like a pair of
scissors, and from that time forth they would travel together. The
oldest man in the world could not make head or tail of the time of
day by such a watch, and so I went again to have the thing repaired.
This person said that the crystal had got bent, and that the main-
spring was not straight. He also remarked that parts of the works
needed half-soling. He made these things all right, and then my
timepiece performed unexceptionably, save that now and then, after
working along quietly for nearly eight hours, everything inside
would let go all of a suddent and begin to buzz like a bee, and the
hands would straightway begin to spin round and round so fast that
their individuality was lost completely, and they simply seemed a
delicate spider's web over the face of the watch. She would reel off
the next twenty-four hours in six or seven minutes, and then stop
with a bang. I went with a heavy heart to one more watchmaker,
and looked on while he took her to pieces. Then I prepared to cross-
question him rigidly, for this thing was getting serious. The watch

had cost two hundred dollars originally, and I seemed to have paid out two or three thousand for repairs. While I waited and looked on I presently recognized in this watchmaker an old acquaintance— a steamboat engineer of other days, and not a good engineer either. He examined all the parts carefully, just as the other watchmakers had done, and then delivered his verdict with the same confidence of manner.

He said—

"She makes too much steam—you want to hang the monkey-wrench on the safety-valve!"

I brained him on the spot, and had him buried at my own expense.

My uncle William (now deceased, alas!) used to say that a good horse was a good horse until it had run away once, and that a good watch was a good watch until the repairers got a chance at it. And he used to wonder what became of all the unsuccessful tinkers, and gunsmiths, and shoemakers, and engineers, and blacksmiths; but nobody could ever tell him.

References

Black, John W., "The Quality of the Spoken Vowel," *Archives of Speech*, 2 (1937), 7-27.

Fairbanks, Grant, *Experimental Phonetics: Selected Articles*. Urbana: University of Illinois Press, 1966.

Laase, Leroy T., "The Effect of Pitch and Intensity on the Quality of Vowels in Speech," *Archives of Speech*, 2 (1937), 41-60.

Lehiste, Ilse, *Readings in Acoustic Phonetics*. Cambridge: M.I.T. Press, 1967.

O'Reilly, Patricia, "The Acoustic Aspects of Vowels Phonated by Children." Unpublished Ph.D. dissertation, The Ohio State University, Columbus, Ohio, 1965.

Peterson, Gordon E., "Parameters of Vowel Quality," *Journal of Hearing Research*, 4 (1961), 10-29.

Russell, G. Oscar, *The Vowel*. Columbus, Ohio: The Ohio State University Press, 1928.

Scripture, E. W., "The Nature of Vowels," *Quarterly Journal of Speech*, 22 (1936), 359-66.

Treviño, S. N., and C. E. Parmenter, "Vowel Positions as Shown by X-Ray," *Quarterly Journal of Speech*, 18 (1932), 351-70.

10

The Consonants of English

The production of one vowel and then another requires only changes in the contour of your vocal tract, that is, a succession of different cavities coupled to the vocal folds. With one configuration you produce one vowel; with another configuration, another vowel. The change from one consonant to another requires more drastic adjustments than these. It may require going from one system of sound production to another, as explained in Chapter 5. Different parts of the oral-nasal structures are brought to bear on the outgoing breath stream with the formation of the several consonants.

A DESCRIPTION OF CONSONANTS

A consonant may be voiced or voiceless, that is, it may or may not be produced with the vocal folds initially modulating the breath stream. A consonant may be oral or nasal, that is, made with the air stream of exhalation through the nose or the mouth. A consonant may be a plosive or a continuant, formed by releasing suddenly a completely blocked airstream or by releasing slowly a partially obstructed pocket of air. Thus, the different consonants occur as a consequence of three factors: (a) where in the vocal tract (b) one degree or another (c) of one or more obstructions occur. The differences between consonants may arise at the vocal folds, lips, or between these sites of possible constriction. These possibilities give a basis for a physiological description of consonants somewhat parallel to that of vowels, and further for a terminology that relates to the way a consonant sounds, for example, plosive, fricative, liquid, glide, and affricative.

The Role of the Consonant

Did it seem to you that the importance of the vowel was slighted in the preceding chapter with respect to its contribution to intelligibility? Is it surprising that you can extract the meaning of a printed sentence even though the vowels are not indicated? Or that an aural sentence is meaningful even though a single vowel quality replaces all of the vowels of the sentence? Why carve a vowel on stone? It can be correctly inferred by anyone familiar with the language! Hence, many ancient inscriptions are without vowels. Consonants are a different matter. Here is the substance of intelligibility. They are indispensable in differentiating the many words that comprise oral language—other than homonyms. Unfortunately for the speaker, there are numerous reasons why some consonants are readily susceptible to being misunderstood, confused. First, their relatively large number (double the number of vowels) adds to the possibilities for confusion. Second, several of the consonants are relatively weak in acoustic power. In the language of Chapter 4, they represent little molecular disturbance. Third, several consonants are relatively similar in their sound waves. And fourth, some consonants are comprised of relatively high frequencies. So it is that the speaker faces the necessity for forming his consonants in as differentiating a manner as possible. This refers to you!

Similarity in Sound

Some consonants are frequently confused with others. This contributes to listeners' misunderstandings of oral language. These mistakes and the substitutions made by children in talking are not random. Phonemes that sound alike are shown in the left-hand column of Table 7. Highly contrasting ones are shown at the right.

Table 7. An enumeration of consonants that appear to listeners to sound most like other initial consonants; also most unlike others (ties indicated by asterisks).

Target Phoneme	Four Most Similar Phonemes				Four Most Dissimilar Phonemes			
ʃ	ʒ	tʃ	dʒ	z	h*	j*	r	l
ʒ	tʃ	dʒ	ʃ	v	k	ʍ	h	l
tʃ	ʒ	ʃ	s	z	k	w	j	l
dʒ	ʒ	tʃ	ʃ	f	g	s	t	k
θ	f	v	s	ð	dʒ	w	l	r
ð	v	f	θ	p	l	j	ʃ	tʃ
f	θ	v	ð	b	tʃ	j	ʃ	g
v	w	m	f	r	t	j	s	k
w	r	v	h	ʍ	k	t	tʃ	s
ʍ	w	h	r	f	ʃ	s	k	g
r	w	ʍ	j	θ	g	ʃ	tʃ	k
l	p	f	ʍ	ð	dʒ	k	g	d
h	z	ʃ	θ	ʒ	t	h	j	l
s	s	ʃ	ʒ	p	t	g	k	l
z	n	h	j	ʍ	k	tʃ	g	ʒ
m	m	ð	v	j	d	ʃ	tʃ	t
n	v	j	θ	g	l	ʒ	w	ʃ
k	k	d	b	v	l	j	h	ʃ
g	d	dʒ	b	v	s	r	j	w
t	j	b	θ	ð	w	dʒ	s	ʃ
d	p	d	v	g	s	l	ʃ	tʃ
b	ʒ	w	r	dʒ	d	t	k	g
j	j	b	v	d	dʒ	w	s	ʒ
p	r	v	z	ʍ	ʃ	tʃ	t	k

Table 6 of Chapter 9 shows another difference among consonants. They occur in strikingly different numbers, varying according to some tabulations by as much as 300 to 1. Thus you are making some of the consonants often and others rarely. How much this difference in the relative occurrence of consonants contributes to appraisals of adequate and inadequate articulation is a matter for conjecture. A poorly articulated sound that recurs often is surely more prominent in an evaluation of speech production than is one that occurs rarely. Table 6 also shows which consonants typically begin and end a word. Only a few /l, n, r/ occur within words in proportions that are comparable to vowels. Obviously, the most frequent syllable in English is consonant-vowel-consonant or consonant-nucleus-consonant.

The Production of Consonants

The speaker who produces clear consonants manages the muscles of his speech mechanism to make firm, rapid closures and sudden releases with the plosive sounds. He achieves partial closures for the fricatives that result in a clearly audible succession of "swishlike" noises. He neither overdoes them nor slights them. He also avoids voicing the sounds that are presumably unvoiced and vice versa. The articulate speaker of English produces a clearly differentiating /l/ and /r/. There is no vestige of a childlike substitution of /w/ with either sound.

The accomplished speaker of English achieves a high degree of fullness of voice, pleasant to the listener, when he gnerates the nasal quality of /m, n, ŋ/ in his normal speech, and he is able to feel a vibration in the region of the cheek bones and the forehead that is unique with the production of these sounds. The speaker adds to the aesthetic pleasure of many of his listeners and especially his speechreaders when he is able to maintain symmetry at the mouth in the production of all consonants.

A conventional classification of consonants is shown in Figure 21.

	Bilabial	Labio-Dental	Lingua-Dental	Lingua-Alveolar	Lingua-Palatal	Lingua-Velar	Glottal
Nasal	m			n			ŋ
Plosive	p b			t d		k g	
Fricative		f v	θ ð	s z	ʃ ʒ		h
Glides	ʍ w			r	j		h
Lateral				l			
Affricates				tʃ dʒ			

Figure 21. A classification of consonants in keeping with their place of articulation (left to right), their dominant characteristic with the listener (top to bottom), and whether a sound is voiced or voiceless (within the cells).

The cells are arranged to show three particulars about consonant production: (a) from left to right the consonants are formed farther back in the mouth; (b) within a cell the left portion is for voiceless sounds, the right for voiced; (c) from top to bottom, in no order that matters, the sounds seem to have a different dominant character.*

---

* Figure 21 could be more complete and precise. For example, the grouping of the fricative sounds is a gross generalization. Some phoneticians divide them on a

Non-Phonemic Consonants

Some consonants are made or not made in English unconsciously or at the discretion of the speaker. In saying /pʌp/ the first /p/ must be exploded or aspirated [pʰ]; the second may or may not be. In some languages the speaker does not have this choice. Another example: in saying /oʊk/ the speaker may begin with a glottal stop /?/, a burst at the vocal folds, or not. But in some languages this stop would signal a unique phoneme.

THE INDIVIDUAL CONSONANTS

/p, b; t, d; k, g/

Six English consonants are plosives. They result from one's stopping the exhalation of breath and then releasing the pent-up air. The stoppage with /p, b/ occurs at the lips; with /t, d/, at the alveolar ridge; with /k, g/ at the palate or roof of the mouth. This divides the group into three subgroups. The three pairs of sounds contain voiceless-voiced counterparts. Thus, another distinction within a pair arises from the fact that one member is voiceless /p, t, k,/ and the other is voiced /b, d, g/. This further subdivides the sounds into six separate and distinct sounds.

Words that contain /b, k, g/ tend to be more intelligible than words that do not contain them; words that contain /p/ tend to be less intelligible. Here is a listing of the sounds that most frequently precede and follow the plosive consonants:

Plosive Phoneme	Preceding Phoneme	Following Phoneme
p:	/ɪ, s, m/	/ɪ, æ, r, l/
b:	/ɑ, r, m, l, e, æ, ɪ,/	/ɪ, r, l/
t:	/ɪ, e, ɑ, f, s, n, r, ɛ, k/	/ɪ, r, e, ʌ, aɪ/
d:	/aɪ, n, l, ,ɪ, ɛ, r/	/ɪ, r, ʌ, ɛ, ɑ/
k:	/e, ŋ, s, ɪ, ɛ, æ/	/r, l, ɪ, w, o/
g:	/r, ɪ, æ, ʌ, ɑ,/	/r, l, ɪ, æ, o/

basis of duration. They might also be divided on a basis of intensity, some being stronger than the others. There is also the possibility of other suspected distinctive features. These are topics for specialized study in phonetics. The present classification suffices for a guide to the analysis and modification of one's habits of articulation. Note, too, the two entries for /h/.

Illustrative Words, /p/

  a. patch peach pierce pitch plus price pump
  b. spade spake spice bump camp damp dump jump lamp limp
  c. lump stoop thump parlor parrot pastor pathway pious
  d. plaid pompous portray precede accept apace compel
  e. comprise depart deprive expire happen impart offspring
  f. rampart repair seaport teaspoon wampum whisper gossip

Illustrative Sentences, /p/*

  a. A lapse of popular support produced a plea for power.
  b. In spite of the low profit, the producers chose to import their supplies for poultry.
  c. The supple spruce saplings produced shapeless sprouts.

Words, /b/

  a. babe blanch bluff branch brave brief cab
  b. club cub rub verb bargain bashful basin beacon beastly
  c. beheld betroth birdie birthplace boiler boldness bracelet
  d. buckwheat burrow abate abbot abyss auburn cable cubic
  e. double fabric gobble hybrid label libel nibble ruby
  f. scribble subject table warbler cherub cobweb

Sentences, /b/

  a. The rubber band around the bundle of bonds surprised the burglar.
  b. Her husband who is a baker bought both the buns and a barrel of butter.
  c. Beneath was a bright bronze tablet.

Words, /t/

  a. taint tank tart throat tint stalk strife
  b. stroke belt bent brought chant chart fort fret late
  c. paint pelt point swept vaunt tunic attic contact
  d. contempt dainty foretell foretold painting parting
  e. plenty portent abbot affect attempt bandit bonnet bullet
  f. carpet create despot effect faucet mallet product receipt

Sentences, /t/

  a. Gaunt and stoicaly they knet at the pulpit.
  b. Dressed in tweeds, all forty awaited the starting trumpet.
  c. It depicted a bandit who was waiting in a penthouse to be sentenced.

---

* Again, as in Chapter 9, *illustrative* will not be used subsequently.

Words, /d/

   a. ditch dive dose dwell abroad birthday
   b. breeder children cider deceit deepen deluge deplace
   c. describe dial discreet disguise duly eastward endless
   d. endure firewood foreward greyhound hidden horrid
   e. hundred idler inward kindred married placid produce
   f. reward sadden shudder steward sundry widely

Sentences, /d/

   a. Suddenly the driver withdrew.
   b. The fiddler waited until midnight to discuss the matter.
   c. Wooden wardrobes are said to be a fad in the old dormitory.

Words, /k/

   a. back bake buck cake calf came cane carve
   b. clang clean clear cliff clown cough crown cure duck
   c. peak peck quaff queen queer rake rook scan scheme
   d. scoff skin tack talk tuck acorn akin chronic collar
   e. context cookie cranny crescent crevice likeness oaken
   f. pucker quarrel scaffold secret thickness

Sentences, /k/

   a. It looks the weakness of the kite is in the back cover.
   b. The baker cut the cake and the queen thanked all of the guests.
   c. Homesick and wakeful, he walked meekly without his falcon.

Words, /g/

   a. bag beg bog brag bug dig drag dug gleam
   b. glove gulf gorge grave grief grieve grudge gruff pig
   c. rug shrug slug stag tug twig vague vogue wig argue
   d. bargain beggar buggy burglar digger druggist foggy
   e. gloomy gravy grievous meager mortgage nutmeg pigment
   f. rigor segment shaggy target tiger vigor

Sentences, /g/

   a. Their daughters gave long gloves and garments to the bride-groom.
   b. Wug and Bug are good linguistic tags.
   c. The handpainted gray jug has zigzag grooves.

/f, v; θ, ð; s, z; ʃ, ʒ/.

Eight English consonants are characterized by the sound of friction, a swishlike sound or the sound of air escaping from a small aperture.

The eight fall into four pairs of sounds. Each pair includes voiceless and voidced counterparts, /f, θ, s, ʃ/ being voiceless and /v, ð, z, ʒ/, voiced. The pairs differ from one another in the distinctive feature of "place [of articulation]." The four partial closures that distinguish the four pairs of sounds physiologically are, respectively,

a. lips lightly against the teeth,
b. tongue against the teeth and nearly blocking the breath stream,
c. tongue approaching the teeth or alveolar ridge leaving a narrow groove centrally on the tongue, and
d. tongue and roof of the front of the mouth leaving a broad aperture between them.

Both /f, θ/ are faint sounds and adversely affect the intelligibility of words that contain them, while /s, ʃ/ apparently enhance intelligibility if *the transmission system is good*. This would include the listener's ears.*

Table 4 shows that the voiceless members of the four pairs of fricative sounds appear more frequently than the voiced members. The sounds also vary in frequency of occurrence from the ever-so-frequent initial /s/ to the very rare /ʒ/.

All of the fricative sounds are troublemakers for speakers who have not learned English in their youth. All require delicate articulatory movements, especially the /s/. Early mismanagement with it sometimes persists as a lisp. The sound /s/ is sensitive to dental irregularities and changes. It is produced with many oral configurations and physiological compensations as baby teeth are replaced by permanent ones. Subsequently, an irregular spacing of teeth or a nicked one may give /s/ yet another acoustic symbolization that ranges from a semiwhistle to a gust of breath from the side of the mouth. Speakers often disagree violently about how /s/ is produced. One supposes that everyone tilts the tip of his tongue upward, and the other that the world follows his practice of tilting the tongue downward! There is considerable leeway in the formation of the fricative sounds of English. Even so, the student who has in mind a lifetime of acting, singing, broadcasting, teaching, public address, or simply excellence in speaking should adopt patterns of acceptable and normal production and differentiation among the fricative sounds.

Sounds that most frequently precede and follow the fricative consonants are:

---

* Here and subsequently please keep in mind that the comparisons of intelligibility were made between the intelligibility scores of words that included a particular sound and words that did not contain it. The outcome should not be interpreted as meaning that a word would be more intelligible if it contained fewer sounds. *Faith* is a relatively unintelligible word, yet it would be less intelligible if it contained only two of the three sounds of which it is comprised.

Fricative Phoneme	Preceding Phoneme	Following Phoneme
f:	/ɪ, æ, ʌ, aɪ, l/	/r, l, t, ɪ, ɔ, aɪ/
v:	/ɪ, aɪ, l, e/	/ɪ, ɔ, æ, ɛ/
θ:	/u, n, l, r, æ, ɔ/	/ɪ, ɔ, ə/
ð:	/ɪ, æ, ʌ, o, r,/	/r, ɛ, ɪ/
s:	/æ, ʌ, i, ɪ, ɛ, k, n/	/t, k, ɪ/
z:	/o, ʌ, e, ɪ, i, u/	/i, ɪ/
ʃ:	/æ, ɪ, ʌ, i, e, ɔ/	/æ, r, ɑ/
ʒ:	/ɪ, ɛ/	/j/

Words, /f/

a. beef bluff buff cliff cuff fault flesh fog
b. fold forge frame gruff half hoof knife leaf loaf
c. lymph scoff sniff snuff affirm artful bashful buffet
d. coffee coffer conform defer differ doleful faithful
e. fallow faulty fearful fervor field fireman follow
f. footman forfeit fortune heifer hopeful peaceful preface

Sentences, /f/

a. From forty-five to fifty coffee colored fox were found in that field.
b. I find that the filter was manufactured in Finland.
c. There were enough fresh fish available to fill the coffer.

Words, /v/.

a. brave crave strive veer verge vice vouch
b. active arrive beaver behave bereave captive convert
c. convex covet cravat devote devour diver divert divide
d. event evil invade invite massive native oval receive
e. reserve revert revive rivet severe valley vanquish
f. vary vesper visit vivid voyage

Sentences, /v/

a. Four left-handed halfbacks were the avowed receivers.
b. Twelve victors wrought vast havoc.
c. That virtue was engraven in every verse.

Words, /θ/.

a. breath broth cloth depth fifth growth health
b. hearth length mirth month north sixth stealth thigh
c. thrall thrive thump troth truth width birthplace

d. birthright deathbed filthy lengthen methinks panther
e. plaything thankful thankless thickness thirteenth
f. thirty thistle thoughtful thousand wrathful zenith

Sentences, /θ/.

a. I though that one third of the throng was thirsty.
b. *Thing* and *bethink* and *thought* and *methought* are not used in the northeast.
c. Earthenware brings wealth to one-ninth or one-tenth of them.

Words, /ð/

a. that then these they those thus although
b. bother brother farther father fathom gather heathen
c. loathsome northern rather rhythm smother themselves
d. thereto therewith therein those thyself within

Sentences, /ð/

a. *They* and *those* are hard for them to bother with.
b. *Then, that,* and *there* trouble all of them.
c. Both the brother and father followed paths that neither thought worthy.

Words, /s/

a. chance scoff skim slat sledge slim snuff sold
b. spouse spray staff stage stem stove swam swerve swoon
c. wince cellar climax crescent dulness gorgeous harvest
d. homesick likeness meekness peaceful precept promise
e. sergeant sever sinful slimy sluggish solar stamen
f. subject suffer weakness

Sentences, /s/

a. Unless those forces pass that fence we can expect peace.
b. Since Sam sharpened his pencil he has sketched six similar subjects.
c. He aspires to see South America soon, perhaps this spring.

Words, /z/

a. bronze wolves applause blazen bosom brazen
b. breeches clumsy crimson dazzle disease earrings
c. espouse exalt expose frozen herdsman husband infuse
d. measles nasal nuzzle plasma poison presence puzzle
e. repose resent reserve resist series surmise thousand
f. topaz townsman weasel zealous zephyr

Sentences, /z/

   a. This is his, this is hers, and these are theirs.
   b. As you examine those eggs look for signs of age.
   c. Do you propose to dispose of a thousand large prisms in one sale?

Words, /ʃ/

   a. sheep sheet shelf shield shift shop shrub shrug
   b. splash ashore assure auction bashful cautious chemise
   c. famish finish function fraction furnish junction
   d. motion nation passion patience patient perish potion
   e. punish racial reddish relish rubbish section shabby
   f. shaggy shatter shiver shorten slavish sluggish social vanish

Sentences, /ʃ/

   a. What a shame that Chicago is not on an ocean.
   b. There is surely a schwa in *surety* as typically spoken in Cheyenne.
   c. Shuffle-board is fashionable on oceanic passenger ships.

Words, /ʒ/

   a. rouge Asia azure fusion garage measure
   b. mirage pleasure prestige treasure vision confusion
   c. enclosure illusion persuasion visual

Sentences, /ʒ/

   a. *Illusion* and *allusion* cause confusion.
   b. Any prestige that arises from leisure is also subject to derision.
   c. To measure the garage will require collusion.

/tʃ, dʒ/

Affricates are called by some lexicographers *consonantal* diphthongs. There are two in English. One is the voiceless counterpart of the other, /tʃ/ and /dʒ/. These symbols are drawn from the two preceding groupings of sounds, the plosives and the fricatives. In saying an affricative the speaker starts with the physiological movements of the first member /t/ or /d/ and glides into the formation of the fricative /ʃ/ or /ʒ/.

Both affricates apparently enhance the intelligibility of words. Frequent phonetic environments follow:

Affricative Phoneme	Preceding Phoneme	Following Phoneme
/tʃ/:	/n, i, ɪ, r/	/ɝ, æ, ɑ, ɪ, ɛ/
/dʒ/:	/ɪ, ɛ, r, n/	/ɝ, ɪ, ɛ, ɑ/

Words, /tʃ/

a. bench branch chaff charge chase choke
b. clutch crouch crutch hunch launch munch parch pinch
c. preach punch quench scorch scratch screech speech
d. staunch stench switch torch trench wrench armchair
e. attach beseech bewitch chapel channel chatter cherish
f. chieftain childhood fortune impeach purchase riches texture

Sentences, /tʃ/

a. Righteous children are at church by their own choice.
b. The chances that a bachelor will marry naturally change.
c. Watch the cellist with the cherry-colored dress.

Words, /dʒ/

a. bridge bulge charge forge gem grange hinge
b. huge jug large lounge range scourge sledge stage tinge
c. adjoin allege angel avenge baggage besiege coinage
d. congeal courage damage drainage enrage gorgeous
e. grandeur hedgehog jingle jostle knowledge largely
f. lodging mortgage package ravage subject tragic vigil

Sentences, /dʒ/

a. George exaggerated the gentleness or gradualness of that ridge.
b. John spent June and July with Jim in Virginia.
c. Generally the agenda has few entries that concern geodesy, geology, geometry, geography, or jurisprudence.

/l, r/

The lateral and glide consonants /l/ and /r/ have some of the properties of vowels. For example, they may be sustained and sung. These two consonants are mastered by a speaker at a later age than the plosive consonants. There is ample opportunity for early substitutions to become habits of long standing and to persist into adult years.

As with some of the fricatives, the /l, r/ phonemes occur with many different acoustic patterns or colorings. Although neither sound is peculiar to the English language, different language cultures have developed the sounds differently, for example, as trilled sounds. The pronunciations of these two sounds in America are somewhat special to this country. One scholar reports more than 100 unique varieties of the /r/. Indicative of the closeness of the sounds to each other, some languages have only one of them. They are also more similar in English than is generally appreciated. For example, as distortion or noise is introduced into a listening channel, the two sounds tend to become confused, one for the other.

Possibly a difficulty in producing the /l/ and /r/ is that neither provides the opportunity for much kinesthetic help in the placing of the tongue. It is not brought close to any oral structure at the moment of articulation. Rather it is suspended in the mouth cavity, somewhat as in vowel production. However, in the saying of different vowels, there is a progression from one quality or one phoneme to another as the speaker changes his cavities. There is no similar progression in the production of /r/ and /l/.

The speaker who has difficulty making the /l/ or /r/ should practice saying the sounds rapidly, in a phonetic context, probably in conjunction with plosive consonants and a closed vowel as /trɪp/, /plɪd/. When he is successful in making /r, l/, he may drop the initial or final consonant, attempting to maintain the /l/ or /r/. As Table 6 indicates, both /l/ and /r/ occur frequently.

The /l/ is apparently detrimental to intelligibility except when it occurs as a syllabic consonant in multisyllabic words. The sound /r/ occurs in combination with all vowels. It frequently precedes /m, d, n, t/ and follows /p, b, t, k, g, f, v, θ, d/. The sound /l/ parallels this usage with the additional combination /sl/.

Words, /l/

   a. bleach blight bluff claim clang clash claw
   b. clear clerk cling cloak cloth cloud clown club filth
   c. fling flute glare glide health lance life plight slang
   d. slope alight allure although artful belie bevel cellar
   e. climax delay delta elude florist glory ladder liquor
   f. naval novel plaything stable teller weasel wholesome

Sentences, /l/

   a. Let's leave the lively little pet in the kennel.
   b. All of the faults here pertain to barks and whelps.
   c. That looking glass is a little brittle.

Words, /r/

   a. barn bring broth crawl cruel frail grape
   b. great growth hearth prowl trill truth screw arbor
   c. barrel bearer darling defraud fairly harness hireling
   d. horror infringe northeast oral parley prelate prior
   e. province reader recur renew riddle rival therewith
   f. thorny wafer wearer whirl wrapper wrestle

Sentences, /r/

  a. The bell on the ferry rang rhythmically for hours.
  b. Quoth the raven, "nevermore."
  c. Recall the crier who roamed about this shire.

/m, n, ŋ/

There are three different nasal sounds in the word *morning.* They include all of the nasal consonants of English. All are voiced. They are spoken with the breath stream directed through the nose. The effect is a nasal timbre. With a normal speech mechanism, this is easily accomplished. Difficulties arise in saying vowel sounds that precede and follow a nasal consonant. There is a strong tendency to make them nasal, too. This nasal quality is generally a poor vocal trait.

The most consistent error among the nasal sounds themselves is the substitution of /n/ for /ŋ/. This is effectively, if colloquially, described as "dropping the g's," and occurs most frequently in the *ing* form of verbs. Henceforth, you may speak more exactly of substituting one consonant for another /ŋ > n/, not "dropping the g's." Another fault, or at least an unusual effect, occurs when /ŋ/ is made to terminate in the explosive manner of /g/. This is a regionalism, not widely evident, and a feature of some foreign dialects. A third odd effect occurs when /n/ is spoken before /v, f/. The articulation occlusion should be made by the tongue behind the alveolar ridge. Usually, however, it is made in the manner of a labio-dental consonant. This effect is so noticeable in Italian and Spanish that the resulting distorted /n/ is given a special phonetic notation.

The intelligibility of a word is enhanced by the presence of /n/. The most probable phonetic environments of the sounds are:

Nasal Phoneme	Preceding Phoneme	Following Phoneme
m:	/ɪ, r, æ, ʌ/	/ɪ, p, æ, ɑ/
n:	/ɪ, ɛ, æ, ɑ, ʌ, r, e/	/tʃ, ɪ, t, d/
ŋ:	/ɪ, æ, ʌ/	/k, θ/

Words, /m/

  a. bloom brim clam crime dream flame frame
  b. groom helm mince muff munch plume prime realm scheme
  c. slam steam swim warm affirm amain autumn climate
  d. fireman footman himself image impress madman meekness
  e. meter mutter remnant segment slimy topmost woodman

Sentences, /m/

  a. My hammer and comb make different musical melodies.
  b. Many mice make sounds that are large in number and volume.
  c. Some men meet on Monday mornings.

Words, /n/

  a. chance hinge launch mince munch nerve pinch
  b. range slain sniff swoon tinge twin whence wrench
  c. adjoin amain anon casement congeal context dolphin
  d. dulness fireman flannel footman likeness lion luncheon
  e. madman margin meekness nephew nutmeg oven planet
  f. rainfall signet walnut witness

Sentences, /n/

  a. When ten lambs are under that canopy one cannot scan the entire pen.
  b. Knights never planned to remain at inns.
  c. Pine knots contain rosin for turpentine.

Words, /ŋ/

  a. bring cling flung sling sprang sting swing
  b. throng awning banking dealing donkeys during finger
  c. hearing hireling jangle kingly language lining
  d. lodging lying meaning meeting methinks ringing
  e. shelling singer sprinkle tangle thankless thinking
  f. tidings

Sentences, /ŋ/

  a. *Angle* and *bring* have one thing in common, a phoneme.
  b. The birds were singing on Thanksgiving Day.
  c. The strength of a single footing depends on the anchor.

/w, ʍ, j, h/

The glides and fricative-glides have limited consonantal character and are sometimes described as merely ways of approaching a subsequent vowel. These four sounds do not occur terminally in a syllable, but for that matter neither does /ŋ/ of the nasal consonants occur initially. These sounds are phonemic, for example, *what* vs. *watt* vs. *hot* vs. *yacht*.

Physiologically the consonantal glides and fricative glides resemble minor coughs. There is a sudden blast of air through an opening that is a bit too small to accommodate the gust without audible friction. The resulting swish is hardly sufficient, however, for all of the sounds to be convincingly classified as fricatives along with /ʃ/ and /f/. A middle-of-the-road adjective *aspirate* is commonly used to describe /h/ and the symbol *h* is written as a superscript to denote aspiration. As explained earlier, the difference between /tɑp/ and /tɑpʰ/ is that the final consonant is aspirated or exploded in the second instance. In Figure 21 /h/ is listed both as a glide and as a fricative.

The principal difficulty encountered in the pronunciation of glidelike sounds by native speakers of English is the substitution of /w/ for /ʍ/. It is somewhat conventional in colloquial speech to hear the sounds said alike, that is *why* = *y* and *where* = *wear*. The phonemic difference is left for the listener to supply on the basic of context. Persons who learn English as a second language have much trouble with the glides.

Words that contain /w/ tend to be more intelligible than ones that do not. The effect of /h/, however, seems to be to reduce intelligibility. The frequent phonetic contexts of these sounds are:

Glidelike Phonemes	Preceding Phonemes	Following Phonemes
/w/:	/k, s/	/ɪ, ɔ, ɛ, e/
/ʍ/:	(another syllable)	/aɪ, ɛ, ɪ, ɑ/
/j/:	/d, k, f/	/ɝ, i, ɑ, u/
/h/:	(another syllable)	/æ, ɛ, ɪ, ʌ, ɑ/

Words, /w/

a. quake queen quote swain swam swerve swing
b. swore sworn twain twig twitch warm width wig wisp
c. world worst await bewitch dweller equal goodwill
d. liquid outweigh query squander sweeten therewith
e. warbler warrant weakness weasel winner wither
f. workman woven

Sentences, /w/

a. The queen led the choir in a quick exquisite waltz.
b. We wished you were with us once we went up the tower.
c. Winston's memoirs awaken one's memories of his persuasiveness.

Words, /ʍ/

a. what wheat which while whilst whirl whisk
b. white why awhile buckwheat nowhere somewhat whereat
c. wherein whirlwind whisker whiskey whisper anywhere

Sentences, /ʍ/

  a. Which wheel is whistling?
  b. Swallow the whole-wheat biscuit when you want it.
  c. *Why, where, who,* and *when* were once covered by a rule.

Words, /j/

  a. cute duke feud yea yearn yeast yes you
  b. young confuse costume cubic deluge demure duly
  c. farmyard junior million pinion senior vineyard

Sentences, /j/

  a. Yet the brickyard had a million cubic yards of clay.
  b. Yes, we yearn to be seniors instead of juniors.
  c. A young duke yelled to you from the vineyard.

Words, /h/

  a. halt hearth helm hence hid hip hoof hot
  b. house hug huge behave behest behoove hanger happy
  c. hardness harmless harness harvest hasty hatred heather
  d. hemlock herald herdsman herring himself hireling
  e. hollow housetop humble hustle hygiene inhale inherit
  f. inhibit

Sentences, /h/

  a. That heifer is held by two hooves.
  b. Who is he, so humble and well behaved?
  c. A huge hedgehog, half grown, huddled helplessly.

Consonantal Affinities: Clusters. Consonants frequently occur in combinations either at the outset or the end of the syllable. These combinations are sometimes called *blends.* The word suggests that the adjacent consonants have a mutual effect on each other, altering the acoustic properties of each. The reasonableness of this approach appears especially true in the light of the experiences of individuals who have difficulty producing a particular consonant. Almost invariably a singular combination of sounds can be found in which the person has no difficulty in making the target phoneme.

The phonetic symbolization of most of the consonant clusters that occur initially in English monosyllables follows:

/bl/	/br/	/dr/	/dw/	/fl/	/fr/
/gl/	/gr/	/gw/	/kl/	/kr/	/kw/
/pl/	/pr/	/sk/	/skr/	/skw/	/sl/
/sm/	/sn/	/sp/	/spl/	/spr/	/st/
/str/	/sw/	/ʃr/	/tr/	/tw/	/θr/

Very frequent phonetic endings of English monosyllables follow. Altogether there are about 160 of these:

/bd/	/bz/	/dz/	/dʒd/	/fs/	/ft/
/gd/	/gz/	/ks/	/kt/	/ld/	/lfθ/
/lʃ/	/lʃt/	/lt/	/lz/	/md/	/mfs/
/mp/	/mps/	/mpst/	/mpt/	/mz/	/nd/
/nt/	/nts/	/nz/	/nzd/	/ŋk/	/ŋks/
/ŋz/	/ps/	/pt/	/pθs/	/rd/	/rgz/
/rmθ/	/rst/	/rθt/	/rz/	/rʒ/	/st/
/sts/	/ʃt/	/ts/	/tst/	/tθ/	
/tθs/	/vd/	/vz/	/zd/	/ʒd/	

APPLICATION

Your desire is to make your spoken consonants conform to your conceptualization of the target consonants. This implies that there will be sharp differentiation from consonant to consonant. That comes with giving the appropriate distinctive features to each one. Your study from this chapter can be turned to immediate intelligibility if used in conjunction with your recently acquired information about voice. You are also aware of which sounds are likely to be confused. This permits you to build some contrasts for your own practice.

The information about the most frequent phonemic environments of sounds can lead to lists of words or nonsense syllables for practice. These can be more realistic if coupled with the probabilities that a sound will occur initially, medially, or finally, found in Table 6.

SUMMARY

Consonants include a wide range of sounds that contribute most of the characteristic of intelligibility to speech. They are formed by placing partial obstructions in the path of the breath stream or by making complete obstructions and then releasing the pent-up air. The place and the degree of the obstruction are of first importance in determining the singular sound of a consonant. It is also important that the vocal folds are used in forming some consonants and not others. Consonants occur with widely differing frequencies. They also occur both singly in a syllable, together with a vowel, and in clusters. There are many perceived substitutions of consonants. Many of these originate with distorted productions on the part of the speaker. However, the language and the listener contribute to the mistakes, for many consonants are similar in sound. Others, fortunately, are highly contrasting.

Unique productions of consonants are one characteristic of pronunciation dialects. Within the United States and among persons to whom English is vernacular there are regional variations of /r and ŋ/, among others. There are also many substitutions of one consonant for another among persons who have spoken another language before English.

Exercises

1 a. Construct sentences of the types of the ones illustrated in this chapter loaded with consonants of particular types: plosives, nasals, glides, fricatives, laterals, and affricatives.

b. Construct sentences that are loaded with consonants that are articulated in the front of the mouth, central portion of the mouth, and in the back of the mouth.

2. You know the sounds that most frequently precede and follow each phoneme. Prepare an enumeration of examples of these combinations. Words for /p/ following /i, s, m/ might be *tip, wasp, bump*.

3. Tally the one-syllable words of two pages of Appendix A, classifying the words according to the number and position of the consonant sounds in the words. Thus, *of* would be classified as vc (vowel-consonant) and *and* as vcc (vowel-consonant-consonant). You will probably find most of the following forms:

		Examples	
v	*a*	cvcc	cccvc
cv	*by*	ccvc	ccvccc
vc	*of*	vccc	cccvcc
cvc	*cup*	cccv	cvcccc
vcc	*and*	ccvcc	cccvccc
ccv	*slow*	cvccc	ccvcccc

The most complex English monosyllable is *strengths*. Where does it fit in the categories of this exercise?

4. You have tried with some success to read a passage substituting a single vowel for all of the vowels of the passage and have found, surprisingly, that your reading is intelligible. Now, try to maintain the vowels of a passage but substitute a single consonant for all consonants in the passage. The result will be gibberish. Side results, however, will include (a) worthwhile vocal

exercise and (b) an awareness of the extent to which your oral reading is a fixed habit, hard to disrupt. This exercise is especially enlightening to parents of children who are trying to be taught to improve their speech.

5. Study the following tongue twisters. Determine whether the feature of the items lies in the vowels or in the consonants.

    a. Peter Piper picked a peck of pickled peppers
       A peck of pickled peppers Peter Piper picked
       If Peter Piper picked a peck of pickled peppers
       How many pickled peppers did Peter Piper pick?

    b. Theopholus Thistle the successful thistle sifter
       In sifting a sieveful of unsifted thistles
       Thrust three thousand thistles
       Through the thick of his thumb.

    c. Betty Botta bought some butter
       "But," said she, "This butter's bitter.
       If I put it in my batter
       It will make my batter bitter
       But a bit o' better butter
       Will make my batter better."
       So she bought a bit o' butter
       Better than the bitter butter,
       Made her bitter batter better.
       So 'twas better Betty Botta
       Bought a bit o' better butter.

    d. Reread Exercise 7, Chapter 6.

6. The last section of the chapter enumerated a list of clusters of consonants that occur initially and terminally in English monosyllables. Prepare five sentences that are loaded with clusters.

7. Say the sounds (not words) that appropriately conclude the following sentences. Classify each as fricative or plosive, and voiced or voiceless. Make the sound. Do not say a word.

    a. The wind in the trees gives (sound) .
    b. Out of oil, the motor sounds (sound) .
    c. Men walking in a swamp sound _____ _____ _____.
    d. Tell me when you hear this combination lock _____.
    e. After the mouse ran up the clock, the clock _____.
    f. Poor gasoline causes some motors to go _____ _____ _____.
    g. As Tom swung his bat, the crowd _____.
    h. The ball hit the glove with a _____.
    i. The fan in the room suddenly _____.
    j. The boy pulled the trigger and the toy gun went _____.
    k. The pen on the paper sounded _____.
    l. The car hit the wall _____.

m. The door opened with _____.
n. The girl lit the firecracker and it went _____.
o. The mouse, seeing the cat, _____.
p. The chalk _____ across the board.
q. The alarm clock went off at 6:00 _____.
r. The hammer hit the nail _____.
s. The sound of one eating celery is _____.
t. When soup is sipped the sound is _____.
u. He was so old his teeth went _____.
v. The sound of brushing teeth is _____.
w. The drill on the tooth went _____.
x. The suction cup was pulled off the window _____.
y. The boy running in his track-shoes across the cinders _____.
z. The ball hit the pane of glass _____.

8. Read the following passage, paying particular attention to the plosive sounds.

On His Blindness

When I consider how my light is spent
Ere half my days in this dark world and wide,
And that one talent, which is death to hide,
Lodged with me useless, though my soul more bent
To serve therewith my Maker, and present
My true account, lest he, returning, chide!
"Doth God exact day-labor, light denied?"
I fondly ask. But Patience, to prevent
That murmur, soon replies: "God doth not need
Either man's work, or his own gifts. Who best
Bear his mild yoke, they serve him best. His state
Is kingly; thousands at his bidding speed,
And post o'er land and ocean without rest;
They also serve who only stand and wait."

John Milton

9. The following laws have been prepared by students with particular relevance to their own speech. Extend this list, with five laws, thinking particularly of the formation of phonemes.

 a. One sound follows another.
 b. It doesn't take much strength to raise a vowel.
 c. The tongue has its ups and downs.
 d. There is more to speaking than meets the ear.
 e. There is more to speaking than opening the mouth.
 f. Articulation is a speaking matter.
 g. Sounds are just a lot of moving air.
 h. The uvula is the gatekeeper to nasality.
 i. You can teach old muscles new tricks.
 j. Now is the time for all good articulators to come to the aid of the speaker.

10. Tally the errors that you have made in intelligibility exercises. Do these tend to fall in a single category with respect to consonants? Final consonants? Voiceless consonants? Any other category of this chapter?

11 a. The following words illustrate some consonant clusters that occur at the outset of one-syllable words. Insofar as possible, match them to the appropriate phonetic transcription of the clusters in the chapter.

(1)	(2)	(3)	(4)
a. black	brown	drop	Dwight
b. fly	front	glide	grade
c. Guam	cloud	crew	quit
d. plane	prime	sphere	sky
e. screw	square	slow	smoke
f. snow	speed	splash	spray
g. star	string	swim	schmoo
h. schnapps	shrill	schwa	sclaff
i. twine	three	thwart	track

b. The following words illustrate terminal consonant clusters of one-syllable words. Insofar as possible, match them to the phonemic transcriptions of clusters of these types in the chapter. Transcribe the remaining clusters.

(1)	(2)	(3)	(4)
a. cubed	midst	beds	lifts
b. begged	oaks	sixth	facts
c. belched	self	twelfth	bulged
d. sulked	realms	helped	welsh
e. faults	healths	wolves	dreamed
f. jump	tempts	pinched	tubes
g. width	hoofs	fifth	digs
h. fixed	sixths	bulb	old
i. gulfs	twelfths	milk	elm
j. pulp	false	welshed	waltzed
k. twelve	eels	lymph	stamps
l. aims	and	touched	breadths
m. gift	fifths	pledged	texts
n. act	gulch	holds	golfed
o. bilge	silks	filmed	alps
p. pulsed	built	wealth	solved
q. nymphs	prompt	inch	changed
r. ounce	points	pins	drink
s. inked	kings	apt	depths
t. barbs	card	scarfs	morgues
u. arc	Carl	arm	storms
v. barns	sharped	harsh	arts
w. wharves	ask	wasp	East
x. eats	faiths		

12 a. From Table 7 enumerate 12 pairs of words that you would expect to be highly confusable.

b. From the same table account for five sound substitutions that you have heard children use.

c. From the same table account in part for the architect's error in Exercise 6, Chapter 8.

References

Black, John W., "The Information of Sounds and Phonetic Digrams of One- and Two-Syllable Words," *Journal of Speech and Hearing Disorders,* 19 (1954), 397-410.

Dewey, Godfrey, *Relative Frequency of English Speech Sounds,* rev. ed. Cambridge, Mass.: Harvard University Press, 1950.

Fairbanks, Grant, *Voice and Articulation Drillbook,* 2d ed. New York: Harper & Row, Publishers, 1960.

French, N. R., C. W. Carter, and W. Koenig, "The Words and Sounds of Telephone Conversation," *Bell System Technical Journal,* 9 (1930), 290-324.

Gemelli, A. and John W. Black, "Phonetics from the Viewpoint of Psychology," *Manual of Phonetics,* L. Kaiser, ed. Amsterdam: North-Holland Publishing Company, 1957.

Jakobson, Roman, C. Gunnar M. Fant, and Morris Halle, *Preliminaries to Speech Analysis, the Distinctive Features and Their Correlates.* Cambridge: M.I.T. Press, 1967.

Moser, Henry, *One-Syllable Words.* Columbus: Charles E. Merrill Publishing Co., 1969.

Thorndike, E. L. and Irving Lorge, *The Teacher's Word Book of 30,000 Words.* New York: Bureau of Publications, Teachers College, Columbia University, 1944.

11

Pronunciation

Chapters 9 and 10 have treated pronunciation, for this topic includes the saying of successive phonemes. Well-formed individual sounds are targets. Yet pronunciation is more than stringing together the individual vowels and consonants of the word. Spoken as a group in a word, they contribute to a semantic aspect. Something beyond vowels and consonants comes into view. What it is, is hardly clear. Some might stress the importance of the morpheme; others, the *word*. The former is a sound or portion of a word that distinguishes it from other words, for example, *man vs. men, bush vs. bushes,* and *like vs. likely.* Surely the syllable is also important. It has a recognizable entity. It is stressed or unstressed, slurred or made clearly, and as a consequence of the way the speaker says successive syllables his pronunciation is or is not clear and acceptable. Theory aside, you should attend to the syllable.

CORRECT PRONUNCIATION

The most frequent query regarding pronunciation seems to be, "Which is the correct way to say the word?" This calls for either a short positive answer or a long explanation that treats among other topics *judgment, alternatives, esthetics, history of language,* and *the development of pronouncing dictionaries.* The former is the easier, the latter the more appropriate. But when the second course is followed, the concluding question is still likely to be, "Yes, I know there are academic quibbles, but *which pronunciation is right?"*

Correct pronunciation is as elusive as the end of the rainbow. Man thought up the concept, and relatively recently! It assumes absolute values in a situation that is aptly described only in relative values. The important criteria for pronunciation are that it convey the intended word and that it be inconspicuous. If the manner in which a word is said distracts listeners, even momentarily, then something defeats the intent of interpersonal communication. This distraction might occur with a faulty articulation, regional dialect, an unusual stress of a syllable, or with a meticulous rendition of the new-found pronunciation.

Of course, you are asking questions about pronunciation and learning about pronunciation continually. The study of foreign languages adds to your perspective about pronunciation. Your foreign language teacher tolerates some deviations from the clearly stated rules of pronunciation of the language and not others. The implication is that some of the rules are more important than others. You ask, "Do his principles also apply to American English?" Your courses in philosophy point to systematic evaluations. You ask, "Do these apply to pronunciation?" Your literature courses are taught by persons who have lived studiously with words for a long time and the selections that are in your anthologies are chosen as excellent examples of the use of words. Your college and university administrators reflect effectiveness, wrought principally by vocal means. Your teachers of art are keenly sensitive to the pleasing and the appropriate, and this sensitivity carries over to their language. These people by the hundreds are heard by you and other asture scholars of oral language. Experts extract from the whole range of pronunciations the one or two that are recorded in a contemporary dictionary. From these entries in dictionaries, from your observations, and from your ever-developing scale of values, you should find the pronunciation that satisfies your notion of *correctness.*

Getting Started With Pronunciation

You are well along in learning your language. Not much remains beyond expanding your vocabulary and developing further your precision in statements. You have habits of pronouncing the language and they are difficult to alter. Fortunately, most of the habits are good ones. You are always eager to check them and a good place to start is not with the new erudite word and not with the multisyllabic one that has several well-recognized pronunciations. Simply as an example, begin with the monosyllable *hope* (you are saying an aspirate plus a vowel or diphthong, plus a plosive which is either aspirated or not). Add a syllable, *hopeful* (there are new sounds and a stressed and unstressed syllable). Add more, *hopefully* (you have a new sound and two unstressed syllables). Put the three syllables in short kernel sentences. Transform the sentences into a query, negative, passive, and other forms. Ideally, you are working with a partner and both of you have dictionaries. Have any questions arisen yet? Now try *cow* (this includes a troublesome diphthong). Add *pen* (now you have a new sound and primary and secondary stress). Make the word plural (you have a farmyard in mind). Now look up the pronunciation of the same word as the name of a town of South Carolina, the site of a battle of the Revolutionary War.

If you feel more comfortable with erudite words—and there are many of them in the exercises of this chapter—beware that the surprises that you find do not lead you to make a mockery of the exercise. This outcome led a columnist to protest the straightjacket that seemed to be enveloping him.

The Dictionary Says—

The Dictionary (ancient terror!)
Tells me that I have been in error
For many years, and very dumbly
Have mispronounced the small word "comely."

The dictionary, judge and jury,
Has also made me blush like fury
By putting in my stubborn skull some
Idea of how I've murdered "fulsome."

O bitter bit of information
Starting a painful cerebration
Of grievous fault without a tiny cure—
The way I have mishandled "sinecure!"

But now the worst is yet to follow;
This beats those small surprises hollow—
Who would have thought the word "remediless"
An almost perfect rhyme of "Daedalus?"

This is no place for jest or laughter;
I'm now announcing that hereafter
The Dictionary, fiend malign,
May go its way, and I'll go mine.

Ted Robinson

Formal Pronunciation.   An oral-aural acoustic recording has a measurable dimension, time. A scheduled radio program has a fixed time. The material to be spoken may have an optimum time. But there is no way of indexing a particular word as falling in a 0.36- or a 0.44-second category. The duration of the word varies with the occasion on which it is said. Spoken in a religious service or eulogy, a word might, and probably would, take up more time than when spoken in casual conversation or at a card table. The individual phonemes, the continuant consonants, and the vowel are longer and have greater quantity on the formal occasion. As each is given more time it also assumes a fuller quality. This formal pronunciation of the word becomes the one that is usually recorded in dictionaries. It befits the stage and often the classroom; it is not the pronunciation of relaxation.

Nonsignificant Variety in Phonetics.   You know a phonetic alphabet and the typical properties of each sound. Also, you know that a sound varies from one pronunciation to another and because of its interaction with adjacent sounds it is spoken somewhat differently in each phonetic environment. For example, /k/ in *keep* is more frontal than the same sound in *cup*. The indifference of aspiration of terminal plosives, of use of the glottal stop, of dark and light /l/—matters of no linguistic significance—contribute to your pronunciation and set it apart from another person's. A similar example follows. On the average the instantaneous intensity of initial consonants exceeds that of final ones; but because the terminal consonants tend to be longer than initial ones, the integrated energy of the final consonants exceeds that of the initial ones. Your mode of pronouncing, however, may be unique in these ratios or in a dozen similar nonphonemic ones.

The Pronunciation of Function Words.   The connectives, prepositions, and articles are typically given only an "identifying pronunciation." This may be a schwa-like syllable or in the instances of *and, in,* and *on,* it may be a syllabic /ṇ/. This practice is sanctioned, comes into teaching of pronunciation to school children, and distinguishes good oral readers and poor ones. Poor readers tend to give a word-by-word rendition of a selection with full-dress or formal pronunciation of the function words. Earlier this slighting of some words was related to the listener's ease in identifying very familiar words and to the contribution of context to speech perception. A reciprocal relationship is easy to envisage in which probabilities of occurrence and the precision of articulation give and take from each other.

Table 2, Chapter 8, enumerated a list of highly frequent English words. Table 8 indicates that there is marked agreement about what the most common English words are, irrespective of the source of the material.

Both the speaker and listener are intuitively well informed about these statistics and expect to process common words correctly with weak pronunciation. Even the frequently used words that are not function words are treated in the manner of function words. The elementary school teacher may represent the other side of this coin *in the clasroom*. Her charges have not yet learned these statistics. She typically pronounces distinctly and does so because she has learned that she must.

Table 8. Six lists of 20 most common English words in speaking and writing.

Written Vocabulary		Spoken Vocabulary			
Dewey	Fraprie	Black-Ausherman	Fossum	Voelker	French, Carter, and Koenig
the	the	the	the	the	I
of	of	and	of	and	you
and	and	of	and	of	the
to	to	to	to	a	a
a	a	a	a	to	on
in	in	in	in	in	to
that	that	that	is	it	that
it	is	is	that	is	it
is	I	it	could	that	is
I	it	they	it	have	and
for	for	you	you	this	get
be	as	this	this	be	will
was	with	we	for	work*	of
as	was	have	have	I	in
you	his	are	are	are	he
with	he	was	be	they	we
he	be	be	they	do	they
on	not	he	he	for	see
have	by	for	we	he	have
by	but	on	as	many*	for

* The topic "Many Hands Make Light Work" affected the frequency of *many* and *work*.

PRONUNCIATION DIALECTS

The target phonemes of a language can be described with considerable precision. However, with semantic units, it is difficult to establish comparable targets. To do so would prescribe rules for pronunciation. The term *correct* would be applied. Conformity would be expected. This would be the standard or correct pronunciation. Current practice does not sanction this view. The authors of *Webster's Seventh New Collegiate Dictionary* write the following paragraphs:

> The term *correct pronunciation* is often used. Yet it is probable that many who use the term would find it difficult to give a precise and clear definition of the sense in which they use it. When the essential facts are considered, *correctness* of prounciation must be a flexible term. It is perhaps as accurate a definition as can be made to say that a pronunciation is correct when it is in actual use by a sufficient number of cultivated speakers. This is obviously elastic, depending both on knowledge—never accurately ascertainable—of the number of users, and on judgment as to the cultivation of the speakers.
>
> The standard of English pronunciation, so far as a standard may be said to exist, is the usage that now prevails among the educated and cultured people to whom the language is vernacular; but since somewhat different pronunciations are used by the cultivated in different regions too large to be ignored, we must admit the fact that uniformity of pronunciation is not to be found throughout the English-speaking world, though there is a very large percentage of practical uniformity.
>
> The function of a pronouncing dictionary is to record as far as possible the pronunciations prevailing in the best present usage rather than to attempt to dictate what that usage should be. In so far as a dictionary may be known and acknowledged as a faithful recorder and interpreter of such usage, so far and no farther may it be appealed to as an authority.*

The target pronunciation is indeed blurred! These paragraphs were written for Webster's *Second New International Dictionary* (1936) and have in some measure survived in successive collegiate editions, survived changes and a rising enthusiasm for description rather than prescription in matters of speech, particularly pronunciation. Your interest at the moment is directed to the words, "somewhat different pronunciations are used by the cultivated in different regions too large to be ignored."

Regional dialects include vocal usages in vocabulary and syntax as well as pronunciation, but, popularly, in the United States *dialect* usually means pronunciation dialect. Regionalisms in pronunciations are far from new. Here is a classical example of one.

---

* By permission. From Webster's Seventh New Collegiate Dictionary © 1967 by G. & C. Merriam Co., Publishers of the Merriam-Webster Dictionaries.

> They said to him, "Then say Shibboleth," and he said, "Sibbo-
> leth," for he could not pronounce it right; then they seized him and
> slew him at the fords of the Jordan. And there fell at that time
> forty-two thousand of the Ephraimites.
>
> Judges 12:6

Commonly, this passage has been referred to in terms of "difficult words" and has given rise to the common use of the word *Shibboleth* to mean "difficult to pronounce." Clearly, the Gileadites were distinguishing the Ephraimites from other Israelites about 1150 B.C. on the basis of pronunciation dialect. Any other word with the sound /ʃ/ would have done as well.

More than a thousand years later regional dialect was recorded in a Christian episode. While Jesus was on trial, Peter was in the courtyard outside. He denied any knowledge of Jesus. Twice he defended himself against the charges of a maid. His Galilean dialect gave him away and the third accusation was telling:

> After a little while, the bystanders came up and said to Peter,
> "Certainly you are also one of them; for your accent betrays you."
>
> Matthew 26:73*

Another thousand years of religious history and it is recorded in the *Sicilian Vespers* (1282), "The French were made to betray themselves by their pronunciation of *ceci e ciceri;* those who pronounced /c/ as in French were hewed down on the spot." Still later when a revolt against the French in Flanders broke out, 1302, the gates were seized, and no one allowed to pass who could not utter, "sclip ende friend"—altogether unpronounceable for a Frenchman. The various pronunciation dialects of the United States were suggested in Chapter 2. How is it that they have developed? There can be no complete answer, however, among the influences are:

a. the origins of the early settlers,
b. the routes of migrations,
c. the fact that large cities tend to dominate surrounding communities,
d. isolation fostered by mountain barriers and river passages,
e. social hierarchies within a community and the yearning for
   status,
f. recent immigration influxes from other countries.

---

* In J. B. Phillips' *The New Testament in Modern English,* this reads, "A few minutes later, those who were standing about came up to Peter and said to him, 'You certainly are one of them, you know; it's obvious from your accent.' "

Although the child has experiences outside the home and these have an effect upon his pronunciation, the principal characteristics of one's pronunciation—and hence his dialect—come from the mother's reinforcement of practices of pronunciation. Fairbanks developed a model that describes the cybernetics of speaking. One monitors his talking with different sensory receptors. These sensations are brought to what Fairbanks designated a *comparator*. The produced speech is compared with the expected speech and adjustments are made so that the two match as well

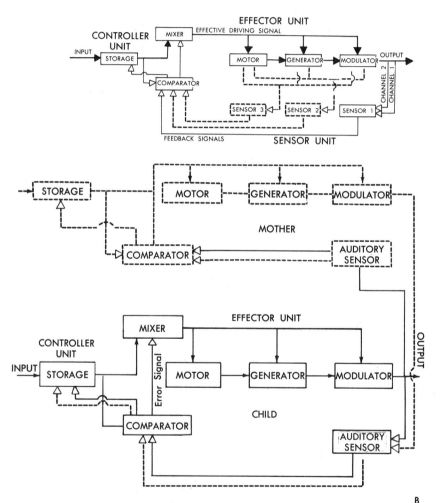

Figure 22. (A) Model of a closed cycle control system for speaking (Fairbanks), and (B) modification of the model to relate to the acquisition of speech.

as possible in successive moments. Figure 22 adds to this model a second monitoring system.* This outside person, perhaps a mother, provides a second comparator, and compares the child's speech with "what the second person expects to hear." This second person may provide positive and negative reinforcement to alter the child's speech to match as closely as possible that of the monitor. Phonemes, stress, intonation, juncture—all of the acoustic aspects of speech are monitored and "corrected." As a consequence, the place of articulation of the consonant; the raised, lowered, or diphthongized vowels; the precision of articulation; the presence or absence of glottal catches; the aspiration or lack of aspiration of terminal plosives are set by the person the child hears. A pronunciation dialect learned from an earlier generation is implanted anew and perpetuated.

Pronunciation dialect is vital on the stage. There, experts render it and listeners momentarily witness a convincing reproduction of life in one or another region of the United States. American dialects also come into literature in a way that calls on you to sense them and interpret them. Here are some examples. James Russell Lowell portrayed the Boston Yankee:

> Dear Sir,—You wish to know my notions
> On sartin pints that rile the land;
> There's nothin' that my natur so shuns
> Ex bein' mum or underhand;
> I'm a straight-spoken kind o' creetur
> Thet blurts out wut's in his head,
> An' ef I've one pecooler feetur
> It is a nose that wunt be led.

> *The Biglow Papers*
> James Russell Lowell

James Whitcomb Riley portrayed the Hoosier:

> Folks in town, I reckon, thinks
> They git all the fun they air
> Runnin' loose 'round!—, 'y jinks!
> We' got fun, and fun to spare,
> Right out here amongst the ash—
> And oak-timber ever'where!
> Some folks else kin cut a dash
> 'Sides town-people, don't fergit!—
> 'Specially in winter-time,
> When they's snow, and roads is fit.

---

* Figure 22 is an extension of the model provided in Figure 5. Please compare the two figures.

In them circumstances I'm
Resig-nated to my lot—
Which putts me in mind o' what
'S call "The Literary."

At "The Literary"
James Whitcomb Riley

Paul L. Dunbar portrayed the uneducated Southern Negro:

Woman's sho' a cur'ous critter, an' day ain't no doubtin' dat.
She's a mess o' funny capahs f'om huh slippahs to huh hat.

*The Turning of the
Babies in the Bed*
Paul Lawrence Dunbar

Many writers of novels illustrate pronunciation dialects. For example, Mark Twain wrote of the dialect of Missouri; Marjorie Rawlings, of Northern Florida; Willa Cather, of Nebraska; George Washington Cable, of New Orleans; Thomas Nelson Page, of the Virginia Plantation; and George and Helen Papashvily, a Russian in the U.S.A. Among writers of short stories, Stephen Vincent Benet and Joel Chandler Harris portray the dialect of the Deep South, and Edward Townsend and Arthur Kober of New York City. Even the comic strip takes note of American pronunciation dialects, as in the Katzenjammer Kids, Abe Martin, and L'il Abner.

The study of dialect is a scholarly activity for many people. For example, some relevant titles of dissertations follow. These show both a student's and his adviser's interest in pronunciation.

a. Some aspects of a Judeo-Spanish dialect as spoken by a New York Sephardic family,
b. The Swabian dialect of Washington County, Michigan,
c. The mid-back vowels in the English of the Eastern United States,
d. The low-central and low-back vowels of the Eastern United States,
e. Features of New England rustic pronunciation in James Russell Lowell's *Biglow Papers,*
f. The dialects of Lunnenburg County, Nova Scotia,
g. A Colorado word geography,
h. A phonological and morphological study of the speech of the Negro of Memphis, Tennessee,
i. Yiddish and English in Detroit,
j. A dialect study of San Antonio, Texas: a bilingual community,
k. The native American English spoken in the Puget Sound area,
l. The usage of stressed front vowels among college freshmen in Ohio.

VOCABULARY

Pronunciation is not apart from the words that are pronounced and as one of these parts of oral language is above average the other tends to be. There is scant virtue in acquiring a vocabulary of size simply for reasons of erudition or working difficult puzzles. However, it would be impossible to restrict the function of vocabulary to these displays. The vocabulary is a resource with which one listens as well as speaks. His experience in saying the words helps him, in turn, to be a more perceptive listener. Here, as in Chapter 8, the contribution of motor activity to speech perception is implicit. Consider the results of three groups of students who were given an intelligibility test. The students heard a word, for example, *grew,* and were asked to identify the word they heard from four optional choices on a response form. The format of the response form is illustrated in the groups of words of Exercise 1, Chapter 8. The students fell into three groups: first, normal-hearing United States students; second, those similar to the foregoing except that they were suspected, as a result of a screening test, of having a mild hearing loss; and third, foreign students preparing to begin their graduate study in the United States. All heard the words of the intelligibility tests under four conditions: quiet and three degrees of interfering noise. The students suspected of having a mild hearing loss did indeed make somewhat lower scores than their normal-hearing peers. Possibly this was attributable to an organic loss in hearing or possibly to a form of poor listening ability, for example, a language deficiency. Notably, the normal-hearing foreign students were quite deficient in identifying the words. This is at least in keeping with the assumption that lack of experience in saying words contributes to lack of skill in identifying them orally.

STRESS

An important part of pronunciation is the fluctuating loudness-pitch (stress) component in the saying of words of more than one syllable. As noted in an earlier chapter, this variety has been quantized into three degrees: primary stress, secondary stress, and minimum stress. The class of a word, noun, adjective, or verb is sometimes suggested by the stressed syllable: present, produce, subject, record, perfect, contract, refuse, proceeds, regress. Usually, however, stress is independent of meaning. It represents either a decision or a habit relative to a speaker's use of a single word.

Habitual stress is hard to alter. A near reflexive control in the nervous system hastens the exhalatory pulse momentarily during the saying of a single syllable and arrests this quickened action for the unstressed syllable.

APPLICATION

Your role in living with a dialect is an active one. Except when deliberately forcing yourself to use a different manner of speaking, you verbalize in the one you acquired with your language. You do more than verbalize in it, however; you also listen in it. Attentive to the train of thought of a speaker, you are perceiving his words in your manner of saying them. Exceptions to this occur when the manner of speaking is so remote from yours that you attend to it rather than the substance.

The view here is not to praise dialect, but to emphasize that it is both inevitable and important. It exists in degrees and seems to be extreme among:

a. less well educated people, rather than more educated ones,
b. single industrial communities rather than diversified ones,
c. people whose livelihood is not very dependent on talking,
d. economically impoverished peoples.

One of your goals, discussed in Chapter 2, is to minimize the regional dialect that you have in your speech. You hold this objective not because there is anything wrong with your home community, but because a dialect is distracting to listeners in another community. Your plans are large ones that relate to state, national, international activity. A cosmopolitan person can ill afford a provincial mannerism of speech.

SUMMARY

If a spoken word conforms to the listener's pronunciation of the same word the matter of its pronunciation is unnoticed. If it deviates slightly he may hear it as though it were said in his manner of speech and pay no attention to it. Wide deviation, however, leads to unintelligibility. In the intervening range between near conformity and wide deviation the listener's attention is diverted as he notes the "mispronunciation" or the regional oddity.

The most common disparity in pronunciation comes with the variety that is appropriate to different occasions. As speaking situations differ in formality and mood, they seem to require one degree or another of precision of articulation and length of vowels.

The second greatest difference in pronunciation comes from regional dialects. These are inevitable. The ambitions of a student of higher learning, however, are usually inconsistent with the shackles of a local dialect.

Exercises

1. Practice reading the following passages.
   a. Evidently to measure an adult abdomen requires a
   b. contractor and some special apparatus. The chic
   c. blackguard has disputable data and his entire material
   d. on eczema is inherently just an embroglio.
   e. It is a grievous and lamentable defect to have
   f. an arctic creek address, especially when vaudeville
   g. experience is gratis.
   h. Joe, tired of Gambier, made a grimace and gave
   i. precedence to a man of great height, an impious
   j. comptroller. Being particularly mischievous he
   k. sacrificed his ragout and with discretion gave his
   l. allies some tea made of special roots which grew along
   m. the route to the tournament.
   n. Mary's respite and romance came when she was
   o. penalized for trying to finance a culinary department.
   p. Is the despicable library rule irrevocable? Let us
   q. put the dictator of the clique in a gondola. It
   r. should be a gala experiment because he lacks height
   s. and has no genuine status. He assumes to be the epitome
   t. of all that is impious, just a flaccid and ribald
   u. Arab. The chameleon bade the sacrilegious brigand
   v. welcome.

2. These eye-catchers are frequently used. Some of them are phonetically correct. Some require latitude on the part of the reader. Evaluate each, pronouncing it carefully.
   a. U drive it
   b. A can-a Hanna paint
   c. E-Z does it
   d. Bar-B-Q
   e. Duz does everything
   f. Y not K C Jones?
   g. C B Yacht Club
   h. A B C D Puppy
   i. U R 2 nice 2 B 4 gotten
   j. Stop 'n shop

3. Bring your plan for improvement up to date. Is this student likely to improve? Critically evaluate the plan.

My Plan for Speech Improvement

My program for the improvement of my speech focuses upon four topics: pronunciation, articulation, loudness, and nasality.

a. Pronunciation. In an attempt to improve my pronunciation, I plan to seek the advice of an up-to-date dictionary. I shall look up the unusual words that come up in my assignments and all of the words that puzzle me in any manner, especially spelling, that I hear in my class lectures. My roommate is going to follow a similar procedure and we shall pool our new words each evening.

b. Articulation. I am practicing all of my new words for clear, precise enunciation. Also, it is fun to watch my 2½-year-old niece as she learns to talk. I repeat her words for her, saying them two or three times. Also, I read children's stories to her, stressing the animal sounds and the sounds of machinery and nature. Finally, I am taking up lip reading.

c. Loudness. My roommate and I are practicing talking to each other from our adjoining rooms. This not only seems to affect our loudness but the precision of our articulation as well.

d. Nasality. For nasality I have written several sentences that have have no nasal sounds and other that are loaded with nasal sounds. I am practicing reading the first set with a mirror held under my nose and trying to see that there is no moisture on the mirror. The contrast with the second set is astonishing.

4. In class, two speakers read alternately. One-half of the class responds to one speaker and the other half of the class to the other. Before reading, each speaker has prepared a program from the following lines of four words. He has selected two words in each of six lines and reads these two words, for example, number 1 *horse hoarse,* number 2 *or or.* His listeners indicate on slips of paper whether the two words are *same* or *different.* The papers are returned to the readers. Please select ones that are difficult for you (you know which ones they are!).

a. fill	fill	feel	feel
b. horse	horse	hoarse	hoarse
c. tin	tin	ten	ten
d. are	are	our	our
e. or	or	oar	oar
f. what	what	watt	watt
g. loose	loose	lose	lose
h. owl	owl	Al	Al
i. tire	tire	tar	tar
j. while	while	wile	wile
k. oil	oil	Earl	Earl
l. key	quay /ki/	coo	coo

m. lore	lore	roar	roar
n. sigh	sigh	thigh	thigh
o. tent	tent	tint	tint
p. tired	tired	tarred	tarred
q. tend	tend	tinned	tinned
r. whale	whale	wail	wail
s. chair	chair	cheer	cheer
t. airs	airs	errors	errors
u. chain	chain	Jane	Jane
v. Jill	Jill	chill	chill
w. look	look	rook	rook
x. file	file	vial	vial
y. bed	bed	bet	bet
z. lend	lend	land	land

5. Discuss the following lines with respect to dialect and cite similar examples from your experience. "The Frenchified and the Italianate Englishman became, as we know, familiar figures in Elizabethan literature, particularly in satire." Sir Thomas More describes such a character, Lalus, a Gallicized Englishman, in a poem of about 50 verses. Two follow:

> ... He keeps
> One only servant.—This man, too, is French;
> And could not, as I think, e'en by the French,
> Be treated more in fashion of the French;
> He clothes him meanly,—that again is French;
> Stints him with meagre victuals,—that is French;
> Works him to death,—and this again is French;
> Belabours him full oft,—and that is French. ...
>
> With accent French he speaks the Latin tongue,
> With accent French the tongue of Lombardy,
> To Spanish words he gives an accent French,
> German he speaks with the same accent French.
> In truth, he seems to speak with accent French
> All but the French itself. The French he speaks
> With accent British. ...*

6. Three explanations were given of speech perception in Chapter 8: the acoustic explanation, a probabilistic explanation, and a motor theory. How do these relate to pronunciation? How do they relate to vocabulary building? Discuss.

7. Practice pronouncing the following words:
   a. abdominal absolute abstract accent acceptable accurate
   b. address adult advantage advertisement airplane allies
   c. alternate alumni another apparatus appreciate argue

---

* From "The Epigrams of Sir Thomas More," in *The Epigram in the English Renaissance,* by Hoyt Hopewell Hudson (Copyright 1947, Princeton University Press). Reprinted by permission of Princeton University Press.

d. armistice artisan assume athlete aviation banquet
e. barrel because beneficial binocular bureaucracy
f. capital caramel carburetor catch catsup century chassis
g. chimney chocolate column contract corps coupon creator
h. culinary deaf decade defect describe detail diaper
i. dirigible discourse division drowned economics emphasize
j. enemy energy envelope era essentially etiquette expert
k. facsimile factories familiar fete finally fish flagrant
l. foliage formidable genius giraffe goal governor gum
m. history horizon hurricane hysteria illustrate influence
n. integral intricate issues juvenile latent leisure lever
o. maintenance measure milk municipal mustache nephew
p. oblique opening orchestra our palm parliament patent
q. perspiration picture policeman popular powerful premier
r. prestige primary program pulpit quote realize really
s. regular reptile response resource revenue revolution
t. roster sacrifice sanitation satire secretary serious
u. silhouette simultaneous sincere since society soot
v. squash stomach strata strength suave suggest suit suite
w. suppose syrup tariff ten theater tiresome tournament
x. typhoid umbrella understand uniform university used
y. vacuum various verbatim veteran veterinary violence
z. virtually wish with wrestle your zero

8. Through reading the following paragraphs, arrive at a definition of Slurvian.

. . . (Excerpt from Slurvian Self-Taught) *

a.   Listening to a well-known Hollywood radio commentator some time back, I heard her say that she had just returned from a Yerpeen trip, and had had a lovely time nittly. I at once recognized her as an accomplished Slurvian linguist and, being a student of Slurvian, readily understood that she had just returned from a European trip and while there (in Yerp) had had a lovely time in Italy.

b.   Slurvian is coming into common use in the United States, but I am, so far as I know, the only scholar to have made a start toward recording it. There is no official Slurvian language, but it is possible, by means of phonetic spelling, for me to offer a brief course of instruction in it. In a short time the student can learn enough to add immeasurably to his understanding and enjoyment of conversation wherever he travels in the country.

c.   I first heard pure Slurvian fluently spoken by a co-worker of mine who told me that his closest friend was a man named Hard (Howard). Hard was once in an automobile accident, his car, unfortunately, cliding with another, causing Hard's wife

---

* Reprinted by permission of Curtis Brown, Ltd. First appeared in *The New Yorker*. Copyright © 1949 by John Davenport.

Dorthy, who was with him, to claps. Dorthy didn't have much stamina but was a sweet woman—sweet as surp.

d. I soon discovered I had an ear for Slurvian, and since I began to recognize the language, I have encountered many Slurvians. At ballparks, they keep track of hits, runs, and airs. On farms, they plow furs. In florist shops, they buy flars. When hard up, they bar money from banks, and spend it for everything from fewl for the furnace to grum crackers for the children.

e. When Slurvians travel abroad, they go to visit farn (or forn) countries to see what the farners do that's different from the way we Murcans do things. While in farn countries, they refer to themselves as Murcan tersts, and usually say they will be mighty glad to get back to Murca. A Slurvian I once met on a train told me he had just returned from a visit to Mexico. He deplored the lack of automobiles down there, and said that the natives ride around on little burrs.

9. Compound words are coming into American English continually. They require unique pronunciations. The following ones are illustrative. Try saying them in sentences. Also, extend the list to include 10 contemporary words of your local campus language.

Let-Up, Coast-Strike, know-how, super-products, Cut-Rite Wax Paper, Glo-coat Floor Wax, Easy-Off, Ginger-Cake, road-louse, glad-hand, hop-head, rah-rah, coffin-nail (cigarette), hot-spot, bug-house, hang-out, pin-head, chair-warmer, canned music, sob-sister, bell-hop, come-back, white-wings, rabble-rouser, college widow, sky-scraper, rubber-neck, loan-shark, high brow, low-brow, hot-dog, joy-ride, love-nest, jay-walker, brain-trust.

10. Here are examples of poems written in dialect. Try to find a selection that reproduces a dialect with which you are familiar and read it to the class.

a. He gotta da bigga, de blacka moustache
   Good clo'es an' good style an' playnta good cash.

Mia Carlotta
T. A. Daly

b. I sha'nt forgit the night
   When I dropped be'ind the fight . . .
   'E lifted up my 'ead,
   An' 'e guv me 'arf-a-pint o' water-green.

Gunga Din
Rudyard Kipling

c. Guid speed and furder to you, Johnie,
   Guid health, hale han's and weather bonie!
   Now, when ye're nickin down fu' cannie
       The staff o'bread,
   May ye ne'er want a stoup o'bran'y
       To clear your head!

To J. Lapraik
Robert Burns

d. Yaw, dot ish so! Yaw, dot ish so!
   "Dis vorldt vas all a fleeting show."
       I shmokes mine pipe,
       I trinks mine bier,
   Und efry day to vork I go;
   "Dis vorldt vas all a fleeting show;"
       Yaw, dot ish so!

> *Yaw, Dot Ish So*
> Charles Follen Adams

11. Note James Russell Lowell's seven rules about Mr. Biglow's pronunciation:

> As regards the provincialisms to be met within this volume, I may say that the reader will not find one which is not (as I believe) either native or imported with the early settlers, nor one which I have not, with my own ears, heard in familiar use. In the metrical portion of the book, I have endeavored to adapt the spelling as nearly as possible to the ordinary mode of pronunciation. Let the reader who deems me over-particular remember this caution of Martial:—"Quem recitas, meus est, O Fidentine libellus; Sed male cum recitas, incipit esse tuus." A few further explanatory remarks will not be impertinent. I shall barely lay down a few general rules for the reader's guidance.

a. The genuine Yankee never gives the rough sound to the *r* when he can help it, and often displays considerable ingenuity in avoiding it even before a vowel.

b. He seldom sounds the final *g*, a piece of self-denial, if we consider his partiality for nasals. The same of the final *d*, as *han'* and *stan'* for *hand* and *stand*.

c. The *h* in such words as *while, when, where*, he omits altogether.

d. In regard to *a*, he shows some inconsistency, sometimes giving a close and obscure sound, as *hev* for *have, hendy* for *handy, ez* for *as, thet* for *that*, and again giving it the broad sound it has in *father*, as *hansome* for *handsome*.

e. To the sound *ou* he prefixes an *e* (hard to exemplify otherwise than orally). The following passage in Shakespeare he would recite thus:
   Neow is the winta uv eour discontent
   Med glorious summa by this sun o' Yock,
   An' all the cleouds thet leowered upun eour heouse
   In the deep buzzum o' the oshin buried;
   Neow air eour breows beound 'ith victorious wreaths;
   Eour breused arms hung up fer monimunce;
   Eour starn alarums changed to merry meetins,
   Eour dreffle marches to delighfle masures.
   Grim-visaged war heth smeuthed his wrinkled front,
   An' neow, instid o' mountin' barebid steeds
   To fright the souls o' ferfle edverseries,
   He capers nimly in a lady's chamber,
   To the lascivious pleasin' uv a loot.

f. *Au*, in such words as *daughter* and *slaughter,* he pronounces *ah.*
g. To the dish thus seasoned add a drawl *ad libitum.*

12. Study the special notes relating to the following words in *The Pronunciation Dictionary of American English* by Kenyon and Knott.

a. acorn	apron	aunt	aye
b. cabbage	caramel	caterpillar	centenary
c. chivalry	clothe	cony	cote
d. cupola	dahlia	dais	directrix
e. disputable	dissoluble	drouth	either
f. elderberry	envelope	ewe	explicable
g. extra	felly	figure	flagstaff
h. flotsam	forge	former	fortnight
i. furthermore	gaol	garage	genealogy
j. glacier	goal	goblin	government
k. governor	granary	greasy	grovel
l. gynecology	harass	hearth	humor
m. indisputable	keg	kettle	kiln
n. library	luxury	mistake	naked
o. neither	nephew	pecan	peony
p. pivot	plait	pumpkin	quaint
q. rarebit	ridden	roof	sacrifice
r. saint	second	sewer	shine
s. steelyard	sumac	surprise	swamp
t. thermometer	thrash	tomato	tremendous
u. valet	visor	voluntary	wake
v. wend	wharf	wheelbarrow	wherewith
w. whoa	wholly	wick	woman
x. wont	yearling	yelk	yule

13. Which word (a, b, c, d) is most nearly a synonym for the first word?
    1. tedious: a. difficult, b. supressive, c. touchy, d. tiresome.
    2. distort: a. deform, b. injure, c. diverge, d. bewilder.
    3. surmise: a. summarize, b. guess, c. conclude, d. overcome.
    4. evoke: a. make, b. elicit, c. annoy, d. release.
    5. revile: a. slander, b. refresh, c. rebel, d. scold.
    6. proscribe: a. condemn, b. designate, c. encircle, d. recommend.
    7. simultaneous: a. concurrent, b. agreeing, c. preceding, d. instantaneous.
    8. acquiescence: a. obtainment, b. confidence, c. adaptation, d. compliance.
    9. succinct: a. blunt, b. concise, c. incessant, d. purposive.
    10. inference: a. deduction, b. degradation, c. category, d. statement.
    11. abject: a. depressing, b. renouncing, c. ignoble, d. subjective.
    12. taunt: a. quiz, b. ridicule, c. betray, d. tighten.
    13. pervade: a. continue, b. overthrew, c. permeate, d. agitate.
    14. vantage: a. abundance, b. respect, c. advantage, d. conceit.
    15. manifestation: a. evidence, b. exhibit, c. variation, d. reality.
    16. veneer: a. gloss, b. antique, c. revenge, d. overlav.

17. retaliate: a. reiterate, b. withdraw, c. revenge, d. reply.
18. biases: a. inclinations, b. proposals, c. influences, d. prejudices.
19. susceptible: a. sensitive, b. conscious, c. suspicious, d. maintainable.
20. dissipate: a. divide, b. disperse, c. abandon, d. decay.
21. intricate: a. tortuous, b. essential, c. complicated, d. inserted.
22. facilitation: a. poise, b. duplication, c. humor, d. aid.
23. diversity: a. duration, b. aversion, c. variety, d. recreation.
24. predicament: a. emergency, b. situation, c. prophesy, d. lesson.
25. analogy: a. metaphor, b. counterpart, c. similitude, d. mysticism.
26. animated: a. reproduced, b. hostile, c. living, d. sensual.
27. paramount: a. entertaining, b. dominant, c. unique, d. constructed.
28. demented: a. insane, b. irrational, c. deceased, d. resigned.
29. propagation: a. diffusion, b. thrust, c. publicity, d. movement.
30. intermittent: a. between, b. immature, c. endless, d. periodic.
31. concomitant: a. ultimate, b. concurrent, c. following, d. respective.
32. orifice: a. lecture, b. prediction, c. production, d. aperture.
33. digress: a. stray, b. rehearse, c. deviate, d. expand.
34. enigmatic: a. obscure, b. doubtful, c. intensified, d. absorbent.
35. enumerate: a. reckon, b. recite, c. articulate, d. count.
36. admonition: a. criticism, b. veneration, c. acceptance, d. warning.
37. imperative: a. dogmatic, b. impenetrable, c. peremptory, d. intangible.
38. abstract: a. sketch, b. summarize, c. refrain, d. mistreat.
39. manipulate: a. handle, b. wave, c. demonstrate, d. fabricate.
40. reiterate: a. repudiate, b. repeat, c. recompense, d. rehearse.
41. dogmatic: a. imperative, b. dictatorial, c. indoctrinated, d. obstinate.
42. oriented: a. popularized, b. systematized, c. designed, d. acquainted.
43. overt: a. ruined, b. sensitive, c. public, d. upset.
44. literal: a. figurative, b. basic, c. readable, d. actual.
45. exclude: a. depart, b. revolve, c. eliminate, d. require.
46. acquire: a. buy, b. demand, c. vindicate, d. gain.
47. perpetuate: a. move, b. mutate, c. continue, d. bewilder.
48. extensive: a. thorough, b. broad, c. dilated, d. premeditated.
49. derive: a. emanate, b. mock, c. disturb, d. eradicate.
50. restrain: a. interrupt, b. saturate, c. retaliate, d. curb.
51. sustenance: a. maintenance, b. hindrance, c. mistrust, d. bread.
52. irrelevant: a. extraneous, b. abnormal, c. profane, d. irregular.
53. paraphernalia: a. translations, b. leeches, c. apparatus, d. tremors.
54. cumulative: a. additive, b. onerous, c. bred, d. fostered.
55. utilize: a. manipulate, b. seize, c. use, d. express.
56. confronted: a. perplexed, b. faced, c. shaped, d. adjusted.
57. verify: a. establish, b. confine, c. confirm, d. broadcast.
58. traversed: a. changed, b. trespassed, c. labored, d. crossed.
59. consequently: a. approvingly, b. protectively, c. accordingly, d. after.
60. valid: a. courageous, b. analytical, c. venturous, d. sound.
61. convey: a. transmit, b. capture, c. summon, d. transform.
62. disparity: a. difference, b. hopelessness, c. crime, d. sorrow.

63. fraught: a. confused, b. laden, c. attacked, d. brotherly.
64. reconcile: a. repay, b. compliment, c. remind, d. adjust.
65. fraudulent: a. irresponsible, b. candid, c. deceitful, d. fragile.
66. appraisal: a. evaluation, b. discovery, c. comprehension, d. date.
67. persistent: a. imitative, b. pursued, c. bothersome, d. persevering.
68. quest: a. interrogation, b. adventure, c. shake, d. prize.
69. pertinent: a. happy, b. timely, c. sarcastic, d. relevant.
70. rigorous: a. athletic, b. rigid, c. excessive, d. burdensome.
71. inquiry: a. audit, b. disturbance, c. oddity, d. investigation.
72. prone: a. addicted, b. declared, c. liable, d. advanced.
73. utility: a. suitability, b. implement, c. process, d. usefulness.
74. impair: a. distort, b. communicate, c. hinder, d. damage.
75. impoverish: a. curse, b. cheat, c. deplete, d. tax.
76. inhibit: a. exclude, b. restrain, c. withdraw, d. flaunt.
77. inherent: a. intrinsic, b. typical, c. prohibited, d. lawful.
78. activate: a. awaken, b. join, c. possess, d. energize.
79. laborious: a. mechanical, b. difficult, c. confusing, d. toilsome.
80. reciprocal: a. identical, b. reverse, c. complementary, d. preceding.
81. vibratile: a. trembling, b. oscillating, c. enthusiastic, d. frail.
82. attenuate: a. intensify, b. weaken, c. affirm, d. alleviate.
83. attribute: a. symbol, b. sorrow, c. money, d. quality.
84. configuration: a. contour, b. limit, c. form, d. secret.
85. anticipate: a. foresee, b. correct, c. hope, d. limit.
86. couch: a. hide, b. secrete, c. recline, d. settle.
87. summative: a. brief, b. cumulative, c. apt, d. enumerate.
88. inevitable: a. appointed, b. avertible, c. passive, d. unavoidable.
89. fluent: a. quick, b. liquified, c. smooth, d. vibrating.
90. premium: a. favor, b. assumption, c. open, d. reward.
91. complacent: a. egotistic, b. self-satisfied, c. amiable, d. suave.
92. deflect: a. twist, b. turn, c. contort, d. determine.
93. arbitrary: a. undecided, b. irrelevant, c. stubborn, d. absolute.
94. abate: a. abolish, b. avoid, c. embarrass, d. resign.
95. annotate: a. lubricate, b. explain, c. oppose, d. criticize.
96. ascertain: a. study, b. discipline, c. discover, d. obtain.
97. discrepant: a. inconsonant, b. different, c. distinct, d. microscopic.
98. innuendo: a. suggesting, b. infusion, c. mystery, d. insinuation.
99. simulate: a. approximate, b. evoke, c. facilitate, d. feign.
100. envisage: a. survey, b. conceive, c. covet, d. pronounce.

14. Read "A Little Learning is a Dangerous Thing," paying particular attention to pronunciation.

A little learning is a dangerous thing;
Drink deep, or taste not the Pierian spring;
These shallow draughts intoxicate the brain,
And drinking largely sobers us again.
Fired at first sight with which the Muse imparts,
In fearless youth we tempt the heights of arts,

While from the bounded level of our mind,
Short views we take, nor see the lengths behind;
But more advanced, behold with strange surprise,
New distant scenes of endless science rise!
So pleased at first the towering Alps we try,
Mount o'er the vales, and seem to tread the sky,
The eternal snows appear already past,
And the first clouds and mountains seem the last;
But those attained, we tremble to survey
The growing labours of the lengthened way,
The increasing prospect tires our wandering eyes,
Hills peep o'er hills, and Alps on Alps arise!

Alexander Pope

15. The following words merit your special attention. Practice saying them in and out of context.

a. acceptable	actually	again	always
b. ambition	another	about you	because
c. being	belittled	catch	cannot
d. Columbus	collapse	comfortable	curriculum
e. definition	desired	despicable	did you
f. eleven	environment	error	feel
g. for example	generally	get	government
h. hundred	I, eye, aye	introduce	imagine
i. industry	intended	just	many
j. nine	now	number	often
k. other	our	out	parents
l. particular	picture	police	poor
m. positive	power	probably	products
n. really	realized	recognized	romance
o. several	sincerity	special	something
p. such	superstition	television	ten
q. this	toward	upon	vicious
r. want	what	when	wishes

References

Allen, Harold B., *Teaching English as a Second Language.* New York: Mc-Graw-Hill Book Company, 1965.

Bronstein, Arthur J., "Let's Take Another Look at New York City Speech," *American Speech,* 37 (1962), 13-26.

Carr, Elizabeth Ball, "Word Compounding in American Speech," *Speech Monographs,* 26 (1959), 1-20.

Chomsky, Noam, *Syntactic Structures.* The Hague: Mouton and Company, 1957.

Dale, Edgar and Donald Reichert, *Bibliography of Vocabulary Studies,* rev. ed. Columbus: The Ohio State University Bureau of Educational Research, 1957.

Fairbanks, Grant, "Systematic Research in Experimental Phonetics: A Theory of the Speech Mechanism as a Servosystem," *Journal of Speech and Hearing Disorders,* XIX (1954), 133-139.

Fossum, Ernest C., "An Analysis of the Dynamic Vocabulary of Junior College Students," *Speech Monographs,* 11 (1944), 88-96.

Fraprie, Frank R., "The Twenty Commonest English Words . . . from a Count of 242,432 Words of English Text taken from Fifteen English Authors and Many Newspapers," *World Almanac and Book of Facts for 1950,* ed. Harvey Hansen. New York: New York World Telegram.

Hudson, Hoyt Hopewell, *The Epigram in the English Renaissance.* Princeton, N. J.: Princeton University Press, 1947.

Malmstrom, Jean and Annabel Ashley, *Dialects U.S.A.* Champaign, Illinois: National Council of Teachers of English, 1963.

Monaghan, Robert, *Pronunciation Guide of Oregon Place Names.* Eugene, Oregon: Oregon Association of Broadcasters, 1961.

Prator, Clifford H., Jr., *Manual of American English Pronunciation,* rev. ed. New York: Holt, Rinehart & Winston, Inc., 1957.

Rahskopf, Horace G., *Basic Speech Improvement.* New York: Harper & Row Publishers, 1965.

Stevens, Leonard A., *The Ill-Spoken Word.* New York: McGraw-Hill Book Company, 1966.

Lawrence, Telete, "An Analysis of the Speech of Twenty Students at Texas Christian University," unpublished master's thesis.

Voelker, Charles H., "The One-Thousand Most Frequent Spoken-Words," *Quarterly Journal of Speech,* 28 (1942), 189-97.

Zimmerman, Jane Dorsey, *Radio Pronunciations.* New York: James Brown Press, 1946.

12

Stabilizing and Integrating Speech Skills In Oral Reading

Specific skills alone do not produce an effective speaking voice. Only when these skills are integrated by a speaker who has a keen desire to communicate will communicatively efficient speech occur. A sincere desire to communicate a message intended by the author, dramatist, or poet will serve as motivation for you to use your speech skills effectively.

In earlier chapters, you learned about the various speech skills desirable for proficiency in speech. You have learned that several processes are involved: respiration, phonation, resonation, articulation, pronunciation, and audition. No one process can work effectively for the production of speech without the harmonious functioning of all parts.

You have practiced and reinforced the necessary speech skills in at least four steps: (a) isolated sounds, (b) words, (c) phrases, and (d) sentences. You may also have had some practice with the specific skill in connected reading or speaking. The purpose of this chapter is to present a brief discussion of oral reading and its use in the stabilization and integration of articulatory and vocal skills. The major part of the chapter will be devoted to the exercises which are graded according to difficulty and purpose.

ORAL READING

The various kinds of oral reading include informational and emotional material represented by prose, drama, and poetry. Oral reading implies the use of the speaking voice and body to convey the meaning of the printed page to the listeners. Oral reading will give you an excellent opportunity to integrate your newly learned speech techniques and your effectiveness will depend largely upon the proficiency with which these techniques are used.

If attention is given to the communication or interpretation of the printed page to the audience, many of the speech skills will be used effectively without any conscious effort to do so. Obviously some selections are more appropriate than others for the practice of certain skills. If the oral reader, for example, feels the emotion conveyed by the meaning in the following selection, his voice may assume the suitable pitch and tempo:

> Break, break, break,
> On thy cold gray stones, O sea!
> And I would that my tongue could utter
> The thoughts that arise in me.

> *Break, Break, Break*
> Alfred Tennyson

If the selection conveys excitement to you, your reading rate may increase; the pitch of your voice may rise. In the reading of "Hail to thee blithe spirit," your voice would probably be softer and higher pitched than if you were reading "The day is cold and dark and dreary." Exercises, organized according to the various aspects of the speaking voice, will be presented at the end of this chapter. You may want to make further selections from other sources according to your particular needs. These may be placed in an appropriate part of your speech notebook as suggested in Chapter 3.

Criteria for Oral Reading

"Good" oral reading involves both impression and expression. You need to ask, "How can I convey the message of the author or poet most effectively through the use of my speech skills?" If one were to establish certain criteria for evaluating oral reading, these questions might be asked:

1. Does the reader convey the meaning intended by the author?
2. Does he pronounce words correctly and appropriately for the selections?

3. Is his diction acceptable?
4. Is his speech intelligible?
5. Are appropriate thought units and pauses used?
6. Is the rate of reading appropriate for meaning of the selection?
7. Is adequate and appropriate inflection used?
8. Is flexibility of voice quality, pitch, rate, and intensity sufficient for the selection and the sustained interest of the audience?
9. Does the reader use visual elements and total bodily activity appropriately and effectively?
10. Is the total effect of oral reading favorable?

Uses of Oral Reading

The ability to read aloud effectively is an asset to anyone, regardless of profession or occupation. The first-grade teacher reads a story to the children; the man of the house reads an editorial or newspaper account to his wife; the minister reads his sermon, the scriptures, or a prayer; the President reads an important speech; and the club woman reads a message at the meeting.

Studying the Selection

The principal purpose for the oral reading of prose, drama, and poetry, so far as this chapter is concerned, is to provide means for the integration and stabilization of speech skills. It is essential, however, to study the selection carefully to ascertain the purpose, meaning, and emotion intended by the author. You may need to answer such questions as: What does the author mean? How do you think he feels about the subject? Is the purpose artistic or informative?

To understand short passages, you will need to go to the original work and read the entire selection. What did Macbeth mean when asked "If we should fail?" How can you read it effectively if you don't know the play? After becoming familiar with the passage, find references which tell you something of the author and, if possible, the reasons and the situation for the writing.

The study of the logical and emotional meanings of words is also necessary for the interpretation of literary selections. To know the full value of words will cause the oral reader to add emphasis through proper inflection, pitch, loudness, and duration. Study, for example, the use of words in "Patterns" by Amy Lowell and "Chicago" by Carl Sandburg.

Punctuation and division of sentences into thought units need study before the oral reading of a passage. Try reading selections, experimenting with different types of punctuations or thought units. Meaning varies according to the location of the pauses. Try saying "Lay on, Macduff" with pause after "on." Now say "Lay on Macduff" with no pause. What is the difference in the meaning? Punctuation often represents pauses in reading; however, you need to understand the meaning before you can pause effectively. The inflection of the voice varies according to the meaning implied. Further discussion on the phrasing will be found later in the chapter.

ARTICULATORY AND VOCAL SKILLS

Speaking skills will be presented in terms of intelligibility, rate, intensity, pitch, vocal quality, and flexibility.

Intelligibility

Intelligibility or the understandability of the oral reader is dependent upon several factors. The articulation of consonants, particularly in the final positions of words, and the enunciation of vowels add to the intelligibility of speech. Accurate pronunciation and other attributes of the speaking voice discussed in this chapter contribute to total communicative effect of the oral reader's words. These topics, discussed here in relation to oral reading, are extensions of discussions in Chapter 7.

Loudness

Through the use of pauses, sufficient breath can be secured to sustain the reader adequately throughout the next phrase. The amount of breath or power necessary will depend upon the size of the room and the audience. The meaning of the material read aloud will also vary and require different degrees of intensity. The oral reader can make the words as loud or as soft as the meaning indicates. To interpret the material adequately, the individual who ordinarily speaks with soft tones may use more force in speaking than he customarily uses. For that reason, and with a therapeutic end in view, selections which suggest power should be chosen for persons with "weak" voices.

How sounds and words are attacked will be affected by the emotional elements involved. For instance, the soft, gentle (effusive) approach will produce an entirely different meaning from the explosive attack. Use the first approach with "Give me what I ask." Now use the explosive attack. One suggests control and the other suggests urgency and possibly impoliteness.

Rate or Duration

Rate involves the consideration of such factors as phrasing, pausing between phrases, and the general rate of speaking phrases and sentences. The duration of vowels and consonants is also part of the overall timing problem in oral reading.

Phrasing.   Proper phrasing is so important in the adequate oral reading of materials that an early study of how to phrase and when to pause is essential. Each phrase contains a unit of thought in which one key word stands out. Many students will read with few or no pauses to indicate thought units.

Pausing.   Pausing at the right places will permit the reader to convey meaning of the passage to the audience. Several purposes of pauses may be indicated: (a) to allow time for the reader to look ahead to see the next phrase; (b) to allow time for the reader to take sufficient breath to sustain speech to the end of the phrase read; and (c) to allow time for the audience to comprehend the phrase or sentence read.

Learning to pause in appropriate places with adequate timing warrants practice to attain skill. Oral reading gives an excellent opportunity to put into practice the use of skills in phrasing and pausing. The symbol (/) is useful to indicate places for pauses to occur. For instance, the symbol for the pause is used in the following sentence: "Speak the speech/ I pray you/ as I pronounced it to you/ trippingly on the tongue."/

A phrase refers to a continuous utterance bounded by pauses. The phrase in speech may not coincide with grammatical groups of words or punctuation marks. During your early practice, some arbitrary marking of phrases may be desirable in order that you may coördinate your breathing and speaking more adequately. As much as possible, the phrases should represent short meaningful units of speech. Fairbanks indicates that "we speak in phrases,/ not in words,/ in thought units,/ not in parts of speech./ A more or less obvious phrase is spoken quickly/ and with reduced emphasis/ so that the important phrases stand out clearly,/ strongly,/ and with real contrast./ The length of phrases varies,/ because speakers vary in their habits of speech/ and in the meaning which they wish to give to phrases./ In other words,/ phrasing depends upon the meaning of what you say/ and also upon your whims as a speaker./ And although there is an element of logic in the process,/ there are no definite rules."*

---

* Grant Fairbanks, *Voice and Articulation Drillbook* (2nd ed.). New York: Harper & Row, Publishers, 1960, p. 145.

Pitch

Oral reading of literature will give the student an opportunity to practice the uses of pitch changes effectively. Changes in pitch, varying from the optimum level, need to be made according to the meaning of the passage read. A variety in pitch will add interest to the speaking voice, making it pleasing to the listener. Variability of pitch is achieved through the use of slides (upward, downward, and a combination) of the upward and downward pitches and steps or changes of pitch between phonations. The key or average product is general pitch level.

Optimum Pitch Level. You now are ready to practice reading material, using the general pitch level best suited to you. To maintain this one level of speaking would lead to monotony; however, you should practice selections first which do not require too much variation of pitch to convey meaning until you are used to the optimum pitch level which you may need to practice. Some selections may require one pitch level to maintain a certain mood. In general, high pitch level will indicate a mood of excitement, happiness, or tension. Extremely high pitch may indicate fear, anger, or unusual excitement. The low pitch may express calmness, sadness, or controlled passions. A medium key may express serenity, possibly indifference, or calmness.

The Slide. The slide is the upward or downward movement of the pitch in a word or syllable. The melody or musical quality of the speaking voice is affected a great deal by the way you use the slides. The upward slide will be represented by (╱) and the downward slide will be shown by (╲). When both upward and downward slides are involved, the symbol (╱╲) will be used. The upward slide is usually used to denote hesitation, questioning, and apology. The downward slide denotes certainty and assurance. If you use both the upward and downward slides, much will be added to the rhythm of the pitch pattern.

Step in Pitch. The step is a change in pitch between phonations. The good speaker has many steps in pitch during oral reading or conversational speech. Extreme changes from the highest notes to the lowest notes are often noted in lively conversation. The student should listen to the speech of others for these changes of pitch. As he listens to members in the class during oral reading assignments, he may note how few steps are made in pitch. The average speaker may not use as many steps as he is capable of using. Through the oral reading of literature, you may consciously practice these changes in pitch according to the meaning of the selection. A wide range in pitch may be cultivated by reading literature which conveys enthusiasm and lively narration. The telling of children's stories provides materials for the practice of flexibility in pitch.

Quality

Pleasing voice characteristics may be cultivated by the application of certain skills to the oral reading of appropriate selections. You will want to give attention to all factors which contribute to a pleasing voice. In earlier chapters, standards for a "good" speaking voice were discussed. Such factors as posture, relaxation, initiation, and reinforcement of tone were also discussed.

Flexibility

Flexibility of speaking involves the use of variety in rate, loudness, pitch, and quality. Before you practice exercises on flexibility, you need to master the use of each of the four attributes of the speaking voice: rate, intensity, pitch, and quality.

SUMMARY

The ability to demonstrate the use of bodily activity, intelligibility, adequate rate, appropriate intensity, suitable pitch, pleasing voice quality, and flexibility in the oral reading of the passages of this chapter does not necessarily mean that your speech is satisfactory in all of the daily uses of speech. To use speech skills effectively in oral reading is one stage in the speech improvement process. Other forms of speech will be discussed in relationship to development of a pleasing and intelligible speaking voice.

Exercises

1. *Practice of Articulate Speech.* In the following exercises, particular attention should be given to clear-cut articulation of final consonants and the use of vowels, extending earlier more microscopic exercises.

    a. Speak the speech, I pray you, as I pronounced it to you, trippingly on the tongue; but if you mouth it, as many of your players do, I had as lief the town-crier spoke my lines.

Hamlet
William Shakespeare

    b. Studies serve for delight, for ornament, and for ability. Their chief use for delight is in privateness and retiring; for ornament, is in discourse; and for ability, is in the judgment and disposition of business.

Of Studies
Francis Bacon

c. The joys of parents are secret; and so are the griefs and fears. They cannot utter the one; nor they will not utter the other. Children sweeten labors; but they make misfortunes more bitter. They increase the cares of life; but they mitigate the remembrance of death.

Of Parents and Children
Francis Bacon

d. Speak not but what may benefit others or yourself; avoid trifling conversation. Resolve to perform what you ought; perform without fail what you resolve.
Wrong none by doing injuries, or omitting the benefits that are your duty.
Avoid extremes; forbear resenting injuries so much as you think they deserve.

Autobiography
Benjamin Franklin

e.   The wind was a torrent of darkness among the gusty trees,
       The moon was a ghostly galleon tossed upon cloudy seas,

The Highwayman
Alfred Noyes

f. The following selection may be read in unison. Consonants should be stressed.

The Kitchen Clock

Knitting is the maid o' the kitchen, Milly,
Doing nothing sits the chore boy, Billy:
"Seconds reckoned, seconds reckoned,
Sixty in it.
Milly, Billy,
Billy, Milly,
Tick-tock, tock-tick,
Nick-knock, knock-nick,
Knockety-nick, nickety-knock"—
Goes the kitchen clock.

Closer to the fire is rosy Milly,
Every whit as close and cosy, Billy:
"Time's a-flying, worth your trying:
Pretty Milly—
Kiss her, Billy!
Milly, Billy,
Billy, Milly,
Tick-tock, tock-tick,
Now—now, quick-quick!
Knockety-nick, nickety-knock,"—
Goes the kitchen clock.

Something's happened, very red is Milly,
Billy boy is looking very silly;
"Pretty misses, plenty kisses:

Make it twenty, take a plenty.
Billy, Milly,
Milly, Billy,
Right-left, left-right,
That's right, all right,
Knockety-nick, nickety-knock,"—
Goes the kitchen clock.

Weeks gone, still they're sitting, Milly, Billy;
O the winter winds are wondrous chilly!
"Winter weather, close together;
Wouldn't tarry, better marry.
Milly, Billy,
Billy, Milly,
Two-one, one-two,
Don't wait, 'twon't do,
Knockety-nick, nickety-knock,"—
Goes the kitchen clock.

Winters two have gone, and where is Milly?
Spring has come again, and where is Billy?
"Give me credit, for I did it:
Treat me kindly, Mind you wind me.
Mister Billy, Mistress Milly,
My-O, O-my,
By-by, By-by,
Nickety-knock, cradle rock,"—
Goes the kitchen clock.

The Kitchen Clock
John Vance Cheney

g. Read "The Naughty Boy" aloud, practicing clear-cut articulation. This selection may also be used for unison reading. The utter nonsense of this verse makes it great fun to do. It must be done very rapidly, and with earnest mock-seriousness. Diction or articulation should be "crisp."

The Naughty Boy,*
A Song About Myself
(from a letter to Fanny Keats)

ALL: There was a naughty Boy,
                A naughty boy was he,
                He would not stop at home,
                He could not quiet be—
FIRST VOICE: He took
                In his Knapsack
SECOND VOICE: A Book
                Full of vowels;

---

* Only Parts I and IV from this selection by Keats were adapted for choral reading.

THIRD VOICE:	And a shirt With some towels—
FOURTH VOICE:	A slight cap For night cap—
FIFTH VOICE:	A hair brush, Comb ditto,
SIXTH VOICE:	New Stockings, For old ones Would split O!
SEVENTH VOICE:	This Knapsack, Tight at 's back, He rivetted close
ALL:	And follow'd his Nose To the North, To the North, And followed his Nose To the North.
ALL:	There was a naughty boy, And a naughty boy was he. He ran away to Scotland The people for to see— And he found
FIRST VOICE:	That the ground Was as hard
SECOND VOICE:	That a yard Was as long
THIRD VOICE:	That a song Was as merry,
FOURTH VOICE:	That a cherry Was as red—
FIFTH VOICE:	That lead Was as weighty,
SIXTH VOICE:	That fourscore Was as eighty,
SEVENTH VOICE:	That a door Was as wooden
ALL:	As in England. So he stood in his shoes And he wonder'd, He stood in his shoes And he wonder'd.

2. Read one of the following selections, giving particular attention to the articulation of consonants.

a.   Silver*

Slowly, silently, now the moon
Walks the night in her silver shoon;

---

* Walter de la Mare, "Silver." Permission to include granted by The Literary Trustees of Walter de la Mare and The Society of Authors as their representative (London, England).

This way, and that, she peers, and sees
Silver fruit upon silver trees;
One by one the casements catch
Her beams beneath the silvery thatch;
Couched in his kennel, like a log,
With paws of silver sleeps the dog;
From their shadowy cote the white breasts peep
Of doves in a silver-feathered sleep;
A harvest mouse goes scampering by,
With silver claws, and silver eye;
And moveless fish in the water gleam,
By silver reeds in a silver stream.

b.   A Sprig of Rosemary**

I cannot see your face.
When I think of you,
It is your hands which I see.
Your hands
Sewing,
Holding a book,
Resting a moment on the sill of a window.
My eyes keep always the sight of your hands,
But my heart holds the sound of your voice,
And the soft brightness which is your soul.

c.   The Creation*
                    (a Negro Sermon)

And God stepped out on space,
And he looked around and said:
I'm lonely—
I'll make me a world.

And as far as the eye of God could see
Darkness covered everything.
Blacker than a hundred midnights
Down in a cypress swamp.
Then God smiled,
And the light broke,
And the darkness rolled up on one side,
And the light stood shining on the other,
And God said: *That's good!*

Then God reached out and took the light in his hands
And God rolled the light around in his hands
Until he made the sun;

** From Amy Lowell, *The Complete Works of Amy Lowell.* Boston: Houghton Mifflin Company, 1955.

* From *God's Trombones* by James Weldon Johnson. Copyright 1927 by The Viking Press, Inc., renewed 1955 by The Viking Press, Inc. Reprinted by permission of the Viking Press, Inc.

And he set that sun a-blazing in the heavens.
And the light that was left from making the sun
God gathered it up in a shining ball
And flung it against the darkness,
Spangling the night with the moon and stars.
Then down between
The darkness and the light
He hurled the world;
And God said: *That's good!*

Then God himself stepped down—
And the sun was on his right hand,
And the moon was on his left;
The stars were clustered about his head,
And the earth was under his feet.
And God walked, and where he trod
His footsteps hollowed the valleys out
And bulged the mountains up.

Then he stopped and looked and saw
That the earth was hot and barren.
So God stepped over to the edge of the world
And he spat out the seven seas—
He batted his eyes, and the lightnings flashed—
He clapped his hands, and the thunders rolled—
And the waters above the earth came down,
The cooling waters came down.

Then the green grass sprouted,
And the little red flowers blossomed,
The pine-tree pointed his finger to the sky,
And the oak spread out his arms,
The lakes cuddled down in the hollow of the ground,
And the rivers ran down to the sea;
And God smiled again,
And the rainbow appeared,
And curled itself around his shoulder.

Then God raised his arm and he waved his hand
Over the sea and over the land,
And he said: *Bring forth! Bring forth!*
And quicker than God could drop his hand,
Fishes and fowls
And beasts and birds
Swam the rivers and the seas,
Roamed the forests and the woods,
And split the air with their wings.
And God said: *That's good!*

Then God walked around,
And God looked around
On all that he had made.

He looked at his sun,
And he looked at his moon,
And he looked at his little stars:
He looked on his world
With all its living things,
And God said: *I'm lonely still.*

Then God sat down—
On the side of a hill where he could think;
By a deep, wide river he sat down;
With his head in his hands,
God thought and thought,
Till he thought: *I'll make me a man!*

Up from the bed of the river
God scooped the clay;
And by the bank of the river
He kneeled him down;
And there the great God almighty
Who lit the sun and fixed it in the sky,
Who flung the stars to the most far corner of the night,
Who rounded the earth in the middle of his hand;
This Great God,
Like a mammy bending over her baby,
Kneeled down in the dust
Toiling over a lump of clay
Till he shaped it in his own image;

Then into it he blew the breath of life,
And man became a living soul.
Amen. Amen.

d. In the following passage, read with particular attention to nasal resonance and the articulation of the /ŋ/ sound at the ends of words. Experiment with variety of rate and intensity for achieving effectiveness.

Retreating and beating and meeting and sheeting,
Delaying and straying and playing and spraying,
Advancing and prancing and glancing and dancing,
Recoiling, turmoiling and toiling and boiling,
And gleaming and streaming and steaming and beaming,
And rushing, and flushing and brushing and gushing,
And flapping and rapping and clapping and slapping,
And curling and whirling and purling and twirling,
And thumping and plumping and bumping and jumping,
And dashing, and flashing, and splashing and clashing;
And so never ending, but always descending,
Sounds and motions for ever and ever are blending,
All at once and all o'er, with a mighty uproar
And this way the water comes down at Lodore.

The Cataract of Lodore
Robert Southey

3. *Exercises for Practicing Rate of Speaking.* In the following exercises, short phrases are clearly indicated for the most part. You may want to use the symbol (/) for the pause, however, to remind you when to pause. Since a short pause usually seems long to the inexperienced reader, you may need to exaggerate the length of pauses. In practice, experiment with the length of pauses for the best effect, the duration of vowels, and the general rate of speaking the phrase.

    a. He who knows, and knows that he knows,
          He is wise . . . follow him.
       He who knows, and knows not he knows,
          He is asleep . . . awake him.
       He who knows not, and knows not he knows not,
          He is a fool . . . shun him.
       He who knows not, and knows he knows not,
          He is a child . . . teach him.

> *Arabian Proverb*
> Anonymous

    b. Flower in the crannied wall,
       I pluck you out of the crannies,
       I hold you here, root and all, in my hand,
       Little flower . . . but *if* I could understand   [use of pause here
                                          for reinforcement]

       What you are, root and all, and all in all,
       I should know what God and Man is.

> *Flower in the Crannied Wall*
> Alfred Tennyson

    c. I will buy with you, sell with you, talk with you, walk with you, and so following, but I will not eat with you, drink with you, nor pray with you.

> *The Merchant of Venice*
> William Shakespeare

    d. Spend all you have for loveliness,
       Buy it and never count the cost;

> *Barter*
> Sara Teasdale

    e. BRUTUS: Not that I loved Caesar less, but that I loved Rome more. Had you rather Caesar were living and die all slaves than that Caesar were dead, to live all free men? As Caesar loved me, I weep for him; as he was fortunate, I rejoice at it; as he was valiant, I honor him; but, as he was ambitious, I slew him. There is tears for his love; joy for his fortune; honour for his valour; and death for his ambition.

> *Julius Caesar*
> William Shakespeare

f. In this selection, the pauses are not so clearly indicated. How would you mark phrases? Read aloud with integration of breathing with speaking and phrasing.

The Little Girl and the Wolf*

One afternoon a big wolf waited in a dark forest for a little girl to come along carrying a basket of food to her grandmother. Finally a little girl did come along and she was carrying a basket of food. "Are you carrying that basket to your grandmother?" asked the wolf. The little girl said yes, she was. So the wolf asked her where her grandmother lived and the little girl told him and he disappeared into the wood.

When the little girl opened the door of her grandmother's house she saw that there was somebody in bed with a nightgown on. She had approached no nearer than twenty-five feet from the bed when she saw that it was not her grandmother but the wolf, for even in a nightcap a wolf does not look any more like your grandmother than the Metro-Goldwyn lion looks like Calvin Coolidge. So the little girl took an automatic out of her basket and shot the wolf dead.

MORAL: IT IS NOT SO EASY TO FOOL LITTLE GIRLS NOWADAYS AS IT USED TO BE.

g. In "I Was Born An American," observe adequate phrasing, pauses, and appropriate inflection.

I Was Born An American

I was born an American; I live an American; I shall die an American; and I intend to perform the duties incumbent upon me in that character to the end of my career. I mean to do this with absolute disregard of personal consequences. What are the personal consequences? What is the individual man, with all the good or evil that may betide him, in comparison with the good or evil which may befall a great country, and in the midst of great transactions which concern that country's fate? Let the consequences be what they will, I am careless. No man can suffer too much, and no man can fall too soon, if he suffer or if he fall in the defense of the liberties and constitution of his country.

Daniel Webster

h. Read "The Loon" with emphasis on prolonging vowels.

The Loon*

A lonely lake, a lonely shore,
A lone pine leaning on the moon;

> All night the water-beating wings
> Of a solitary loon.
>
> With mournful wail from dusk to dawn
> He gibbered at the taunting stars . . .
> A hermit soul gone raving mad,
> And beating at his bars.

i.   First Bull Fight*

As I watched the bull wheel and start to charge, the horrible thought struck me: this was not a friend of mine pushing a mechanical bull . . . this was a real and vicious wild beast that was charging to kill me. I froze for a fraction of a second. My first reaction was, God, he's going at this cape, so if I clutch it to me he won't see it and then he'll go away and leave me alone! This would have been fatal, of course, as the bull, following the movement of the cape, would have crashed straight into me. My next reaction was, God, he's going at the cape so if I fling it from me he'll attack it and leave me alone! And as I watched the animal bear down on me I thought, Mother help me, this idea of being a bullfighter was complete insanity! Mother!

But so intense had been my training that my natural reactions were nullified . . . like those of a well-trained soldier going into combat for the first time. Instinctively, fighting my impulses, I held the cape out properly for the bull and made myself stand straight and as gracefully as possible, as though Maestro Solis were watching to see if I were keeping my back flat against that fence. Then as the horns came almost to my body I somehow swung the cape in front of the animal's nose and guided him past me, the horns just a foot or so away from my legs.

Later I learned that the crowd yelled "Ole!" but I was too absorbed in what I was doing to hear anything. So it worked! It actually worked the way the Maestro said it would. The bull went by without hitting me!

j. Read the first paragraph of MacArthur's speech* with the slow deliberate rate required for halls of Congress and the dignity of the occasion.

Mr. President, Mr. Speaker, and the distinguished members of the Congress: I stand on this rostrum with a sense of deep humility and great pride. . . . humility in the wake of those great American architects of our history who have stood here before me, pride in the reflection that this home of legislative debate represents human liberty in the purest form yet devised.

---

* From Carlos Arruza with Barnaby Conrad, *My Life as a Matador*. Boston: Houghton Mifflin Company, 1956.

* Address to Congress by Douglas MacArthur, April 19, 1951. Printed in *Vital Speeches of the Day,* May 1, 1951.

k. (a continuation)

I am closing my 52 years of military service. When I joined the Army, even before the turn of the century, it was the fulfillment of all my boyish hopes and dreams. The world has turned over many times since I took the oath at West Point, and the hopes and dreams have all since vanished, but I still remember the refrain of one of the most popular barracks ballads of that day which proclaimed most proudly that old soldiers never die; they just fade away. And like the old soldier of that ballad, I now close my military career and just fade away, an old soldier who tried to do his duty as God gave him the light to see that duty. Goodby.

l. Read the following passage from the Gettysburg Address to an assumed audience of about five hundred people. Where would you place the pauses? Would length of pause vary with size of audience? How is the rate of speaking affected?

Fourscore and seven years ago our fathers brought forth on this continent a new nation conceived in liberty and dedicated to the proposition that all men are created equal.

The Gettysburg Address
Abraham Lincoln

m. Read Madame Chiang Kai-shek's message* as you might to the United States Senate.

Mr. President, members of the Senate of the United States, ladies and gentlemen: I am overwhelmed by the warmth and spontaneity of the welcome of the American people, of whom you are the representatives. I did not know that I was to speak to you today at the Senate except to say, "How do you do? I am so very glad to see you," and to bring greetings of my people to the people of America. However, just before coming here, the Vice President told me that he would like to have me say a few words to you.

I am not a very good extemporaneous speaker; in fact, I am no speaker at all. But I am not so very much discouraged, because a few days ago I was at Hyde Park and went to the President's library. Something I saw there encouraged me and made me feel that perhaps you will not expect overmuch of me in speaking to you extemporaneously.

What do you think I saw there? I saw many things, but the one thing which interested me most of all was that in a glass case there was the first draft of one of the President's speeches, a second draft, and on and on up to the sixth draft. Yesterday I happened to mention this fact to the President, and told him that I was extremely glad that he had to write so many drafts when he is such a well known and acknowledgedly fine speaker. His reply to me was that sometimes he writes twelve drafts of a speech. So my remarks here today being extemporaneous, I am sure you will make allowances for me. . . .

---

* Delivered before the United States Senate, February 13, 1943.

I came to your country as a little girl. I know your people. I have lived with them. I spent the formative years of my life among your people. I speak your language, not only the language of your hearts, but also your tongue. So coming here today I feel that I am also coming home.

4. *Exercises for controlling intensity.* In reading the following selections aloud, try to adjust your intensity to suit the meaning of the selection and the situation in which you speak.

a.

> King: I am the King of all this land:
> I hold a scepter in my hand;
> Upon my head I wear a crown;
> Everybody stands when I sit down.*

b. The Alarm

> Awake, awake! . . .
> Ring the alarum-bell. . . . Murder and treason! . . .
> Banquo and Donalbain! . . . Malcolm! awake!
> Shake off this downy sleep, death's counterfeit,
> And look on death itself! up, up, and see
> The great doom's image! . . . Malcolm! Banquo!
> As from your graves rise up, and walk like sprites,
> To countenance this horror! Ring the bell.

> > *Macbeth*
> > William Shakespeare

c. Use an even attack or steadiness of approach on the following passage:

> Mirage
> The hope I dreamed of was a dream,
> Was but a dream; and now I wake
> Exceeding comfortless, and worn, and old,
> For a dream's sake.
>
> Lie still, lie still, my breaking heart;
> My silent heart, lie still and break;
> Life, and the world, and mine own self, are changed
> For a dream's sake.

> > Christina Rossetti

5. Exercises for the reinforcement of skills in the use of pitch.

a. Read the following passage, using your optimum pitch.

> The Lord is my shepherd; I shall not want.
> He maketh me to lie down in green pastures;
>   he leadeth me beside the still waters.
> He restoreth my soul; he leadeth me in
>   the paths of righteousness for his name's sake.

---

* From *Two Slatterns and a King.* Copyright © 1921, 1949 by Edna St. Vincent Millay.

Yea, though I walk through the valley of the shadow
of death, I will fear no evil; for thou art with me;
Thy rod and thy staff they comfort me.
Thou preparest a table before me in the presence of mine
enemies; thou anointest my head with oil:
my cup runneth over.
Surely goodness and mercy shall follow me all the days
of my life: and I shall dwell in the house of the
Lord forever.

                                                    Psalms 23

b. Read the following selections aloud and listen to the variations of
   pitch. How adequate is your use of pitch?

My heart's in the Highlands, my heart is not here;
My heart's in the Highlands, a-chasing the deer:
A-chasing the wild deer, and following the roe
My heart's in the Highlands, wherever I go!

                                        My Heart's in the
                                        Highlands
                                        Robert Burns

Once upon a midnight dreary, while I pondered weak and weary,
Over many a quaint and curious volume of forgotten lore
While I nodded, nearly napping, suddenly there came a tapping,
As of someone gently rapping, rapping at my chamber door.

                                        The Raven
                                        Edgar Allan Poe

How they tinkle, tinkle, tinkle,
    In the icy air of night!
While the stars that oversprinkle
All the heavens seem to twinkle
    With a crystalline delight;

                                        The Bells
                                        Edgar Allan Poe

And out of the houses the rats came tumbling,
Great rats, small rats, lean rats, brawny rats,
Brown rats, black rats, gray rats, tawny rats,
Grave old plodders, gay young friskers,
Fathers, mothers, uncles, cousins,
Cocking tails and pricking whiskers,
    Families by tens and dozens,
Brothers, sisters, husbands, wives . . .
Followed the Piper for their lives.

                                        The Pied Piper of
                                        Hamelin
                                        Robert Browning

When icicles hang by the wall
And Dick the shepherd blows his nail,
And Tom bears logs into the hall,

And milk comes frozen home in pail;
When blood is nipt, and ways be foul,
Then nightly sings the staring owl
        Tu-whoo!
To-whit, Tu-whoo! A merry note!
While greasy Joan doth keel the pot.

Winter
William Shakespeare

A Madrigal

Crabbed Age and Youth
Cannot live together:
Youth is full of pleasance,
Age is full of care;
Youth like summer morn,
Age like winter weather,
Youth like summer brave,
Age like winter bare:
Youth is full of sport,
Age's breath is short,
Youth is nimble, Age is lame:
Youth is hot and bold,
Age is weak and cold,
Youth is wild, and Age is tame:—
Age, I do abhor thee,
Youth, I do adore thee;
O! my Love, my Love is young!
Age, I do defy thee—
O sweet shepherd, hie thee,
For methinks thou stay'st too long.

William Shakespeare

Blow, Blow, thou winter wind,
Thou art not so unkind
As man's ingratitude;
Thy tooth is not so keen
Because thou art not seen,
Although thy breath be rude.
Heigh ho! sing heigh ho! unto the green holly:
Most friendship is feigning, most loving mere folly:
        Then, heigh ho! the holly!
        This life is more jolly.

Amiens' Song
William Shakespeare

6. Read the passage which follows in two different ways. Explain how slides affect the meaning.

MACBETH: If we fail?

LADY MACBETH: We fail. But, screw your courage to the sticking-
place and we'll not fail.

Macbeth
William Shakespeare

7. Read one of the following paragraphs aloud. What speech skills are useful in portraying meaning of paragraph?

    a.   Then the sky grew black and the air filled with the deep still roar of many wings beating against each other, and upon the land the locusts fell, flying over this field and leaving it whole, and falling upon that field, and eating it as bare as winter. And men sighed and said . . . so Heaven wills, but Wang Lung was furious and he beat the locusts and trampled on them and his men flailed them with their flails and the locusts fell into the fires that were kindled and they floated dead upon the waters of the moats that were dug. And many millions of them died, but to those that were left it was nothing.*

    b.   She was not more than fifteen. Her voice, form, and manner belonged to the period of transition from girlhood. Her face was perfectly oval, her complexion more pale than fair. The nose was faultless; the lips slightly parted, were full and ripe, giving the lines of the mouth warmth, tenderness, and trust; the eyes were blue and large, and shaded by drooping lids and long lashes; and, with harmony with all, a flood of golden hair, in the style permitted to Jewish brides, fell unconfined down to the pillow on which she sat. The throat and neck had the downey softness seen which leaves the artist in doubt whether it is an effect of contour or color. To these charms of features and person were added others more indefinable . . . an air of purity which only the soul can impart, and of abstraction natural to such as think much on things impalpable. Often, with trembling lips, she raised her eyes to heaven, itself not more deeply blue; often she raised her head like one listening eagerly for a calling voice. [This paragraph is a description of Mary as she was going to Bethlehem.]**

    c.   It was a cloudy, misty night and there he saw it! Something white gliding in! He heard the still rustle of its garments. It stood still by his bed; a cold hand touched his; a voice said, "Come"! three times in a low fearful whisper. And while he lay sweating in terror he knew not when or how, the thing was gone.***

    d.   Now I know what makes you so different from other women. It's having that wonderful mother! She . . . she . . . well, she's one woman in a million; I don't have to tell you that! It's something to thank God for, a mother like that! It's something to know her. I've been watching her all day, and I've been wondering what she gets out of it . . . that was what puzzled me; but now, just now, I've found out! This morning, thinking what her life is, I couldn't see what repaid her, do you see? What made

---

* Copyright © 1931, 1949 by Pearl S. Buck; renewed 1958 by Pearl S. Buck. Reprinted from *The Good Earth* by Pearl S. Buck by permission of the John Day Company, Inc., publisher.
   ** Lew Wallace, *Ben Hur.* New York: Harper & Row, Publishers, 1922, p. 35.
   *** Harriet Beecher Stowe, *Uncle Tom's Cabin.* Boston: Houghton-Miflin Company, 1899, pp. 472-473.

up to her for the unending, unending effort, and sacrifice, the pouring out of love and sympathy and help . . . year after year after year. . . .*

8. *Dramatic Selections.* Play reading is an excellent medium for developing proficiency in the use of vocal and articulatory skills. Work for variety in pitch, loudness, and rate.

    a. Read and practice a part in the short conversational passage taken from "The Second Mrs. Tanqueray" by Sir Arthur Wing Pinero.

MISQUITH: Aubrey, it is a pleasant yet dreadful fact to contemplate, but it's nearly fifteen years since I first dined with you. You lodged in Piccadilly in those days, over a hat-shop. Jayne, I met you at that dinner, and Cayley Drummle.

JAYNE: Yes, yes, What a pity it is that Cayley isn't here tonight.

AUBREY: Confound the old gossip! His empty chair has been staring us in the face all through dinner. I ought to have told Morse to take it away.

MISQUITH: Odd, his sending no excuse.

AUBREY: I'll walk round to his lodgings later on and ask after him.

MISQUITH: I'll go with you.

JAYNE: So will I.

AUBREY: (Opening the cigar-cabinet) Doctor, it's useless to tempt you, I know. Frank . . . (Misquith and Aubrey smoke) I particularly wished Cayley Drummle to be one of us to-night. You two fellows and Cayley are my closest, my best friends. . . .

MISQUITH: My dear Aubrey!

JAYNE: I rejoice to hear you say so.

AUBREY: And I wanted to see the three of you round this table. You can't guess the reason.

MISQUITH: You desired to give us a most excellent dinner.

JAYNE: Obviously.

AUBREY: (Hesitatingly) Well . . . I . . . (Glancing at the clock) . . . Cayley won't turn up now.

JAYNE: H'm, hardly.

AUBREY: Then you two shall hear it. Doctor, Frank, this is the last time we are to meet in these rooms.

JAYNE: The last time?

MISQUITH: You're going to leave the Albany?

---

* Kathleen Norris, *Mother.* New York: Grossett and Dunlap, 1916, p. 178.

AUBREY: Yes. You've heard me speak of a house I built in the country years ago, haven't you?

MISQUITH: In Surrey.

AUBREY: Well, when my wife died I cleared out of the house and let it. I think of trying the place again.

MISQUITH: But you'll go raving mad if ever you find yourself down there alone.

AUBREY: Ah, but I shan't be alone, and that's what I wanted to tell you. I'm going to be married.

MISQUITH: Married?

AUBREY: Yes . . . to-morrow.

JAYNE: Tomorrow?

MISQUITH: You take my breath away! My dear fellow, I . . . I . . . of course, I congratulate you.

JAYNE: And . . . and . . . so do I . . . heartily.

AUBREY: Thanks . . . thanks.
(There is a moment or two of embarrassment.)

MISQUITH: Er . . . ah . . . this is an excellent cigar.

JAYNE: Ah . . . um . . . your coffee is remarkable.

b. Read a part in the following passage from *Lady Windermere's Fan* by Oscar Wilde. Observe opportunities for developing variety in inflection, rate, and volume.

PARKER: Is your ladyship at home this afternoon?

LADY W: Yes . . . who has called?

PARKER: Lord Darlington, my lady.

LADY W: (Hesitates for a moment) Show him up—and I'm at home to anyone who calls.

PARKER: Yes, my lady.

LADY W: It's best for me to see him before to-night. I'm glad he's come.
(Enter Parker with Lord Darlington)

PARKER: Lord Darlington.

LORD D: How do you do, Lady Windermere?

LADY W: How do you do, Lord Darlington? No, I can't shake hands with you. My hands are all wet with these roses. Aren't they lovely? They came up from Selby this morning.

LORD D: They are quite perfect.

c. The class may be divided into two sections with each section reading one part of "The Meticulous Customer" by Percival Wilde.* Atten-

---

* Percival Wilde, *Three-Minute Plays*. New York: Greenburg Publisher, 1927.

tion must be given to variety in inflection and precise articulation. If you need to reinforce the use of the /s/ sound, the selection has many of the sounds.

The Meticulous Customer

CHARACTERS: The Customer
The Baker

SCENE: A Bake Shop

THE MASTER OF CEREMONIES (as the curtain rises): The scene is a bake shop on a Monday. This is a Baker. (He indicates the door through which a young man now enters). This is a Customer: a meticulous customer. If you don't know what "meticulous" means just watch him, and you will learn.

THE CUSTOMER (elegantly attired in a walking coat, silk hat, and spats, and carrying a cane and a monocle): My good man.

THE BAKER: Yes, sir?

THE CUSTOMER: Is this a bake shop?

THE BAKER: Yes, sir, It says so on the program.

THE CUSTOMER: Quite so. Quite so. That's why I came in here. (He gazes at the shelves, and his glance returns to the Baker) I wonder—I wonder—if you could make me something very special.

THE BAKER: With great pleasure, sir.

THE CUSTOMER: I want a little bun—about so long and about so wide, and about so high—and I'd like it to be decorated with the letter "S" in white icing.

THE BAKER: (Writing down the order) The letter "S". That will cost . . .

THE CUSTOMER: (Interrupting, and handing him a banknote) It doesn't matter what it costs.

THE BAKER: Yes, sir, Thank you, sir. The bun will be ready tomorrow.

THE CUSTOMER: Good day.

THE BAKER: Good day, sir.

THE MASTER OF CEREMONIES: A day elapses. It is now Tuesday.

THE CUSTOMER: (Re-entering) Ah, good afternoon.

THE BAKER: Good afternoon, sir.

THE CUSTOMER: I gave you an order yesterday . . .

THE BAKER: I remember! A bun with the letter "S".

THE CUSTOMER: Exactly. Is it ready?

THE BAKER: (Producing a bun from the shelf behind him) Here it is, sir.

THE CUSTOMER. Ah! But that won't do at all!

THE BAKER: No, sir?

THE CUSTOMER: The length is right, and the width is right, and the height is right; but the initial "S" is all wrong. You see, I wanted something plain, and chaste, and severe; just a block letter. You've gone to work and given me something much too rococo—oh, much! I believe you call this fancy script?

THE BAKER: Yes, sir.

THE CUSTOMER: Well, it's not what I want.

THE BAKER: (Taking back the bun) I shall have another bun ready at this time tomorrow. (Writing) Block letter "S".

THE CUSTOMER: Yes; block letter. Good day.

THE BAKER: Good day, sir.

THE MASTER OF CEREMONIES: Another day elapses. It is now Wednesday.

THE CUSTOMER: (Re-entering) Ah, good afternoon.

THE BAKER: Good afternoon, sir.

THE CUSTOMER: I gave you an order yesterday——

THE BAKER: I remember! A bun with the letter "S".

THE CUSTOMER: Exactly.

THE BAKER: The block letter "S".

THE CUSTOMER: Quite so. Is it ready?

THE BAKER: (Producing the bun) Here it is, sir.

THE CUSTOMER: Ah!

THE BAKER: Is the length correct? (Customer nods) And the width? And the height? And the block letter "S"?

THE CUSTOMER: Perfect! Plain, chaste, severe: just what I wanted!

THE BAKER: (Taking the bun, and beginning to wrap it up) Thank you, sir. Thank you. We aim to please. And now, sir, where shall I send it?

THE CUSTOMER: Send it? Send it? Send it? Why, don't send it anywhere. I'm going to eat it right here. (He does)

d. Dramatic Speech: Roosevelt on the Radio*

My friends! I am not going to try to be funny tonight, because what I am going to ask you to do is not very funny. But, first, I want to introduce to you two young friends of mine, who can perhaps explain, better than I can, the purpose of this White House Jamboree. Miss Peggy Jones and Mr. Philip Barker.

---

* From the play, "I'd Rather be Right," George S. Kaufman. New York City: Random House, Inc., p. 117-18. The play is a "take-off" on President Roosevelt and family as well as cabinet members.

(whispers) Sing your song. The way you did it for the Cabinet. (they do) My friends, the reason I asked you to listen to that little love song is that those two young folks are in love. And I've made them a promise that I will see them married and happy . . . but alas! my friends, that takes time. More time, I am afraid, than I shall have. And so I am asking the American people, who have always believed in love and marriage, to give time to weld as one these star-crossed lovers, to give me . . . a third term. You've given me two terms . . . give me one more. Think what you get, folks, a balanced budget, some great radio programs, and anything I can think up during my third term. So, be sure to listen in next week at this same hour, to hear Jim and Cordell, Frances and Henry, the Hillbilly Swing Band, and the latest news of Phil and Peggy and my third term.

I am asked to remind you that Lady Esther's Face Powder is on sale at all neighborhood drug stores.

e.   The First Client*

CHARACTERS: The Lawyer
                  The Stenographer
                  The Client

SCENE: His Office

THE MASTER OF CEREMONIES: (As the curtain rises) A young lawyer's office. (He waves his hand) Everything is new—so new that it hurts. The bookcases are new; the law library in them is new; the desk and the inkwell and the swivel chair and the wastebasket and the carpet are new.

Our hero—(He indicates the young man who paces up and down the office)—started in business for himself at nine o'clock this morning. It is now exactly one minute past nine. (He bows and retires)

THE LAWYER: (Interrupts his promenade to strike a legal pose. Then he resumes his peregrinations. The telephone, piled in a corner and wrapped in its wire, attracts his attention. He picks it up, unrolls the wire, and places the instrument in a strategic position on his desk. The end of the wire he tucks into a drawer. He finds a bell push in another corner. He places this, too, on his desk, and striking a pose, pushes the button)

THE STENOGRAPHER: (Entering) Did you ring for me, sir?

    THE LAWYER: (With surprise) The bell push isn't connected yet.

THE STENOGRAPHER: I know it. I was watching through the keyhole. Would you like to dictate a letter?

    THE LAWYER: Would I like to? I'd love to" (She seats herself eagerly, and flips open a notebook). Yes, I'd love to dictate a letter to a client. I'd do it, but for one reason—

---

* Percival Wilde, *Three-Minute Plays*. New York: Greenburg Publisher, 1927.

THE STENOGRAPHER:	That you have no clients?
THE LAWYER:	Exactly. (Their eyes meet. They laugh)
THE STENOGRAPHER:	Maybe there'll be one soon. (A bell rings) What did I say?
THE LAWYER:	It can't be! What, it can't be! The sign on the door isn't dry yet!
THE STENOGRAPHER:	Maybe he hasn't noticed! (She rushes out. She is back in a moment) It's a client!
THE LAWYER:	(Swallowing hard) What does he look like?
THE STENOGRAPHER:	Middle-aged; respectable, prosperous—
THE LAWYER:	A bank-president?
THE STENOGRAPHER:	I shouldn't be surprised.
THE LAWYER:	A capitalist?
THE STENOGRAPHER:	Maybe.
THE LAWYER:	Keep him waiting a few minutes, and then send him in. (Correcting himself) NO: when you hear me strike a match, send him in.
THE STENOGRAPHER:	Yes, sir. (She goes out)
THE LAWYER:	(Yanks half a dozen books out of the cases, opens them and strews them about. He places a box of cigars on the desk, takes one himself. He takes up the telephone. Then he strikes a match)
THE STENOGRAPHER:	This way, sir. (She ushers in an important looking individual, who carries a small satchel and effaces himself. The caller, at a gesture from the lawyer, sits down)
THE LAWYER:	(Over the telephone) Yes: I expect him to compromise for a hundred thousand. It's cheap at that . . . I'm glad you're pleased with me . . . Thank you; thank you. (He steals a glance at the Client's face; it is impassive) Sorry, but I'll be busy all day tomorrow: one conference after another. Make it Thursday? . . . At eleven o'clock? . . . I can give you from eleven to eleven-twenty . . . All right. Good by. (He hangs up, and pushes the cigars toward the Client)
THE CLIENT:	Um. (He takes one)
THE LAWYER:	A light?
THE CLIENT:	Um. (He draws a few whiffs) Good cigar.
THE LAWYER:	Glad you like. Now, what can I do for you?

THE CLIENT: (Rises, and to the Lawyer's astonishment, removes his overcoat, his coat, and his vest. He places his valise on the desk, opens it, and produces a variety of tools. Then he smiles gently) I'm from the telephone company. I was sent here to hook up your instrument.

f. Dialogue from

"The Importance of Being Ernest" by Oscar Wilde
(Enter Lady Bracknell)

LADY BRACKNELL: Mr. Worthing! Rise, sir, from this semi-recumbent posture. It is most indecorous.

GWENDOLEN: Mamma! (He tries to rise, she restrains him) I must beg you to retire. This is no place for you. Besides, Mr. Worthing has not quite finished yet.

LADY BRACKNELL: Finished what, may I ask?

GWENDOLEN: I am engaged to Mr. Worthing, mamma.
(They rise together)

LADY BRACKNELL: Pardon me, you are not engaged to anyone. When you do become engaged to someone, I, or your father, should his health permit him, will inform you of the fact. An engagement should come to a young girl as a surprise, pleasant or unpleasant, as the case may be. It is hardly a matter that she could be allowed to arrange for herself. . . . And now I have a few questions to put to you, Mr. Worthing. While I am making these inquiries, you, Gwendolen will wait for me below in the carriage.

GWENDOLEN: (Reproachfully) Mamma!

LADY BRACKNELL: In the carriage, Gwendolen! (GWENDOLEN goes to the door. She and JACK blow kisses to each other behind LADY BRACKNELL's back. LADY BRACKNELL look vaguely about as if she does not understand what the noise was. Finally turns round) Gwendolen, the carriage!

GWENDOLEN: Yes, mamma.
(Goes out, looking back at JACK)

LADY BRACKNELL: (Sitting down) You can take a seat, Mr. Worthing.
(Looks in her pocket for note-book and pencil)

JACK: Thank you, Lady Bracknell, I prefer standing.

LADY BRACKNELL: (Pencil and note-book in hand) I feel bound to tell you that you are not down on my list of eligible young men, although I have the same list as the dear Duchess of Bolton has. We work together, in fact. However, I am quite ready to enter your name, should your answers be what a really affectionate mother requires. Do you smoke?

JACK: Well, yes, I must admit I smoke.

LADY BRACKNELL: I am glad to hear it. A man should always have an occupation of some kind. There are far too many idle men in London as it is. How old are you?

JACK: Twenty-nine.

LADY BRACKNELL: A very good age to be married at. I have always been of opinion that a man who desires to get married should know either everything or nothing. Which do you know?

JACK: (After some hesitation) I know nothing, Lady Bracknell.

LADY BRACKNELL: I am pleased to hear it. I do not approve of anything that tampers with natural ignorance. Ignorance is like a delicate fruit; touch it and the bloom is gone. The whole theory of modern education is radically unsound. Fortunately in England, at any rate, education produced no effect whatsoever. If it did, it would prove a serious danger to the upper classes, and probably lead to acts of violence in Grosvenor Square. What is your income?

JACK: Between seven and eight thousand a year.

LADY BRACKNELL: (Makes a note in her book) In land, or in investments?

JACK: In investments, chiefly.

LADY BRACKNELL: That is satisfactory. What between the duties expected of one during one's lifetime, and the duties exacted from one after one's death, land has ceased to be either a profit or a pleasure. It gives one position, and prevents one from keeping it up. That's all that can be said about land.

JACK: I have a country house with some land, of course, attached to it, about fifteen hundred acres, I believe; but I don't depend on that for my real income. In fact, as far as I can make out, the poachers are the only people who make anything out of it.

LADY BRACKNELL: A country house! How many bedrooms? Well, that point can be cleared up afterwards.

You have a town house, I hope? A girl with a simple, unspoiled nature, like Gwendolen, could hardly be expected to reside in the country.

JACK: Well, I own a house in Belgrave Square, but it is let by the year to Lady Bloxham. Of course, I can get it back whenever I like, at six months' notice.

LADY BRACKNELL: Lady Bloxham? I don't know her.

JACK: Oh, she goes about very little. She is a lady considerably advanced in years.

LADY BRACKNELL: Ah, now-a-days there is no guarantee of respectability of character. What number in Belgrave Square?

JACK: 149

LADY BRACKNELL: (Shaking her head) The unfashionable side. I thought there was something. However, that could easily be altered.

JACK: Do you mean the fashion, or the side?

LADY BRACKNELL: (Sternly) Both, if necessary, I presume. What are your politics?

JACK: Well, I am afraid I really have none. I am a Liberal Unionist.

LADY BRACKNELL: Oh, they count as Tories. They dine with us. Or come in the evening, at any rate. Now to minor matters. Are your parents living?

JACK: I have lost both my parents.

LADY BRACKNELL: Both? That seems like carelessness. Who was your father? He was evidently a man of some wealth. Was he born in what the Radical papers call the purple of commerce, or did he rise from the ranks of the aristocracy?

JACK: I am afraid I really don't know. The fact is, Lady Bracknell, I said I had lost my parents. It would be nearer the truth to say that my parents seem to have lost me. . . . I don't actually know who I am by birth. I was . . . well, I was found.

LADY BRACKNELL: Found!

JACK: The late Mr. Thomas Cardew, an old gentleman of a very charitable and kindly disposition, found me, and gave me the name Worthing, because he happened to have a first-class ticket for Worthing in his pocket at the time. Worthing is a place in Sussex. It is a seaside resort.

LADY BRACKNELL: Where did the charitable gentleman who had a first-class ticket for this seaside resort find you?

JACK: (Gravely) In a hand-bag.

LADY BRACKNELL: A hand-bag?

JACK: (Very seriously) Yes, Lady Bracknell. I was in a hand-bag—a somewhat large, black leather hand-bag, with handles to it—an ordinary hand-bag in fact.

LADY BRACKNELL: In what locality did this Mr. James, or Thomas, Cardew come across this ordinary hand-bag?

JACK: In the cloack-room at Victoria Station. It was given to him in mistake for his own.

LADY BRACKNELL: The cloak-room at Victoria Station?

JACK: The Brighton Line.

LADY BRACKNELL: The line is immaterial. Mr. Worthing, I confess I feel somewhat bewildered by what you have just told me. To be born, or at any rate bred, in a hand-bag, whether it had handles or not, seems to me to display a contempt for the ordinary decencies of family life that remind one of the worst excesses of the French Revolution. And I presume you know what that unfortunate movement led to? As for the particular locality in which the hand-bag was found, a cloak-room at a railway station might serve to conceal a social indiscretion—has probably, indeed, been used for that purpose before now—but it could hardly be regarded as an assured basis for a recognized position in good society.

JACK: May I ask you then what you would advise me to do? I need hardly say I would do anything in the world to ensure Gwendolen's happiness.

LADY BRACKNELL: I would strongly advise you, Mr. Worthing, to try and acquire some relations as soon as possible, and to make a definite effort to produce at any rate one parent, of either sex, before the season is quite over.

JACK: Well, I don't see how I could possibly manage to do that. I can produce the hand-bag at any moment. It is in my dressing-room at home. I really think that should satisfy you, Lady Bracknell.

LADY BRACKNELL: Me, sir! What has it to do wth me? You can hardly imagine that I and Lord Bracknell would dream of allowing our only daughter— a girl brought up with utmost care—to marry into a cloak-room, and form an alliance with a parcel? Good morning, Mr. Worthing! (LADY BRACKNELL sweeps out in majestic indignation)

9. Read aloud one or more of the following selections. Make an effort to demonstrate the use of stress and flexibility of pitch, rate, and intensity.

a. The Rebellious Vine

One day, the vine
That Clomb on God's own house
Cried, "I will not *grow,*"
And, "I will *not* grow,"
And, "I *will* not grow,"
And, "*I* will not grow."
So God leaned out his head,
And said:
"You need not." Then the vine
Fluttered its leaves, and cried to all the winds:
"Oh, have I not permission from the Lord?
And may I not begin to cease to grow?"
But that wise God had pondered on the vine
Before he made it.
And, all the while it labored *not* to grow,
It grew; it grew;
And all the time God knew.

Harold Monro

b. Ulysses

. . . Come, my friends,
Tis not too late to seek a newer world.
Push off, and sitting well in order smite
The sounding furrows; for my purpose holds
To sail beyond the sunset, and the baths
Of all the western stars, until I die.
It may be that the gulfs will wash us down:
It may be we shall touch the Happy Isles,
And see the great Achilles, whom we knew.
Tho' much is taken, much abides; and tho'
We are not now that strength which in old days
Moved earth and heaven; that which we are, we are;
One equal temper of heroic hearts,
Made weak by time and fate, but strong in will
To strive, to seek, to find, and not to yield.

Alfred Tennyson

c. PHIL: (Calling softly) Alice. Alice. Bob is walking in his sleep.

ALICE: Oh, Phil, wake him before he gets hurt.

PHIL: I don't want to startle him. Bob (softly) Bob. Bob. Bob (increasingly loud). He won't awaken.

ALICE: You *must* make him hear.

PHIL: (Quite softly) Bob. Bob. He's turning around. He's coming back.

ALICE: (Softly) He's still asleep. Maybe we can get him to bed without waking him.

> Taken from *Foundations of Speech*
> (edited by O'Neill, p. 221)

d.   God's World*

O world, I cannot hold thee close enough!
> Thy winds, thy wide grey skies!
> Thy mists that roll and rise!
Thy woods, this autumn day, that ache and sag
And all but cry with colour! That gaunt crag
To crush! To lift the lean of that black bluff!
World, World, I cannot get thee close enough!

Long have I known a glory in it all,
> But never knew I this:
> Here such a passion is
As stretcheth me apart. Lord, I do fear
Thou'st made the world too beautiful this year.
My soul is all but out of me, . . . let fall
No burning leaf; prithee, let no bird call.

e. In the oral reading of the passage from *The Tell-Tale Heart,* observe variety of rate and intensity particularly. Remember to maintain breath control through adequate pauses.

The officers were satisfied. My *manner* had convinced them. I was singularly at ease. They sat, and while I answered cheerily, they chatted of familiar things. But, ere long, I felt myself getting pale and wished them gone. My head ached, and I fancied a ringing in my ears: but still they sat and still chatted. The ringing became more distinct:—it continued and became more distinct: I talked more freely to get rid of the feeling: but it continued and gained definitiveness—until, at length, I found that the noise was *not* within my ears.

No doubt I now grew *very* pale;—but I talked more fluently, and with a heightened voice. Yet the sound increased—and what could I do? It was a *low, dull, quick sound—much such a sound as a watch makes when enveloped in cotton.* I gasped for breath—and yet the officers heard it not. I talked more quickly—more vehe-

---

mently; but the noise steadily increased. I arose and argued about trifles, in a high key and with violent gesticulations; but the noise steadily increased. Why *would* they not be gone? I paced the floor to and fro with heavy strides, as if excited to fury by the observation of the men—but the noise steadily increased. Oh God! what *could* I do? I foamed—I raved—I swore! I swung the chair upon which I had been sitting, and grated it upon the boards, but the noise arose over all and continually increased. It grew louder—louder—*louder!* And still the men chatted pleasantly, and smiled. Was it possible they heard not? Almighty God!—no, no! They heard!—they suspected!—they *knew!*—they were making a mockery of my horror!—this I thought, and this I think. But anything was better than this agony! Anything was more tolerable than this derision! I could bear those hypocritical smiles no longer! I felt that I must scream or die! and now—again!—hard! louder! louder! louder! *louder!*

"Villains!" I shrieked, "dissemble no more! I admit the deed! —Tear up the planks! here! here!—It is the beating of his hideous heart!"

Edgar Allan Poe

f. The passage from *Acres of Diamonds** provides material suitable for experimenting with flexibility of the various attributes of voice. The following paragraphs represent a conversational style of speaking. Try to make your speaking effective as you read the selection aloud through the use of short phrases, flexibility, and variety in pitch, loudness, and rate. Make your speech intelligible for a class of twenty-five.

But your wealth is too near. I was speaking in New Britain, Connecticut, on this very subject. There sat five or six rows from me a lady. I noticed the lady at the time, from the color of her bonnet. I said to them, what I say to you now, "Your wealth is too near to you! You are looking right over it". She went home after the lecture and tried to take off her collar. The button stuck in the buttonhole. She twisted and tugged and pulled and finally broke it out of the buttonhole and threw it away. She said: "I wonder why they don't make decent collar buttons?"

Her husband said to her: "After what Conwell said tonight, why don't you get up a collar button yourself? Did he not say that if you need anything other people need it; so if you need a collar button there are millions of people needing it. Get up a collar button and get rich. 'Wherever there is a need there is a fortune' ".

Then she made up her mind to do it; and when a woman makes up her mind, and doesn't say anything about it, she does it! And she invented this "snap button", a kind of button that snaps together from two pieces, through the buttonhole. That very woman

---

* Russell H. Conwell, *Acres of Diamonds.* John C. Winston Co.

can now go over the sea every summer in her own yacht and take her husband with her. And if he were dead she would have enough money left to buy a foreign count or duke, or some such thing. . . .

g.   Speech in the Convention of Delegates, March 23, 1775

. . . Gentlemen may cry, peace, peace, . . . but there is no peace. The war is actually begun! The next gale that sweeps from the north will bring to our ears the clash of resounding arms! Our brethren are already in the field! Why stand we here idle! What is it that gentlemen wish? What would they have? Is life so dear, or peace so sweet, as to be purchased at the price of chains and slavery? Forbid it, Almighty God! I know not what course others may take; but as for me, give me liberty, or give me death!

Patrick Henry

h.   Read "Enoch's Secret" for practicing variety in rate, loudness, and pitch. You should read the entire poem, "Enoch Arden" by Tennyson, in order to understand the meaning of this passage.

Enoch's Secret

He called aloud for Miriam Lane, and said,
"Woman, I have a secret—only swear,
Before I tell you—swear upon the book,
Not to reveal it till you see me dead."
"Dead" clamor'd the good woman; "hear him talk!
I warrant, man, that we shall bring you round."
"Swear," added Enoch, sternly, "on the book".
And on the book, half-frighted, Miriam swore.
Then Enoch, rolling his gray eyes upon her,
"Did you know Enoch Arden, of this town?"
"Know him?" she said; "I knew him far away.
Ay, ay, I mind him coming down the street;
Held his head high, and cared for no man, he."

Alfred Tennyson

i.   Read aloud "The Terrestrial Globe." Others may join you on the "roll on" refrains. Prolong vowels. Observe variety in rate, pitch, and intensity.

To the Terrestrial Globe
(by a Miserable Wretch)

Roll on, thou ball, roll on!
Through pathless realms of Space
     Roll on!
What though I'm a sorry case?
What though I cannot meet my bills?
What though I suffer toothache's ills?
What though I swallow countless pills?
     Never you mind!
          Roll on!
Roll on, thou ball, roll on!
Through seas of inky air

Roll on!
It's true I've got no shirts to wear;
It's true my butcher's bill is due;
It's true my prospects all look blue—
But don't let that unsettle you!
Never <u>you</u> mind!
Roll on!
(It rolls on.)

W. S. Gilbert

10. Select one of the following exercises.

a. Read an anecdote to the class. Make an attempt to use eye contact and to interest the audience. Practice telling the story several times before class, experimenting with variety in pitch, intensity, rate, and quality.

b. Present excerpts from several types of reading materials which might be used in daily life. Explain when each is used. Is any type easier to read than others? Why?

c. Present orally several illustrations of materials which you have collected in your notebook. Why did you make the selection? Tell how each would be useful in practicing the use of specific speech skills which you need to practice.

d. Read a selection which you like. In the introduction preceding the reading, comment upon the author and what you think he means by the passage. Allow three minutes for complete performance.

e. Present some child's story to the class. Condense the story to three minutes or less. Tell the story in your own words. Work for variety in pitch, intensity, and rate. Observe whether your audience is interested.

References

Armstrong, Chloe, and Paul D. Brandes, *The Oral Interpretation of Literature.* New York, McGraw-Hill Book Company, 1963.

Brooks, Keith, Eugene Bahn, and L. Lamont Okey, *The Communicative Act of Oral Interpretation.* Boston: Allyn & Bacon, Inc., 1967.

Lee, Charlotte I., *Oral Interpretation,* 3rd ed. Boston: Houghton Mifflin Company, 1965

Parrish, Wayland Maxfield, *Reading Aloud,* 4th ed. New York: The Ronald Press Company, 1966.

Sarett, Alma Johnson, Lew Sarett, and William T. Foster, *Basic Principles of Speech,* 4th ed. Boston: Houghton Mifflin Company, 1966.

13

Stabilizing and Integrating Speech Skills in Speaking Situations

In the preceding chapter, you studied and practiced the use of speech skills in oral reading. You are now ready to consider the application of your new skills to various types of controlled or spontaneous speaking. Such speaking events are illustrated by such activities as structured conversations, role playing, informal and formal conversations, and platform speaking. The more spontaneous speech is, the less you are able to think about the application of your new skills. So in the beginning, you will need to start with structured or practiced speech activities and gradually increase the difficulty until you are able to apply your speech skills somewhat automatically. The final step in the total process is the ability to speak spontaneously using your speech skills effectively.

CONVERSATIONAL SITUATIONS

Conversational situations are either controlled or spontaneous. The controlled or structured type of conversation is better for the initial practice of speech techniques than conversation which is spontaneous. Spontaneous speaking requires the ability to apply speech skills quickly and with little thought. In other words, informal or spontaneous conversational situations should be practiced after you have mastered the application of speech skills in oral reading or structured situations.

Structured Conversations

Conversation is the "informal interchange of thoughts by spoken words" or "social intercourse." By its nature, conversation implies two or more people. Intimate acquaintances may not require the same precision of enunciation that strangers need for understanding. Social conversation at a formal gathering may involve the use of more careful speech than that used by close friends drinking coffee in the living room.

The most common types of conversations are those involving greetings and leave-takings. Such conversations could be structured for practice during the initial stages of application of speech skills to speaking. For example, a common interchange of greeting might be, "Hello there. How are you?" The response may be "Fine, thank you." In this exchange of greetings, you could practice any new speech skill which needs reinforcing. A somewhat more complex structured conversation might appear as follows:

Q. "Won't you have lunch with me today?"
R. "Why yes, where shall we meet?"
Q. "The Union at 12:00."
R. "I'll be there."

Additional short structured conversations are represented in role playing. For the purposes of this chapter, role playing shall refer to situations in the personal life of the individual which are acted out and discussed. Psychologists use the method to assist individuals in understanding themselves. The person assumes a role, either as himself in a certain situation or as someone else. He plays the character, speaks as he feels the person would talk, and acts the role as he thinks the person would act.

Although the major purpose of the role playing in a voice and diction class is to provide a medium for the practice of speech skills in a somewhat structured situation, a very important function of role playing may be to furnish outlets for you to express your fears relative to speech. In the beginning, therefore, playing of roles may be designed as a mental hygiene exercise. Two or three students, for example, may discuss or enact a speaking activity which affected one of the members unfavorably. This conversation, followed by discussion, is expected to lead to the improvement of attitudes toward speaking.

A simple activity might be the ordering of a meal in a restaurant. One student plays the waitress and another plays the customer. Some discussion precedes the role playing in order that the conversation to be practiced is structured so that optimum gains may be made in the practice of speech skills. It may even be desirable to write out the anticipated speeches so that major attention may be given to the practice of speech. As you gain ability in the application of specific skills, you may try creating the role more spontaneously.

A more elaborate type of role playing than the imagined conversations is the dramatization of short scenes. Again, it is wise to plan rather carefully ahead of time the words which will be used so you may direct your attention to the application of speech skills. Imagine, for example, that you want to play a scene concerned with eating breakfast. What are some of the words you might use? Many of these words, such as *egg*, *toast*, *syrup*, *pass*, would give you an opportunity to improve your pronunciation of vowels. The choice of certain phrases may also provide means for using intelligible connected speech which is devoid of substandard patterns. In role playing, much opportunity for developing flexible vocal qualities will be provided. Doing the same exercise over several times in different ways will help you to use your speech most effectively.

Informal Conversational Situations

After sufficient practice of the structured type of conversation, you are ready for the informal type of discussion. Conversations and discussions in informal situations are not too different. Only two or three persons are usually involved in a conversation. Topics are not organized and several subjects may be discussed in a short period. A "good" conversationalist will also be a "good" listener, giving others a chance to talk. Asking questions or observing ideas in the speech of others will add to the speaker's material for conversation. Talking briefly, and not too often, is always desirable in conversations involving more than a few people. Although an opinion often is necessary for interesting talking, the use of "to me, ..." and "according to my point of view. . . . ," is recommended as a means of avoiding argument.

Some of the following topics will provide ideas for conversational practice: hobbies, social standards, television programs, working while in college, and "my home town." As a member of a conversational team, you may spend a few minutes thinking about your contribution, so that you can apply the techniques of speech which you have been practicing. These conversational exercises may be very short. As the listening member of the class, you may observe if the speakers are successfully applying the skills and techniques which they have studied.

INFORMAL DISCUSSION

Discussion is problem-solving conversation. There is a purpose to discussion, whereas conversation occurs spontaneously according to the ideas of the persons involved. Informal discussion is not as formally prepared as is the type which utilizes the panel, debate, or lecture as presentations of ideas. An informal discussion may take place in committees or parent-teacher groups. The committee may be concerned, for example, about the ethical practices of its members. Consequently, the purpose of the discussion revolves around one topic: ethical practices. In the case of parent education meetings, the discussion might be concerned with speech development.

In preparation for informal discussion, the leader may (a) define the problem, (b) outline the various phases of the problem, (c) predict the possible solutions, (d) make suggestions, and (e) summarize the problem and its solutions. At the meeting, the leader's major problem is to encourage people to contribute ideas to the solution of the problem. The leader presents the issues involved and the value of the topic to the members of the group. During the discussion, the leader needs to keep the discussion related to the topic, resolve differences of opinion, and encourage all members to participate.

As methods for opening the discussion, the leader may use one of the following methods: (a) review a case history, (b) use a question as presentation of the problem to solve, (c) review a book or article which applies to the problem, (d) use a film related to the topic, or (e) give a talk presenting the issues.

PUBLIC DISCUSSION

Public discussion refers to the cooperative deliberation for the solving or understanding of problems by two groups: the audience and the source of stimulation (panel, debate). Public discussion is much more formal than is the face-to-face type of discussion described earlier in this chapter. The use of public discussion as a means of applying speech skills may be easier for you than the use of the informal conversational type of discussion. As has been stated previously, you need to make thorough preparation before speech skills can be applied without thought. Consequently, the use of the prepared or written and well practiced speeches in the panel, debate, or dialogue may have advantages for you.

Types of Public Discussion

For the purposes of utilizing public discussion as an opportunity for the practice of articulation and voice, the following types will be described: (a) the symposium, (b) the panel, (c) the dialogue, (d) the lecture-form, and (e) the debate.

The Symposium. The public-speaking approach is used by the three to five persons who present various aspects of the problem. Each participant may present a viewpoint or each may give a certain phase of the subject. The topics, for instance, might be as follows: definition of terms and problems, analysis of subject, and possible solutions.

Following the formal presentations, some questions and answers from members of the symposium may take place. Although the major part of the talk may be prepared ahead of time, the participant must be able to speak extemporaneously in order to fit his remarks into the discussion of the other members on the panel as well as to contribute during audience discussion. As in other forms of public discussion, the symposium is usually followed by audience participation. The moderator or leader of the symposium will serve as chairman of the meeting.

The Panel. The panel is similar to the symposium, except for the use of a conversational approach instead of the public-speaking method in the presentation of ideas of the panel members. The four to six members hold a conversation for the benefit of an audience. The main function of the panel is to present the various phases of the topic. After some definite pattern for discussion of ideas has been established by the panel, the audience is encouraged to participate.

The Dialogue. The dialogue refers to a discussion between two persons for the benefit of an audience. One person asks questions; the other one answers. Again, the main function is to present the principal issues of the problem. The audience usually participates when the questioner who also serves as leader feels the topic has been "aired" enough.

Lecture-Forum. A public speech, defining and interpreting the problem is presented. The lecture is the basis for discussion by members of the audience. The speech may be organized according to the five steps already suggested above: (a) definition, (b) analysis, (c) possible solutions, (d) comparison of solutions, and (e) activation of solutions.

Debate. The debate is a formal means of presenting two sides of a controversial issue. Two speakers for the affirmative and two speakers for the negative usually present one main speech and one rebuttal. A suitable topic for debate might be "Woman's place is in the home." Other topics are presented in the exercises at the end of the chapter. One, two, or three members talk *for* and an equal number talk *against* the topic.

The prepared speeches provide the voice and diction student an opportunity to use certain skills which he wants to practice.

Aims of Discussion

In all forms of discussion, the major aims are to develop understanding of the problem and to choose appropriate forms of solution.

Techniques of Discussion

Need for Preparation. Panel participants need to study the topic under discussion. With the aid of the leader, a plan is made. Each speaker will study a certain phase of the problem. Some research may be necessary.

In the preparation for a discussion, the following steps may be taken: (a) make an agenda or outline, (b) assign topics to panel members, (c) gather material and information to verify points of view, (d) observe activities concerned with the problem when necessary, and (e) organize information for presentation to the group.

Responsibilities of Chairman. The chairman is a professional guide of a discussion and does not usually become involved in it. In some cases, however, the leader is also the resource person. When this is true, the factual data may be given in an introductory discussion. Then, the speaker shifts his role to that of the leader of the discussion.

The chairman of a discussion will (a) state the problem clearly, (b) introduce the speakers and their topics, (c) guide the discussion, and (d) summarize at appropriate points. In his preliminary introduction, the leader may present the problem, the facts out of which the problem arises, and the objectives of the discussion. Each speaker is selected with the idea of presenting various points of view or phases of the problem. The speaker's name, activity, and subject will be stated by the chairman. Transitional comments may also be needed by the chairman as each speaker of a panel and symposium speaks.

After the panel members are through speaking, the leader assumes major responsibility of guiding the discussion. In order to avoid some confusion, the following four-step outline of procedures may be followed:

1. Exploring the problem; find out various points of view.
2. Evaluating the situation:
   a. Points of agreement
   b. Points of disagreement.
3. Discussion of disagreement; disagreeing members asked to give reasons.

4. Summarizing conclusions:
   a. What is problem?
   b. What are facts?
   c. What are objectives of discussion?
   d. What progress made on points of disagrement?

The recorder makes an outline of the main points of the discussion, including detailed notes. He may be called upon by the discussion leader to summarize at appropriate times throughout the meeting.

Responsibilities of Panel Members. Each member of the panel, symposium, debate, or dialogue speaks according to rules of designated procedure by the chairman. A "good" panel member speaks to the point and concisely. As audience participation increases the panel member decreases his amount of speaking.

Responsibilities of Members of Audience. Each member in the discussion group is encouraged to participate. No one member should monopolize the discussion. A knowledge of one's own weaknesses or prejudices will aid in understanding a problem. Coöperation with others in a discussion group is needed if solutions are to be attained.

PUBLIC SPEAKING

Speaking from a platform is not too different from speaking in a formal discussion. Speech used in platform speaking is really a one-sided conversation. The techniques used in speaking will vary according to the formality of the situation, the size of the room, the composition of the audience, the physical attributes of the situation, and the purpose of the speech.

Application of Speech Skills

Platform speech usually requires a slower tempo; more precise articulation; greater variety in pitch, loudness, timbre, and rate; and more volume than ordinarily used in discussion or conversational speech. In some respects, the application of speech skills to platform speech is easier than to informal spontaneous speech forms. Except for impromptu speaking, platform speaking is usually well planned and rehearsed before presentation. Such preliminary preparation provides an opportunity for the student to think about the application of one or more of the speech skills he needs to practice.

In public speaking, you may obtain practice in developing flexibility of pitch, loudness, rate, and quality. In practicing passages or speeches for flexibility of pitch levels, you should not hesitate to experiment with the use of your voice. This was termed "voice stretching" in earlier chapters. In adding emphasis to certain words, greater intensity is used than on other words. Pausing before an important word will also help to emphasize a thought. A change in pitch for a word or phrase will serve to bring out an idea or mood. Inflection of the voice through various pitch changes or glides will add interest to the speaking voice as well as help to convey the meaning of the speaker. The use of various rates will also affect the meaning and moods of the speaker. As you experiment with platform speaking, you will also want to try using various vocal qualities to convey your meanings. Flexibility in pitch, loudness, rate, and quality will occur as the result of much experience and practice in the use of the voice.

Voice and diction in platform speaking involve the effective use of loudness, phrasing, emphasis, and articulation of sounds. The speaker must be able to use consciously the desirable attributes of voice while addressing an audience from the platform. The speaker's voice should be flexible and adjustable according to the changes in content of the subject matter of the speech. Voice and articulation also should be adjustable to the situation.

Loudness will vary according to the size and the acoustics of the room. In large rooms, the speaker needs to increase his intensity without straining his voice. Ordinarily, a good rule is to try to speak so the people in the back rows can hear. As an exercise in adjusting to the various types of rooms, you may give the same speech in different situations. First of all, you might pretend to speak to only six or seven people in a small sitting room at home; the next room may be the regular speech classroom with the students sitting in the back of the room; and last, the room may be a small theatre which seats about five hundred people. You may imagine you are talking in these situations as you practice your speech. Any of the exercises at the end of this chapter may be used in this manner.

Although loudness may be adequate to be heard by the people in the last rows, the intelligibility of spech may be inadequate. Merely speaking louder does not guarantee intelligibility. An important part of understandability is the clear-cut articulation of consonants. In large audiences, the speaker must exaggerate the articulation, particularly, of the voiceless consonants such as /p, t, k/. Consonants in final positions of words also need special attention. Prolonging vowels will add "carrying" power to the voice in a large room.

Adequate phrasing is important for the understandability of the speaker. Platform speaking provides an excellent opportunity for the student of voice and diction to practice speaking in short phrases. The larger the room, the shorter the phrases and longer the pauses between phrases. Closely related to understandability is the rate of speaking. Too rapid speech may decrease intelligibility. There is no set rule for rate of speaking, however, as some very intelligible speakers speak quite rapidly, for example, in radio and television programs.

The purpose of this discussion is to present platform speaking as a means of providing an opportunity for the improvement of voice and diction. Only the necessary fundamentals of public speaking will be presented. The discussion will be developed under these major headings: types of speeches, approach to the speech situation, and mechanics of speech preparation.

Types of Speeches

You will have a choice of several types of platform speaking: written speeches, extemporaneous speeches, and impromptu speeches. You will want to practice your speech skills in these types of speeches in the same order as indicated above.

Written speeches. The first materials used in platform speaking should probably be speeches which have been written. These written speeches are of two types: those prepared by others and those prepared by you. In studying the written speeches of others for oral presentation, you will use many of the same techniques discussed in Chapter 12 on oral reading. Your first original speeches may be written and practiced as oral readings. Such a procedure allows for an easy transition to the more difficult types of speaking, extemporaneous and impromptu.

Extemporaneous Speeches. As soon as you have mastered the use of specific speech skills in the written type of speech, you are ready to apply the skills to extemporaneous speaking. Speaking extemporaneously involves enough preparation to allow you an opportunity to reinforce the speech skills which you are learning. Through the use of an outline, you will practice the speech several times. If possible, record your speech on a tape recorder. As you replay, you can evaluate how the skills have been applied. Each time you rehearse the speech, your speaking will probably improve. No attempt is to be made to memorize any set wording of the speech.

Impromptu Speaking. Impromptu speeches are ones which are given on the spur of the moment, without any preparation. You may try impromptu speaking after you have improved your speech with other types of speaking. Quotations, riddles, epigrams, and popular topics are useful in suggesting subjects for impromptu speaking.

Members of your class might make the list for the impromptu speeches. Each member may write down at least one topic which he thinks would be suitable for a one-minute speech. These slips of paper are then collected and placed on the desk at the front of the room. You draw two slips, decide which one you want, and return the other one to the desk. Each member of the class will draw a slip in a similar manner. Preparation of the talk is limited to the time required for picking up the slip with the topic. Your only preliminary direction may be to suggest that you try to apply at least one of the skills which you have practiced in class. To remember to use one's skills, such as proper phrasing for instance, would be enough to remember during your first experience in impromptu speaking. Until you have mastered the speech skills, some preparation is necessary in order to apply the techniques successfully.

Approach to the Speaking Situation

Some attention has already been given to the mental attitude of the speaker in earlier chapters. Special consideration to fear as related to public speaking is needed, however, since so many students appear more frightened to appear in front of a group than to appear as members of discussion or role-playing groups. A gradual introduction to the platform speaking situation may be made through the use of discussion and role-playing situations. As you become acquainted with other members of the group, you will lose much of your fear of speaking before them. Going from informal to formal discussion situations is a step toward helping you to feel at home on the platform.

Thinking of public speaking as a one-sided conversation will also help to alleviate fear. Looking directly at the individuals in the class with the purpose of sharing ideas with them is an aid in overcoming any feelings of inadequacy and fear. In formal audiences outside the classroom, the speaker may pick out a few friendly faces in the audience.

Speaking from a platform is a normal activity and speech should be used in a conversational way. This is one time that the speaker has a chance to do all the talking. His main objective will be to make his audience hear and understand his ideas. If the attention is placed upon the ideas which are to be expressed rather than upon "what the listeners will think of me," much of the stage fright of public speaking will be eliminated.

Being well prepared is a *must* if you expect to reduce your fear. Although your speech may be short, sufficient preparation needs to be made so that your mental attitude is favorable for the most efficient practice of speech skills. A positive point of view, having faith in the ability to speak well, is also necessary for developing confidence in the speech situation.

Some bodily activity before speaking is always helpful in removing any mounting tensions which often occur at the thoughts of speaking before a class. If fear is a great factor, the first speeches should involve subject matter which requires some bodily activity.

It is not unusual for the most experienced speakers to feel some fear before the speech is given. For even the most experienced speaker, fear is expressed through various bodily sensations, such as dry mouth or moist hands. This fear usually gradually diminishes as the speaker becomes involved in the speaking. His ideas supersede his fear of speaking. With experience in speaking, symptoms of extreme fear of speaking will decrease

Mechanics of Speech Preparation

The preparation involved in speech making will depend upon the purpose and form of the speech given. For the student interested in the improvement of his vocal and articulatory skills, attention to these skills is of primary importance in the practice of speeches.

Choosing a Topic. In choosing a topic for your speech, you may consider such purposes as the following: What do I want to accomplish? What skills do I want to practice? Do I want to inform, impress, entertain, or actuate? The simple informational speech may be the easiest type of speech for the beginning speaker. The speech, however, which serves to move the audience to action will indirectly stimulate the speaker to use his speech more effectively. The speech designed to impress the audience is also an excellent medium for stimulating the best use of vocal attributes. In the speech for entertainment, an opportunity is usually provided for variety in rate, intensity, and pitch. Ideas for subjects are often suggested from articles which appear in magazines, such as the *Atlantic Monthly, Harpers,* or *Reader's Digest.* Quotations are also sources for short speeches.

Outlining the Speech. In the short speech, the outline will have an introduction, two parts in the main body of the speech, and a conclusion. The introduction is designed to arouse interest and to state the purpose of the speech. The conclusion provides an opportunity for summary or reinforcement of the two main points. A quotation or short story is often utilized at the end of a speech.

Style of the Speech.   Simple language with short words and sentences is preferable to complex sentence structure. As much as possible, the words should be concrete, specific, and pictorial. Short words instead of long words will add to the communicative effectiveness of your speech. For example, you might use "gifts" instead of "donations," or "begin" for inaugurate," or "try" for "endeavor."

SUMMARY

In this chapter, various types of speaking situations have been discussed: structured conversations, role playing, informal and formal discussions, and informal and formal public speaking. These activities were presented for the purpose of providing procedures for the transfer of speech skills to meaningful and useful situations.

At first, you are advised to use fairly well controlled speech activities, such as structured conversations and role playing. Informal conversational situations follow those which are controlled. As skill is developed in speaking, the effective use of speech may take place somewhat automatically. A gradual progression, however, must occur from the use of structured speaking to the spontaneous type in order for the student to learn how to apply his skills. Exercises are included for the logical development of practice.

Exercises

1. In the following exercises, two persons may assume the roles in each of the structured conversations. Observe how speech skills are applied.

   a. I'm going down town, won't you come along?
      Yes, I believe I will.
      Good, get your coat.
      O.K.

   b. I'm going bowling tonight, why don't you come too?
      Sorry, but I can't tonight.
      Too bad, another time.

   c. Let's go out and have a cigarette.
      Can't now, I have a class.

   d. Betty, would you like to go to the dance Friday?
      Yes, I'd like to very much.

Fine, I'll see you about 8:30.
Thanks for calling.

e. Peggy, I'm sorry but I can't keep the appointment this noon.
That's too bad.
Let's make it Monday instead.
Sorry, but I'm busy then.
Well, maybe later in the week.
We'll see.

f. I've got two tickets for the play—would you like to go?
Oh, yes, I want to see it.
I'll see you Friday night then.
Fine.

g. Come in, Agnes.
Do you have company?
No, I'm all alone.
Good, I thought I'd drop in for a bit.

h. Good evening, is Mr. John home?
Yes, come in. I'll call him.

.   .   .   .

Mr. John, I'm Tom Cain.
Glad to know you; what may I do for you?

i. Oh, Helen, I'm sorry to be late.
That's all right, come in.
Have I held things up?
No, lunch is ready right now.

j. My, it's nice to be here!
How long can you stay?
A week if it's all right?
Of course it is!

k. I better go. It's getting late.
Don't hurry.
It has been a very nice evening.
I'm glad you could come—do stop again.
Thank you.

l. Good night, Mrs. Brown.
Good bye, Jane.
It was a lovely party.
Thank you, I'm glad you could be here.

m. May I help you?
Yes, I'd like a two-ring notebook.
That will be fifty cents.
Thank you.

n. Do you have any blue curtains?
Yes, we do.
How much are these?

Two-ninety five a pair.
I'll have two pairs.

o. Five gallons of regular.
Anything else?
Check the oil, please.
It's all right.
Thank you, that's all.

p. I'd like to look at coats.
What color?
Red.
Size 14?
Yes.

q. May I help you?
I'm just looking, thank you.
Go right ahead.

2. In the following role-playing situations, you may practice the use of speech techniques. Each situation chosen should be studied as to the kind of person speaking and the exact words he will speak. Some freedom of expression is allowed at first in the development of natural conversational expressions. Then you should practice the same exercise several times to reinforce the skills you wish to practice.

Imagine yourself in one of the situations suggested below. Develop short conversations. Practice situation with one or two other students as participants.

a. You are Dean of Men. The students have just been celebrating May Week and have destroyed some property. You address the students and attempt to calm them.

b. You are the football coach. Your players are not doing as well in studies as they should. You talk to them about scholastic standing.

c. You are the college instructor telling the class to contribute to the community fund.

d. You are a parent talking to a son about improving his grades.

e. You are a psychologist addressing a group of women relative to the effects of television on young children.

f. You are a salesman for stainless steel cookware. You address a group of women about the values after you have cooked a dinner for them.

g. You are talking to your husband or wife about the advisability of buying a new house.

h. You are a teacher talking to a parent about her child's slow speech development.

i. You are a student talking to a professor about the values of graduate work.

j. You are a student talking to the landlady about your rent. She wants her money and you have to wait for your next allowance from home.

3. Be prepared to discuss one of the following topics with four of your classmates. After the discussion, evaluate the application of speech skills.
   a. Comic Books
   b. Leisure Time Activities
   c. Speech Standards
   d. Highway Safety
   e. World Understanding

4. Be prepared to discuss the pro or con of one of the following statements. Ask a classmate to discuss the opposite side of the question.
   a. Membership in a fraternity or sorority is advantageous.
   b. Comic strips contribute to crime.
   c. Woman's place is in the home.
   d. Small colleges should be selected by undergraduate students in preference to large universities.
   e. The grading system in the university should be improved.
   f. Students should have voting power in making the policies of the university.
   g. The drafting system for wars should be changed.
   h. General American speech should be adopted universally in the United States as standard speech.
   i. Policies concerning wars in foreign countries should be changed.
   j. Money is the measure of success.

5. Read aloud the following selected paragraphs from "Too Much Football." With two or three classmates, discuss the pros and cons of collegiate football.

Too Much Football

A significant little adage which circulates in Michigan athletic circles says in effect that there are three aspects of college life at Michigan . . . intellectual, social, and athletic . . . but that the student has time for only two. This idea can circulate only where athletics have become, or are thought to become, as important as the academic work of the University. The student who plays football is expected to sacrifice his studies. When after one Saturday game I limped off the field with a twisted ankle, I knew that I would be expected to spend a good deal of Sunday in the training room taking treatment for the injury. But since Sunday was the only time that I was able to study for the coming examination, I stayed away from the training room. As a result the ankle stiffened and on the practice field I was made to feel guilty for the rest of the week. The coaches are aware that in theory studies come first, but they are also aware that, in a big-time league, if studies actually come first, second-rate teams are likely to be the result.

. . . .

A word must be said about the rabid football alumni and the over-zealous football fans. I find no fault with anyone who has a normal interest in athletics, but the perverted bigness of football produces people with a perverted interest in sport. Although the number of the most adhesive of these hangers-on to the football scene is not large, their presence is distressing because they are undoubtedly the articulate representatives of a much larger group whose interest in and attitude toward big-time football allows the unhealthy and prolonged hysteria which permeates the college football scene each fall.

. . . .

So, after four years of seeing everything there is to see in big-time football . . . victories, defeats, publicity, hospitals, championships, and bowls . . . of being known as a "football player" rather than a human being, of seeing myself and my teammates misrepresented and misquoted by sportswriters who seldom attempted to know the players personally, of playing in a 97,000 seat stadium in which my non-paying student friends were forced to sit in the end zone, of having my natural desire for physical exercise corrupted and commercialized, of giving up pleasant afternoons in favor of kicking and rolling in the dust and muck of the practice field . . . I have decided that big-time football is a poor bargain for the boys who play the game.*

6. Prepare and present a two-minute demonstration speech which requires considerable bodily movement. Use speech skills as effectively as you can. Suggested topics follow.
   a. Strokes in playing golf
   b. How to put on a coat
   c. How to fold blankets
   d. Drawing a picture
   e. How to play baseball

7. Make an outline for a two-minute extemporaneous speech on one of these topics. Practice the speech aloud, using the outline. Give attention to phrasing, breath control, suitable intensity, adequate intelligibility or articulation.
   a. Why I have selected my profession
   b. If I had a million dollars
   c. On taking myself too seriously
   d. Art with a camera
   e. A book which has influenced my life
   f. My favorite poet
   g. If I were president of this university
   h. My plan for speech improvement
   i. Honesty is the best policy
   j. Installment buying

8. Combine reading and speaking in the same assignment (three-minute talk). Present a poem or quotation which expresses a thought which may be the basis for a short talk. Suggestions are as follows:
   a. "Patterns" by Amy Lowell
   b. "My Last Duchess" by Robert Browning
   c. "The Ballad of the Harp Weaver" by Edna St. Vincent Millay

---

* Allen Jackson, "Too Much Football." Copyright © 1951, by The Atlantic Monthly Company, Boston, Mass. Reprinted with permission.

   d. "Richard Cory" by Edwin Arlington Robinson
   e. "A poor life this if, full of care,
      We have no time to stand and stare" from *Leisure* by W. H.
      Davies.

9. Give an impromptu two-minute speech on one of the following topics:
   a. Pride goes before a fall.
   b. Friends in fine weather only are not worth much.
   c. Honesty is the best policy.
   d. Look before you leap.
   e. Do not let anything turn you from your purpose.
   f. Well begun is half done.
   g. Haste makes waste.
   h. Prevention is better than cure.
   i. Make hay while the sun shines.
   j. Take the bull by the horns.

References

Baird, A. Craig and Franklin H. Knower, *General Speech,* 3rd ed. New York: McGraw-Hill Book Company, 1963.

Barnes, Harry G. and Don Streeter (eds.), *Speech Handbook,* 2nd ed. New Jersey: Prentice-Hall, Inc., 1959.

Black, John W. and Wilbur E. Moore, *Speech: Code, Meaning and Communication.* New York: McGraw-Hill Book Company, 1955.

Monroe, Alan H., *Principles and Types of Speech,* 6th ed. Glenview, Illinois: Scott, Foresman and Company, 1967.

Sanford, William Phillips and Willard Hayes Yeager, *Principles of Effective Speaking,* 6th ed. New York: The Ronald Press Company, 1963.

APPENDIX A

Selections for Reading Aloud and Discussion

I

20,000 Cycles Under the Sea*

a. Recordings of underwater sounds of biological origin would have little meaning if we were content to file them simply as a document of science. Yet when related to the past, they stand for more than this: they stamp with absolute authenticity some of the wildest dreams of our ancestors; they corroborate our prophets; they stand back of our poets.

b. This is not a new thing for science. Men scoffed at Daedalus, airborne, and grounded him with wings of wax; there was a terrible to-do when a handful of men began prattling about an earth that was round; it was difficult for Heyerdahl to find backers when he wanted to cross the Pacific on a raft. The proof often comes plodding after the pudding, and we are used to that. But it is not often that a scientific document suddenly lights up grayed-out pages or gives status to gibberish.

c. The recordings which make up the scientific document owe their existence to a war and to an accident. "During the Second World War,"

---

* Frederick Ramsey, Jr., "20,000 Cycles Under the Sea." Reprinted by permission of John Cushman Associates, Inc., New York, New York. Copyright © 1953 by Frederick Ramsey, Jr.

we read in Rachel Carson's *The Sea Around Us,* "the hydrophone network set up by the United States Navy to protect the entrance to Chesapeake Bay was temporarily made useless when, in the spring of 1942, the speakers at the surface began to give forth, every evening, a sound described as being like 'a pneumatic drill tearing up a pavement.' . . . Eventually it was discovered that the sounds were the voices of fish known as croakers, which in the spring move into Chesapeake Bay from their offshore grounds."

d. If these songs of fish produced consternation and incredulity when reported to the high command, the secret has been well guarded. But the next step, when all memoranda were in and the information had been somewhat uncomfortably digested, was to find out what fish were saying amongst themselves.

e. Researchers at the Scripps Institution of La Jolla, California, were set to work on a new project, marine eavesdropping. Laying down their microphones for the first undertaking of its kind in the history of ichthyology, they tapped sounds that grew "curiouser and curiouser" with each day of listening. Reports came in that a chorus of croakers was living off the pier of the Institution, and that this particular chorus had a particular time for singing. Every year, the eavesdroppers discovered, from May until late September, the evening song began about sunset, increasing "gradually to a steady uproar of harsh froggy croaks, with a background of soft drumming." The tanks at the Institution already contained croakers gathered for other studies; by comparing their song with that of the "wild" fish, they could be fairly certain that these, too, were croakers. But the drummers heard at this ichthylogical listening post were still anonymous.

f. New sounds came in over the wires every day.

g. Earphones and loudspeakers crackled with "a sizzling sound, like dry twigs burning or fat frying." It was soon learned that "mammals as well as fishes and crustaceans" were holding submarine colloquy. Hydrophones were set up (or rather, dropped down) in an estuary of the St. Lawrence River. Hydrophones are a waterproofed, seagoing, pressure microphone. They had originally been developed by our navy to detect submarine motor noises; but they are a scientific instrument, and nothing on earth or undersea will induce them to shut up when other sounds come in range.

h. So the hydrophones dropped into the St. Lawrence estuary brought up "high-pitched resonant whistles and squeals, varied with the ticking and clucking sounds slightly reminiscent of a string orchestra tuning up, as well as mewing and occasional chirps . . ." These things were hard to believe; but this was science, and these were hydrophones, responding to and reproducing given stimuli. The question of who gave the stimuli was urgent.

i. It continues to be urgent. Many of the animals producing sounds have been isolated in tanks, as were croakers in the first experiment, and their song positively verified. Still other stimuli remain to be identified. Their source confronts us with a mystery as challenging as the origin of matter or the conquest of space, flying saucers notwithstanding.

j. This brings us to the recordings and the form in which they have been made available for home record players. The two sides of the long playing record (Folkways Science Series FPX 121) are distinct, in that the second side contains recordings of sounds taken in tanks, while the first side reproduces underwater sounds of biological origin taken at various depths in the Atlantic and Pacific Oceans. When the source of sound is known, it is given; we learn from the labels that a cast of croakers, toadfish, snapping shrimp, sea robins, drum fish, cat fish, crabs, and spot fish has produced the lively show of thumps, mews, drumbeats, coughs, snaps, barks, and pneumatic rattles.

k. The bands of the first side are arranged in a sequence that lowers the armchair listener gently down to the bottom. The curtain rises above the sea, with the first salty gurglings of surface water, then the listener goes below with the hydrophone to the rather foreboding business that transpires at 2,000 fathoms (a little over 2¼ miles) *down*. It is doubtful whether any listener can stay fixed in his chair at this depth; the moaning picked up here—no man has ever managed to get down this far, and no man knows what animal is involved—is possibly the most mysterious, probably just plain most frightening, sound man has ever heard.

l. In concert music, everyone is familiar with the sumptuous, programmatized heavings and rollings of nature-pieces like Debussy's "La Mer." There is the modest thunderstorm of the Beethoven Sixth Symphony; there is the drawing-room elegance of Haydn drumbeats; the shrilling of crickets and other natural sounds of Transylvania are suggestively mimicked in certain works by Béla Bartók. There is in the concluding section of Alban Berg's somber "Wozzeck" an arresting passage which Ernest Newman has described as "the downward slither of some twenty consecutive ninths." Ravel's "L'Enfant et Les Sortilèges" gives us a delightful musical miauing, as imagined by a little boy in a nightmare about a cat he has tortured. Milhaud's "Création du Monde" is jazzy and danceable, and contains passages that suggest the primeval heavings which gave birth to the world; the dynamics of railroad sounds have been carried over into a range of compositions that might begin with

Lumbye's frothy "Jernbane Galop," roar down the tracks with Honegger's "Pacific 231," and grind into the roundhouse with Duke Ellington's "Daybreak Express" and "A Train."

m. But these are, essentially, man-made and man-abstracted sounds. They are relatively familiar; we are even a bit cozy with them. But with an unknown sound piped from 2¼ miles below surface, we are brought directly to the mystery of the sea, and of our origin. "The mysteriousness, the eerieness, the ancient unchangingness of the great depths," Rachel Carson has written, "have led many people to suppose that some very old forms of life—some 'living fossils'—may be lurking undiscovered in the deep ocean."

n. Let us now see how close man has come, alone and without the hydrophone, to the idea of life—and sound—beneath the surface.

o. Perhaps of all tales told of the sea, those of Rabelais were most entertaining. For Rabelais, in a period of teratogenic scientific investigation and momentous voyages of discovery, maintained a sense of humor. As background to Rabelais' stories, it is pertinent to turn to two distant points: Florida and the east coast of Malay. Fishermen off the Florida coast have reported hearing strange sounds when large schools of fish have come close to the surface. The men were in small, open boats, and their story comes to us before the days of the airplane and motor launch.

p. Their story might be dismissed as simply another case of *cafard* on the high seas were it not for an article recently published in *The New Yorker* ("Crocodiles and Human Radars") which tells how Malay fishermen track down schools of fish. The *juru selam* are men who go beneath the surface and listen for sounds made by the schools, then direct other boats to them.

q. "The art of *juru selam*," Christopher Rand tells us, "is based on the development of the senses to an exceptional degree, together—or so it is believed by the Malays—with a touch of the supernatural. . . . The underwater hearing of Malay fishermen must be unequaled among human beings anywhere. An Englishman on the east coast who has a motorboat told me that they could hear him coming eighteen miles away, long before they could see him or hear his engine through the air."

r. Then Rand talked with one of the men whose hearing rivaled the hydrophone: "He said he told the fish apart chiefly by the kind of noise they made in their throats—'clucking' or 'grunting' was how Che Osman expressed it. The *lelemah* was loudest, he said, and made a noise like 'kha, kha.' One fish, whose name I didn't catch, said 'ah . . . oh . . . ah'— the sounds were nasal and well separated—when it was alone but something like 'ump . . . ump' when swimming in a shoal. Another fish said 'gho-ho-ho-oow.' *Beliak mata* made a sound like 'tikatikatika-socosoco-soco'; the old man whispered this softly, as if to himself, rocking his head back and forth."

s. It is possible that fishermen long ago heard sounds at sea, and reported them ashore; of all persons, Rabelais is most likely to have picked up this fish tale and amplified it to suit his whim. A ghoulish parallel is supplied by the fact that Rabelais' sounds are of war and the engines of war; it was to the engines of war that our naval hydrophones were tuned when they first picked up the Chesapeake Bay croakers.

t. This is Rabelais' story: "When we were at sea, Junketing, Tipling, Discoursing, and telling Stories, Panatagruel rose and stood up to look out; then ask'd us, Do you hear nothing, Gentlemen? . . . At last we began to fancy that we also heard something, or at least that our Ears tingled; and the more we listen'd the plainder we discern'd the Voices, so as to distinguish Articulate Sounds. This mightily frighted us, and not without cause, since we could see nothing, yet heard such various sounds and Voices of Men, Women, Children, Horses, etc., insomuch that Panurge cry'd out, Cods Belly, there's no fooling with the Devil . . . let's fly. There is some Ambuscado hereabouts . . .

u. "The Skipper made answer; Be not afraid, my Lord, we are on the Confines of the Frozen Sea, on which, about the beginning of last Winter, happen'd a great and bloody Fight between the Arimaspians and the Nephelibates. Then the Words and Cries of Men and Women, the hacking, slashing, and hewing of Battle-Axes, the shocking, knocking, and joulting of Armours and Harnesses, the neighing of Horses, and all other Martial Din and Noise, froze in the Air: And now the Rigor of the Winter being over, by the succeeding Serenity and Warmth of the Weather, they melt, and are heard.

v. "By jingo, quoth Panurge, the man talks somewhat like; I believe him; but couldn't we see some of 'em? Methinks I have read, that on the edge of the Mountain on which Moses received the Judaic Law, the People saw the Voices sensibly.—Here, here, said Pantagruel, here are some that are not yet thaw'd. He then throw'd us on the deck whole handfuls of frozen Words, which seem'd to us like your rough Sugar-Plumbs, of many Colors . . . and when we had somewhat warm'd them between our Hands, they melted like Snow, and we really heard them, but could not understand them, for it was a Barbarous Giggerish; one of them only that was pretty big, having been warm'd between Fryar John's Hands, gave a sound much like that of Chestnuts when they are thrown into the Fire without being first cut, which made us all start.

This was the Report of a Fieldpiece in its time, cry'd Fryar John . . .

w. "When they had been all melted together, we heard a strange Noise, Hin, hin, hin, hin, his, tick, tock, taack, brededin, brededack, frr, frr, frr, bou, bou, bou, bou, bou, bou, bou, bou, track, track, trr, trr, trr, trrr, trrrrrr, on, on, on, on, on, on, ouououououon, gog, magog, and I do not know what other barbarous Words, which, the Pilot said, were the Noise made by the Charging Squadrons, the Shock and Neighing of Horses.

x. "Then we heard some large ones go off like Drums and Fifes, and others like Clarions and Trumpets. Believe me, we had very good sport with them."

y. It is just possible that to Rabelais, a man who wrote so persuasively of frozen sounds, the idea of hydrophones, 2,000 fathom cables, and tape recording might seem a little tame. His eyes might twinkle on hearing of them, however, and he might state, with some justice, that all this paraphernalia could do was document things as they exist; that his frozen sounds were enormously superior, because they could also take us into the past; the People who saw Voices sensibly as Moses received the Judaic Law were at least one step ahead of televiewers (he might have a kind word here for Aldous Huxley, who put "feelies" in his "Brave New World"); and that strange sounds from the deep were no newer than the Old Testament, wherein it had been doubtfully enquired, "Canst thou draw out Leviathan with a hook?"

z. And since it would be only fair to set down both sides of this conversation, perhaps it should be reported that our scientists replied (by Frozen Words shot backward) that "We haven't yet drawn out Leviathan with a hook, but we may have caught him with a hydrophone."

II

Curfew Must Not Ring Tonight

a.
England's sun was slowly setting
O'er the hills so far away,
Filling all the land with beauty
At the close of one sad day;
And the last rays kissed the forehead
Of a man and maiden fair—
He with a step so slow and weakened,
She with sunny, floating hair;
He with sad bowed head, and thoughtful,
She with lips so cold and white,
Struggling to keep back the murmur,
"Curfew must not ring tonight."

b.   "Sexton," Bessie's white lips faltered,
      Pointing to the prison old,
      With its walls so dark and gloomy—
      Walls so dark, and damp, and cold—
      "I've a lover in that prison,
      Doomed this very night to die,
      At the ringing of the curfew,
      And no earthly help is nigh.
      Cromwell will not come till sunset"
      And her face grew strangely white,
      As she spoke in husky whispers,
      "Curfew must not ring tonight."

c.   "Bessie," calmly spoke the sexton—
      Every word pierced her young heart
      Like a thousand gleaming arrows,
      Like a deadly poisoned dart—
      "Long, long years I've rung the curfew
      From that gloomy shadowed tow'r;
      Every evening, just at sunset,
      It has told the twilight hour.
      I have done my duty ever.
      Tried to do it just and right;
      Now I'm old, I will not miss it;
      Girl, the curfew rings tonight!"

d.   Wild her eyes and pale her features,
      Stern and white her thoughtful brow,
      And within her heart's deep center,
      Bessie made a solemn vow.
      She had listened while the judges
      Read, without a tear or sigh,
      "At the ringing of the curfew
      Basil Underwood must die."
      And her breath came fast and faster,
      And her eyes grew large and bright;
      One low murmur, scarcely spoken—
      "Curfew must not ring tonight."

e.   She with light step bounded forward,
      Sprang within the old church door,
      Left the old man coming slowly,
      Paths he'd often trod before;
      Not one moment paused the maiden,
      But with cheek and brow aglow,
      Staggered up the gloomy tower,
      Where the bell swung to and fro;
      Then she climbed the slimy ladder,

Dark, without one ray of light,
Upward still, her pale lips saying,
"Curfew shall not ring tonight."

f.   She has reached the topmost ladder,
O'er her hangs the great dark bell,
And the awful gloom beneath her,
Like the pathway down to Hell.
See, the ponderous tongue is swinging,
'Tis the hour of curfew now;
And the sight has chilled her bosom,
Stopped her breath, and paled her brow.
Shall she let it ring? No, never!
Her eyes flash with sudden light,
As she springs and grasps it firmly—
"Curfew shall not ring tonight."

g.   Out she swung, far out, the city
Seemed a tiny speck below;
There twixt heaven and earth suspended,
As the bell swung to and fro;
And the half-deaf sexton ringing
(Years he had not heard the bell)
And he thought the twilight curfew
Rang young Basil's funeral knell;
Still the maiden clinging firmly,
Cheek and brow so pale and white,
Stilled her frightened heart's wild beating—
"Curfew shall not ring tonight."

h.   It was o'er—the bell ceased swaying,
And the maiden stepped once more
Firmly on the damp old ladder,
Where for hundred years before
Human foot had not been planted;
And what she this night had done
Should be told in long years after:
As the rays of setting sun
Light the sky with mellow beauty,
Aged sires with heads of white,
Tell the children why the curfew
Did not ring that one sad night.

i.   O'er the distant hills came Cromwell;
Bessie saw him, and her brow,
Lately white with sickening terror,
Glows with sudden beauty now.
At his feet she told her story,
Showed her hands all bruised and torn;

And her sweet young face so haggard,
With a look so sad and worn,
Touched his heart with sudden pity,
Lit his eyes with misty light;
"Go, your lover lives!" cried Cromwell;
"Curfew shall not ring tonight."

Rose Hartwick Thorpe

III

Chauncey A. Goodrich to Rufus Choate

Yale College
November 25, 1852

My dear Sir,

I have taken the liberty to send you, through our friend Henry Hill, a book which I have recently published, designed to aid the young men of our country in the study of eloquence.* A glance at the preface will show you my plan, and will explain my reason for confining the present volume to the orators of Great Britain. The copy sent you is the one originally intended as a tribute of respect and veneration for the greatest of our New England orators. I have felt that it ought to pass into your hands; especially as the City of Boston and Dartmouth College have called upon you to speak of his greatness and his virtues.

There is a passage in one of the early pages of this work (21st) which reminds me of what I heard from Mr. Webster, when I first listened to his eloquence. It is Lord Belhaven's application of the words *"Et tu quoque, mi fili"*, to Scotland, when "attending the fatal blow and breathing—her last," (as he considered it) under the compulsion which drove her into a legislative union with England. Mr. Webster applied them still more beautifully at the close of his argument at Washington in the case of Dartmouth College. In publishing his speech, however, he left out the entire peroration, giving in its place an extract from Cicero, which he probably regarded as a more appropriate conclusion of a strictly legal argument. No hand but his could ever reproduce it; but I am sure you will be interested in a slight sketch of the circumstances as they will always live in my memory.

Before going to Washington (which I did chiefly for the sake of hearing Mr. Webster) I was told that in arguing the case at Exeter, N. H., he had "left the whole court room in tears" at the conclusion of his speech. This, I confess, struck me unpleasantly—any attempt at pathos on a purely legal question like this, seemed hardly in good taste. On my way to Washington I made the acquaintance of Mr. Webster; we were together for some days in Philadelphia at the house of a common friend; and as the "College Question"

---

* Chauncey A. Goodrich, *Select British Eloquence*. New York: Harper and Row, Publishers, 1852.

was one of deep interest to literary men, we conversed often and largely on the subject. As he dwelt upon the leading points of the case in terms so calm, simple, and precise, I said to myself, more than once, in reference to the story I had heard, "whatever may have seemed appropriate in defending the College at *home,* and on her own ground, there will be no appeal to the feelings of Judge Marshall and his associates at Washington." The Supreme Court of the United States held its session that winter in a mean apartment of moderate size, the Capitol not having been rebuilt after its destruction in 1814. The audience, when the case came on, was therefore small, consisting chiefly of legal men, the elite of the profession throughout the country. Mr. Webster entered upon his argument in the calm tone of easy and dignified conversation. His matter was so completely at his command that he scarcely looked at his brief, but went on for more than four hours with a statement so luminous and a chain of reasoning so easy to be understood and yet approaching so nearly to absolute demonstration, that he seemed to carry with him every man of his audience without the slightest effort or weariness on either side. It was hardly eloquence in the strict sense of the term, it was pure reason. Now and then for a sentence, his eye flashed and his voice swelled into a bolder note as he uttered some emphatic thought, but he instantly fell back into the tone of earnest conversation which ran throughout the great body of the speech. A single circumstance will show you the clearness and absorbing power of his argument. Judge Story, as I remarked at the opening of the case, prepared himself pen in hand, to take copious minutes. Hour after hour I saw him fixed in the same attitude but *not a note on his paper.* The argument closed and *he had not taken a single note.* To one who spoke to him afterwards of the fact with surprise, he remarked, "Everything was so clear, so easy to remember, that not a note seemed necessary; in fact, I thought nothing about my notes."

"Sir, you may destroy this little institution; it is weak, it is in your hand! I know it is one of the lesser lights in the literary horizon of our country. You may put it out! But if you do so, you must carry through your work! You must extinguish, one after another, all those great lights of science which for more than a century have thrown their radiance over our land! It is Sir, as I have said, a small college. And yet *there are those* who love it!" There the feelings which he had thus far succeeded in keeping down, broke forth. His lips quivered; his firm cheeks trembled with emotion; his eyes were filled with tears, his voice choked; and he seemed struggling to the utmost, simply to gain that mastery over himself which might save him from an unmanly burst of feeling. I will not attempt to give the few broken words of tenderness in which he went on to speak of his attachment to the college. What he said seemed to be mingled throughout with the recollections of father, mother, brother, and all the trials and preventions through which he had made his way into life. Everyone saw that it was wholly unpremeditated—a pressure on his heart which sought relief in words and tears. Recovering himself, after a few moments, and turning to Judge Marshall, he said, "Sir, I know not how others may feel (glancing at the opponents of the college before him), but for myself, when I see my *Alma Mater* surrounded, like Caesar in the senate house, by those who were reiterating stab upon stab, I would not for this right hand have her say to me, '*Et tu quoque, mi fili!*' "

He sat down, and I need not tell you that the whole court room at Washington, as at Exeter, was in tears. It has always struck me, in looking back at that scene, that the pathetic depends not so much on the words themselves, as upon the estimate we put on him who utters them. No one was ashamed to weep when he saw before him the man who had made such an argument, melted into the tenderness of a child.

I am with much respect
Very truly yours
CHAUNCEY A. GOODRICH

Hon. Rufus Choate
Boston, Massachusetts

IV

These passages have been used frequently in experimental surveys and experimental and diagnostic work. They are well made. Some contain all of the sounds of English; others are weighted with sounds that vary markedly among the pronunciation dialects of America. Record the passages and, with the help of "a trained ear," listen to the recordings critically. Try to identify the unique properties of each.

a. *The Rainbow Passage*

When the sunlight strikes raindrops in the air, they act like a prism and form a rainbow. The rainbow is a division of white light into many beautiful colors. These take the shape of a long round arch, with its path high above, and its two ends apparently beyond the horizon. There is, according to legend, a boiling pot of gold at one end. People look, but no one ever finds it. When a man looks for something beyond his reach, his friends say he is looking for the pot of gold at the end of the rainbow.

Throughout the centuries men have explained the rainbow in various ways. Some have accepted it as a miracle without physical explanation. To the Hebrews it was a token that there would be no more universal floods. The Greeks used to imagine that it was a sign from the gods to foretell war or heavy rain. The Norsemen considered the rainbow as a bridge over which the gods passed from earth to their home in the sky. Other men have tried to explain the phenomenon physically. Aristotle thought that the rainbow was caused by reflection of the sun's rays by the rain. Since then physicists have found that it is not reflection, but refraction by the raindrops which causes the rainbow. Many complicated ideas about the rainbow have been formed. The difference in the rainbow depends considerably upon the size of the water drops, and the width of the colored band increases as the size of the drops increases. The actual primary rainbow observed is said to be the effect of superposition of a number of bows. If the red of the second bow falls upon the green of the first, the result is to give a bow with an abnormally wide yellow band, since red and green lights when mixed form yellow. This is a very common type of bow, one showing mainly red and yellow, with little or no green or blue.

b. *Arthur the Rat*

Once there was a young rat named Arthur who never could make up his mind. Whenever the other rats asked him if he would come out with them, he wouldn't say "Yes" or "No" either. He would always shirk making a choice.

One day his aunt Helen said to him, "Now look here, no one is going to care for you if you carry on like this. You have no more mind than a blade of grass."

c. *My Grandfather*

You wished to know all about my Grandfather. Well, he is nearly ninety-three years old; he dresses himself in an ancient, black frockcoat, usually minus several buttons; yet he still thinks as swiftly as ever. A long, flowing beard clings to his chin, giving those who observe him a pronounced feeling of the utmost respect. When he speaks, his voice is just a bit cracked and quivers a trifle. Twice each day he plays skillfully and with zest upon our small organ. Except in the winter when the ooze or snow or ice prevents, he slowly takes a short walk in the open air each day. We have often urged him to walk more and smoke less, but he always answers, "Banana oil!" Grandfather likes to be modern in his language.

d. *The Navy*

The navy was once made up of wooden ships with cloth sails. Then came iron ships, but the sails were still of cloth. When the wind blew, the navy could attack. Years later boilers and engines were invented, and the sailors could strike their enemy at will. You might think it is easy to figure out a new idea, but changes come slowly. When great changes occur, history is made. Not little changes, but great changes are a measure of our progress.

e. *Horrid Day*

One horrid rainy day, rather late in February, we started south along a desolate road through the forest. Now and then we heard frogs in the swamps on the peninsula. Later a goose honked, and fog rolled in from the water. After three or four miles the road came out onto a barren sandy stretch. Here and there was a barnyard, with a donkey and a few hogs. Some orange flowers grew beside the road. Suddenly the rain came down in torrents, and the roof of the car began to leak. We were sorry that we hadn't fixed it before leaving home, but our plans had involved so many details that we hadn't bothered. Our clothes absorbed so much dampness that we felt cold, so we hurried to the next village. After leaving our car to be greased at a garage we found a restaurant where we ordered coffee and pancakes with maple syrup. We waited for lunch by a huge fireplace, where a cheerful log fire was burning. The walls and floor were made with heavy pine boards, which were black with suet. We were surprised to see various queer things in the corners. There was a glass case filled with dolls, some of which were from foreign lands. Next to the chimney was a calendar that advertised a laundry, and beyond it was a horrible old parrot on a perch. We watched this absurd scene until a waiter brought our lunch through a narrow sort of corridor from the kitchen. Meanwhile, we tried to solve a cross-word puzzle, but our hands were so greasy that we had to wash and rinse them first. When we finished we found that the rain had cleared up enough to warrant our going on. We borrowed a cloth to clean our car windows, and hoped that tomorrow would bring better weather. The route number seemed to correspond with the one on our road map, and we followed it past an old stone quarry near the lane. That night we slept in a tourist cabin, and listened to a windmill which revolved slowly and noisily outside our door.

f.   Willie White had a new white wheel. Being a robust athlete, Willie decided to set a precedent and ride his new wheel to New York. He thought he could enjoy nature, pick a few apricots, and maybe do a little zoological research on the way. So on Tuesday, he put on his chic new outfit his spouse had given him and started out. His itinerary took him over a circuitous route through Illinois and across the boundary to Indiana. He rode over gravel, asphalt, and cement highways. One time he had to take a detour and it almost turned into chaos because Willie nearly had an accident when he hit a culvert on this alternate route. Willie was compiling data about the hydrangea, the elm trees, the various rock strata, reptiles, and nature and geography in general. Whenever Willie felt his protein level was low, he would worry and eat a chocolate almond bar and resume his journey. Willie was miserable. Upon inquiry he found his daily ration contained only carbohydrates. This would never do because he needed a huge amount of energy for the herculean task of riding his white wheel over the mountain heights. Meanwhile Willie had received no mail because his mischievous Mrs. had put the wrong address on the envelopes. Willie was harrassed and his morale so low that he had the hiccoughs until the perspiration rolled off his forehead. He rode as fast as his new white wheel would carry him to an unfrequented country bridge where he jumped into the creek and drowned. Thus ends the poignant story of Willie White and his new white wheel. Do you think he was an ignoramus?

V

The following excerpts taken from speeches given by John Mason Brown and Al Capp at the Town Meeting of the Air are presented for the purpose of stimulating controversial discussion. Details for preparing for such an assignment are given in Chapter 13. One student may present one viewpoint; another may give the opposing side of the issue. Following the presentations, evaluating of speaking performances would be appropriate.

a. What's Wrong With the Comics*

The comics, alas, like death and taxes, are very much with us and to my way of thinking, they are equally unfunny. Why they are called comics when people who read them, young and old, always look like so many undertakers during the reading, eludes me. But we'll let that pass, just as most of us parents have had to let comics pass into our homes, against our will, against our wishes, against our better judgment.

I love comedians, the highest, the lowest, and the toughest, and I love cartoons, too, but my allergy to comics is complete, utter, absolute. I *know* there are bad comics and I am *told* there are good comics. I have read them . . . a few of both, and only a few, fortunately . . . under protest, but I regret them both. I deplore them and, to continue the understatement, I abhor them.

---

* (Taken from a speech by John Mason Brown, *Town Meeting Bulletin,* Vol. 13, No. 45.)

So far as I am concerned, they might as well be written in a foreign language for which no dictionary has ever been published, and I wish they had been.

Let me quickly admit that I am low enough and sometimes defeated enough as a parent to make use of comics. I mean in desperate moments when, of a rainy Sunday morning or afternoon, I want peace in the home. Or when I'm travelling with my two sons on a train and I need to subdue them. Then . . . yes, I'll confess it . . . I do resort to comics, without shame, without conscience.

b. What's Wrong With the Comics*

There must have been a lot of innocent little kids who listened and I'm sure they were frightened to death listening to Mr. Brown tell them what's wrong with their comics.

I'd like to hear a Town Hall forum of the same kids on the subject, "What's Wrong with Dramatic Critics?" They might, with complete righteousness, make the same complaints about dramatic critics that Mr. Brown makes about comic strips, like, for instance, "Dramatic critics are a waste of time." "Dramatic critics are very unfunny; they're bad for the eyes; they're untrue to life; they're horrible to think about." "Dramatic critics are not only the bane of the bassinet, they're the didey service of the nursery."

Of course, any fool can plainly see, these kids would be wrong, because kids just aren't the best judges of dramatic critics. And this point occurred to me during Mr. Brown's speech: dramatic critics just aren't the best judge of kids.

(Capp refers to a typical family to illustrate his points. In the following section, he presents his argument.)

"Look," she (Mrs. Kinsey) screams at Mr. Kinsey. "Look at what your child is reading."

"It's only Dick Gravey," replies little Kingsblood.

. . . .

"Only Dick Gravey, my eye," snarls his mother. "Why, this thing is full of murder, crime, violence, and look, why there's even a boy in it who doesn't think that a girl in it is repulsive, so its full of S-E-X, too."

Mr. Kinsey speaks, "Yes, I've been reading several articles lately by several psychologists, or psychiatrists, or something, that state that these stories of murder, crime, and violence and S-E-X are very bad stuff for kids."

---

* (Taken from Al Capp's speech which was delivered on America's Town Meeting of the Air at the same time that John Mason Brown spoke. Entire speech found in *Town Meeting Bulletin,* Volume 13, No. 45.)

He says, "Why do you bother with that old comic page, anyhow, son? Why don't you read the news?"

"I did, Pop," replies the lad. "And, oh boy, it's all full of murder, and crime, and violence and S-E-X too, Pop."

Mr. Kinsey looks over the front page of the paper and he has to admit the kid is right. He tears the newspaper up, cancels his subscription. . . .

    .   .   .   .

"Son," Mr. Kinsey said, pulling a volume off the bookshelf, "why don't you read a good book instead, like *Oliver Twist?*"

"I read it," reports little Kinsey. "It's all about a kid who falls in with a criminal named Fagin who teaches him how to commit crimes. There's a big gorilla in it named Sikes, who beats a girl to death."

"Stop," cries his father. "Stop! I can see now that the work of Charles Dickens is very bad for kids." So he tears the works of Dickens all up. He feels he owes this to the psychologists.

    .   .   .   .

Comic strippers are story tellers, just the same as people who write radio shows, books, and movies. Some of us are right and some of us are wrong. It's the same with psychologists . . . and even dramatic critics. Some of them are right, some are wrong. But don't worry about the kids. They're usually right.

APPENDIX B

Audio-Visual Aids and Suggestions for the Study of Applied Phonation and Phonology

Audio-Visual Aids

Films, transparencies, tape recorders, and language laboratories may be used to supplement the teaching of voice and diction. Some suggestions follow.

Films

1. "Ears and Hearing" (Encyclopedia Britannica Films, Inc., 1150 Wilmette Ave., Wilmette, Illinois), 11 min.
2. "The Speech Chain" (Bell Telephone Laboratories, 463 West Street, New York, New York), 20 min.
3. "Your Voice" (Brooklyn College: Department of Speech).
4. "The Search: Hearing" (Young America Films Inc., 18 East 41st Street, New York 17, New York), 25 min.

*Transparencies**

Transparencies are used on overhead projectors. Information concerning transparencies and overhead projectors may be secured from Visual

---

* References from which suitable diagrams for transparencies may be found are as follows:
Arthur J. Bronstein, *The Pronunciation of American English*. New York:

Products, 3M Company, 2501 Hudson Road, St. Paul, Minnesota 55119. They may be made by the instructor or an audio-visual department. The following illustrations may be used to accompany the factual material presented in the lectures to the class.

Slide   1. The Mechanism for Articulation
Slide   2. The Palate and Oral Cavity
Slide   3. The Vibrating Source
Slide   4. Passageway for Energy Source for Speech
Slide   5. Diagrams of the Ear
Slide   6. Diagram of the Process of Hearing
Slide   7. Diagram of the Auditory Feedback Loop
Slide   8. Audiogram Illustrates Conductive-Type Hearing Loss
Slide   9. Consonant Chart
Slide 10. Articulatory Adjustments for Nasal Consonants /m, n, ŋ/
Slide 11. Articulatory Adjustments for Plosives /p, b, t, d, k, g/
Slide 12. Articulatory Adjustment for /l/
Slide 13. Articulatory Adjustment for /f, v, θ, ð/
Slide 14. Articulatory Adjustment for Fricatives /s, z, ʃ, ʒ/
Slide 15. Articulatory Adjustment for /t, d/
Slide 16. The Physiological Vowel Diagram
Slide 17. Articulatory Adjustments for Vowels
Slide 18. Articulatory Adjustment for /ɝ, ɜ, ʌ/
Slide 19. Retroflex and Non-Retroflex Forms of /ɝ/.

The Tape Recorder

The following excerpt from "Audio-Aids in Modern Language Teaching" will provide some suggestions for the use of the tape recorder.

The Tape Recorder*

The tape recorder has now found its way into the majority of schools and in many ways it is potentially the most useful teaching aid available to us today. It takes only a few minutes to master the

---

Appleton-Century-Crofts, Inc., 1960.
Hilda B. Fisher, *Improving Voice and Articulation.* Boston: Houghton-Mifflin Company, 1966.
James Carrell and William R. Tiffany, *Phonetics.* New York: McGraw-Hill Book Company, Inc., 1960.
Harold M. Kaplan, *Anatomy and Physiology of Speech.* New York: McGraw-Hill Book Co., 1960.
* An excerpt from "Audio-Aids in Modern Language Teaching" by S. R. Ingram. Reprinted by permission from *Visual Education,* June, 1961, pp. 5-8. Also printed in *Teaching English as a Second Language,* Harold B. Allen, ed. New York: McGraw-Hill Book Company, 1965.

technique of operating one. There are very few knobs, very little can go wrong and no more maintenance is required than for a radio set. It is usually best to record loudly and play back under control. If handled correctly, the machine will faithfully record the sound and reproduce it almost immediately. The same tape can be used indefinitely if the recording is not meant to be permanent, for any material can simply be erased by recording again on top of it. On the other hand, permanent recordings varying from a few minutes to several hours can be made on tape and these can be reproduced an almost infinite number of times without wearing out. Always mark your tapes carefully with adhesive paper. Keep them in boxes and label these boxes clearly.

The most obvious use of the tape recorder in the classroom is to give pupils the salutary lesson of hearing their own voices. Until we have heard ourselves on a tape, we have little real idea of what our voice sounds like to other people. The first impact on the hearer is one of shock, for undoubtedly most pupils just do not believe us when we tell them about their mistakes. When the children have got over this initial impact and the fun of hearing each other, the real work can begin. Although you can use the tape recorder for class oral work, its best remedial function is with small groups. If by some arrangement you can achieve a smallish teaching unit, outstanding progress can be made in the elimination of personal faults in pronunciation, intonation and rhythm. The technique of using the recorder with young beginners has to be learned by experience. Do not use it too much or too often.

Choose your material carefully—say two sentences illustrating certain points of pronunciation or intonation. Practice them with a small number of pupils before you record—this is to give them confidence as well as practice—then record their voices straight off. Play the recording back straight through and let the whole group hear the accurate record of what took place. Either let the group criticise or do so yourself, stopping the machine at appropriate points. The same recording can be used several times to illustrate different points and the interest can thus be maintained quite a long time, as the participants are both present and known to the rest of the group. Next, re-record, hoping you have improved on the original, and, of course, using the same speakers. Finally, play the original and the second recording and try to learn from it all.

Many variations of this basic technique will suggest themselves. The teacher can make criticisms as the lesson proceeds, his voice coming in immediately he hears a mistake; the pupil repeats the word or phrase, the teacher does and so on. The whole recording is then played again, and comment is invited from everyone present. Finally an attempt is made to produce a really good version. Most pupils are prepared to work very hard at this kind of exercise.

The Language Laboratory

The language laboratory may be used effectively for the teaching of skills in phonation and phonology. Suggestions which may be adapted to use by the instructor of voice and diction may be found in the following article.

The Language Laboratory*

If we believe, as I suppose most of us now do, that much of language learning is the learning of complicated skills, and that learning skills is largely a question of adequate and effective practice, then any means by which the time our students spend on such practice can be increased without, of course, prejudice to their other proper activities—whether study or play—must be desirable. In other words, if we can get more practice done in the time we have available for language learning, then we shall have achieved considerable economies and a notable intensification of the learning process. This is precisely what the language laboratory should be able to do for us, if we use it properly.

Basically a language laboratory is a language classroom in which the students are isolated from each other by soundproof walls. These walls prevent the sounds made by one student from reaching his neighbours. This leaves him free to practise speaking without disturbing them and he, in his turn, can listen to speech undisturbed by them. The result of this should be that a whole class of students can practice speaking at the same time instead of one after another as in the conventional classroom. In this way the language laboratory can help us to save time. Instead of sitting quiet (but not necessarily idle), while all the other members of the class practice an item of language one by one, the student can be busy practicing himself.

Of course, this is a rather simplified description of a language laboratory. There is, in fact, a large variety of possible ways of using a laboratory and different types of practice to be done in one, but we should do well constantly to bear in mind that in essence a language laboratory is no more than a special classroom where a large number of students can practice oral-aural language skills at the same time without disturbing one another. If we do this we shall avoid falling into the error of thinking that the language laboratory is the final answer to all language–learning problems, that it will ease the teacher's burden, that it will magically speed the learning process, and so on. All these claims and many others have been made for the laboratory, but now, after many years' experi-

---

* S. Pit Corder, "The Language Laboratory," *English Language Teaching*, 16 (1962), 184-188. Also in *Teaching English as a Second Language*, Harold B. Allen, ed. New York: McGraw-Hill Book Company, 1965.

ence, it is being valued at its true worth and has its accepted place amongst the various aids available to the language teacher—a powerful aid if properly used, a waste of time and money if improperly used. The language laboratory is a tool and, like any tool, useful only in the hands of a craftsman who know how to use it.

Language laboratories may have quite simple equipment, in which case the sort of practical work possible in them is limited; or they can be very lavishly equipped and thus very versatile in their use. The more versatile they are, however, the more complicated they tend to be for teacher and student to operate and the more liable they are to mechanical breakdown. For this reason I should recommend that anyone setting up a laboratory should start with the simpler equipment. As the teacher through practice and experience gains confidence in handling it, and if he is convinced that he is getting useful results, he can then think of extending the equipment to undertake more complicated tasks. Experience has shown that the initial installation of the most complicated form of language laboratory has often been followed by confusion and discouragement on the part of the teacher and loss of interest on the part of students. The laboratory is neglected or misused, or used at less than its full potential capacity, that is, uneconomically.

There are three stages in the development of a laboratory from the simplest to the most complex. In the first stage it consists of a number of soundproof booths, each containing a set of headphones connected to a microphone in front of the teacher. In this set-up the students can listen to the teacher and carry out his instructions, copy his speech, answer his questions and so on, all at the same time. The first refinement within this stage is to connect the students to the output of a gramophone or tape recorder. This leaves the teacher free while the students continue to practice. The weakness of this arrangement is, of course, that the teacher cannot check up on the students' work. He does not know whether they are practicing correctly, persisting in their mistakes, or indeed practicing at all! Clearly the advantage of setting the teacher free in this way is lost unless he can be freed for useful work. This leads us to the next stage of development.

In the second stage, the teacher has earphones and is connected with a microphone in each student's booth. We now have two-way communication. The teacher and the individual student can speak to each other and the teacher can now listen to and monitor any student's production and advise him how to improve. The student also can speak to the teacher and ask for an explanation or help. At this stage, then, we have a sort of electronic copy of the ordinary classroom situation with the advantage that the teacher can deal individually with any student without all the other students remaining silent. Much useful work can be done with no more equipment than this. Beginners using a language laboratory would be well advised to master the uses of a laboratory of this sort before passing on to the next stage, of new and expensive equipment which certainly increases the versatility of the installation but which for many ordinary school users might perhaps be of only marginal use.

The third stage of development then sees the introduction into each student's booth of a tape recorder. Now the student can record his practice efforts together with those of the model. He can then play back the results and make comparisons. The teacher, too, is able (given time!) to monitor the individual work of all his class, if he wishes. Furthermore, the tape recorders in the individual booths can now play back prerecorded practice tapes to the student independently of what all the other members of the class are doing, or even out of class-time. But in this case, of course, the teacher cannot monitor the students' work except during class-time, nor can the student compare his efforts with the model on the prerecorded tape.

At this point the last refinement is introduced: special dual-track tape recorders in the students' booths on which the master's model can be played and the student's copy recorded all in one operation. The student has now achieved complete independence from the teacher and, given suitable pre-recorded tapes and the special dual-track tape recorder, might almost as well be at home!

To sum up so far, we have three stages of development:

Stage 1.
   (a) The teacher can speak direct to all students together.
   (b) The teacher or the recorded material can speak to all students.
Stage 2.   In addition to facilities available in Stage 1,
   (a) Individual students can speak to the teacher and the teacher can monitor their practice.
   (b) The teacher can now speak to any student individually.
Stage 3.   In addition to the facilities in Stages 1 and 2,
   (a) Students can record the teacher's and their own voices on their single-track tape recorders.
   (b) Students can play individual tapes on their dual-track recorders and simultaneously record their own responses.

The opportunity for the student to hear his own efforts in pronunciation and compare them with the model was originally thought to be the great contribution of the dual-track tape recorder: it was thought that by this means the necessity for a teacher was to some extent done away with. This hope has not been realized in practise. It is in fact doubtful whether a student is any better able to monitor and correct his own production by this means than he is in a live teaching situation; in which case the use of dual-track tape recorders for this type of work may actually be dangerous, since students will be doing a lot of inexact repetition which remains uncorrected because the teacher cannot monitor all the students all of the time. Needless to say, this does not apply to the practice of grammatical material, where self-monitoring presents fewer problems.

I said earlier that the language laboratory could be a powerful tool *if effectively used,* and now we come to the crux of the matter. All the expensive equipment will be wasted if the techniques of using the laboratory and, even more important, the linguistic materials are not appropriate, adequate, or properly prepared.

At this point we must go back to first principles: the complicated patterns of sound which we call "language" only have meaning in relation to the situation or context in which they are uttered. In our classroom work we always try to retain meaning in the language drills we rightly introduce by relating them to a situation, whether it be the classroom, and conversation we have had, reading we have done, or a scene we have acted. Drilled material is meaningless, and hence boring, in the degree it is not related to a context. If we are to avoid largely meaningless repetition in the drills in the language laboratory (and drill is what we must call much of the laboratory work), they must be directly related, and recognized by the students to be so related, to work done in the classroom. Uncontextualized language practice material used in the laboratory has been the reason for so much of the boredom and lack of motivation so frequently mentioned in reports on the use of laboratories. Work in the laboratory is only a part, and not even a major part, of the whole teaching/learning process; whatever we do in the laboratory must remain an integral part of that process. As the student's sophistication increases with maturity, and an understanding of the purposes of the different work done in language learning develops, the laboratory becomes more useful. Adults will tolerate a greater degree of sheer donkey-work because they are aware of the need for it and its place in the learning process. Their long-term aims in learning are clearer and sustain them in situations where the short-term motivation of the younger pupil will not.

The laboratory is for practicing the aural-oral skills. These skills are more especially applied to learning language-material in the fields of pronunciation and grammar. Any materials and methods used for practicing the oral skills in these fields in the classroom are appropriate and can be adapted to the language laboratory. Thus procedures such as listening to, indentifying, distinguishing between, and copying sounds, stresses, tones, and tone patterns in pronunciation practice and ear training are possible. In grammar the familiar drills of substitution, completion, prepared conversation and the like, are appropriate. The laboratory can be used for asking and answering questions, informal oral testing, and more formal oral examination. The inventive teacher can find a use for the laboratory in practising out difficulties of any sort which have arisen in his classroom work. It has its place in the earliest stages of language learning as also in its most advanced stages, but never can it replace the teacher or take over the whole teaching burden. It must always be a tool, not a master.

It will be clear, and it is as well to recognize it early, that the possession of a laboratory does nothing to lighten the teacher's work. On the contrary, and precisely because more work by the students is being compressed into the same amount of time as formerly, the preparation of materials for use either "live" or recorded in the laboratory increases the teacher's work considerably. The teacher cannot improvise in the laboratory; he cannot find *ad hoc* practise material in the course of the lesson as he can in the classroom; he cannot rely on intuition, and, if his inventiveness runs dry, turn to some other activity. Laboratory work must be more carefully and more fully prepared even than classwork. Nor must the teacher imagine that material prepared for one year can be used unchanged the next. The laboratory is voracious of the teacher's time and energy. Unless the teacher is prepared to do this extra work and spend this extra time, the laboratory will be improperly, uneconomically, or ineffectually used.

Listening and Practice Centers

In some colleges and universities, listening centers may be available where the student may work independently to reinforce information or skills. Dual-track tape recorders are usually available in individual booths. The master's model may be imitated by the student on the tape so that on playback the student may compare his production with that of the model. On other master tapes, only listening is required. For some, the listening may be tested by requests to make judgments of sounds, voices, or intonation.

Master tapes might include such titles as the following:
1. Sound Discrimination Test
2. Word Sound Recognition Test
3. Voice Analysis (twenty voices)
4. Improvement of Vocal Rate
5. Pitch Variability
6. The Consonants—Plosives
7. The vowels—/i, ɪ/
8. Pronunciation

The tapes would probably fall under these headings: (1) listening activities, (2) tests, (3) voice, (4) articulation of sounds, and (5) pronunciation.

A log of listening and practice sessions at the listening center may be kept by the student. The examples in Table B-1 are taken from the logs of students:

Table B-1.   Examples of Logs of Listening Activities

No.	Record-ing No.	Descriptive Title	Date	Time, min.	Comments
2	S417-A5	Word-sound recognition test	1/13/66	20	I learned to pronounce my words more clearly and to sound out my words. It made me listen carefully.
4	S417-B15 B16	Voice analysis (20 excerpts)	1/13/66	30	I enjoyed listening to voices of other students, trying to evaluate their voices. It helped me to evaluate my own voice.
9	S417-B11	Vocal stress	1/26/66	18	This tape emphasizes importance of vocal stress in speaking. I learned to stress certain syllables in words.
13	S417-C2	Pronunciation	2/23/66	20	This tape was very helpful to me. I tend to pronounce such words as fish, dish, push, and bush incorrectly. This tape made me aware of differences which I am trying to improve.

Table B-1. (Cont.)

No.	Record-ing No.	Descriptive Title	Date	Time, min.	Comments
23	S417 D-15	Fricative con-sonants	2/11/66	15	These exercises were helpful in learning the importance of precise articulation. They also supplemented class notes. The /s, z/ was especially good for me as I could practice my /s/ sound. As I repeated the /s/ sound, I noticed and felt a definite improvement. This to me was a valuable exercise.

SUGGESTIONS FOR ANALYSIS OF SPEECH NEEDS AND ABILITIES

The assessment of the voice and articulation of the students may include information pertinent to speech skills, as well as the actual evaluation of the samples of the student's speech.

History

The following topics might be included in the questionnaire designed to obtain information which may be helpful in the assessment of needs and abilities or planning of instruction:

Speech History. Indicate what experiences or instruction you have had in speaking.

Attitudes Toward Your Speech and Speaking. Such questions as these may be asked: Do you like to talk? Are you afraid to talk in class? Describe how you feel when you speak to a group. Has anyone ever made fun of your speech? Why? What is your attitude toward this course?

Describe your speech (articulation) and voice. Do you stutter? Have you ever stuttered? Any other speech problems? Do people understand you? Do you like your voice?

Personal History. Places where you lived. Experiences in school. Employment. Any special problems? Travel. Reading. Social. Hobbies. Major in college and expected vocation.

Family History. Parents. Siblings. Language spoken in home. Always live in home or with other persons? Occupation of father or guardian.

Assessment of Articulation and Voice

Passages for the students to read may be found in Appendix A. These paragraphs are suitable for the evaluation of specific sounds as well as for the study of vocal factors. Conversational speech may consist of responses to such questions as (1) If I had a chance, I'd like to _____, (2) When I graduate, I expect to _____, (3) I am taking voice and diction so _____. Check sheets for use by the instructor or the student may include the consideration of vocal factors, such as time or rate, loudness, pitch, and quality; of articulation, including general inaccuracy, oral inactivity, omissions, substitutions, and distortions. A simple form for use in the analysis of voice and articulation might appear as follows:

Rating of Voice and Articulation

Key to the scales: (1) exceptionally satisfactory, (2) very satisfactory, (3) adequate, (4) unsatisfactory, and (5) clinical. (Draw a circle around the number which best describes your reaction.)

I. *Voice*

Voice pleasantness 1   2   3   4   5
Loudness of voice 1   2   3   4   5
Pitch of voice 1   2   3   4   5
Flexibility of voice 1   2   3   4   5
General reaction to voice 1   2   3   4   5

II. *Articulation*

Intelligibility 1   2   3   4   5
Rhythm 1   2   3   4   5
Pronunciation 1   2   3   4   5
Accuracy of sound production 1   2   3   4   5
Rate 1   2   3   4   5

Specific sounds inaccurately made _____
Vocal inadequacies noted _____
Date_____ Observer_____

The student may use the same form as suggested above. A self-evaluation form which might be used at any time during the instructional period may include some of the following questions: Do you like your voice? How do you think others react to your voice? What are your good points? What are your weak characteristics? In making your check sheet, consider these items: pitch, rate, loudness, resonance, variety, articulation, and pronunciation. Is your pitch too high, too low, or adequate? Is your rate of speaking too fast, too slow, or monotonous? Is the speech singsong? Monotonous? Are you easily heard? Too loud? Are all your sounds distinct and accurately made? Do you slur or omit any sounds? Are you too precise in your articulation? Indicate the sounds which you made indistinctly or inaccurately. List the words which you think you mispronounced. If you do not like the sound of your voice, describe in terms of breathy, harsh, nasal, or hoarse.

Listening to Voices of Others

As you listen to voices of those who speak on the radio or television, on the platform, or in your class, you may want to use a guide with some of the following topics and questions:
I like the voice _____ do not like the voice _____.
I would like (would not) to know the speaker _____.
The voice sounds good _____ fair _____ poor _____ to me. The outstanding characteristics of the voice are _____.
(describe in terms of pitch, quality, variety, etc.)
If the voice appears unpleasant, it is nasal, harsh, high pitched, low pitched, weak, loud, breathy, hoarse, or _____.
I was influenced by other characteristics than the voice _____ (dress, facial expression, content or speech, etc.)

Evaluation of Individual Progress

This questionnaire used at the end of the term may be constructed with the intent of determining to what extent the voice and diction course has been successful in improving your speech. You will want to indicate what you have done in terms of attendance at class, outside practice, reading, and study. Include such topics and questions as these:
   1. Speech is about the same _____ better _____ worse _____ than at the beginning of the course.

2. If better, it is probably due to _____ (indicate in terms of all of the types of possible activities).
3. Others have (have not) made favorable comments about my speech. (What have they said?)
4. In what specific ways have you improved? What do you need to do yet?

Index